008008

P9-EAX-372

Spiritual

Sydney Smith

GANDHI AND NON-VIOLENCE

by William Borman

STATE UNIVERSITY OF NEW YORK PRESS

Published by State University of New York Press, Albany
© 1986 State University of New York
All rights reserved
Printed in the United States of America

Cover drawing is by Sydney Smith © Copyright 1986.
Cover and text design by Sushila Blackman.
No part of this book may be used or reproduced in any manner whatsoever
without written permission except in the case of brief quotations embodied
in critical articles and reviews.

For information, address State University of New York Press,
State University Plaza, Albany, N.Y., 12246

Library of Congress Cataloging-in-Publication Data

Borman, William, 1948–
  Gandhi's non-violence.

(SUNY series in transpersonal and humanistic psychology)
  Bibliography: p.
  Includes index.
  1. Gandhi, Mahatma, 1869–1948. 2. Nonviolence.
I. Title. II. Series.
HM278.B63   1986   303.6′1   86-1889
ISBN 0-88706-330-6
ISBN 0-88706-331-4 (pbk.)

To *Kumar Maharaj*

For the Path of

Pax, Shalom, and Shanti

SUNY Series in Philosophy
Robert C. Neville, Editor

SUNY Series in Transpersonal and Humanistic Psychology
Richard D. Mann and Jean B. Mann, Editors

NOTE: Citations to Gandhi's writings and speeches customarily include date of publication or date of statement or both. Gandhi's many compilers and editors differ in the style in which these dates are given, viz., order of month and day. Sources for this book have been chosen largely for comprehensiveness and availability and the style of the compiler in each source has been retained. Thus, of the five main compilers used, Kumarappa, Kher and Desai cite by day/month/year; Kripalani and Hingorani cite by month/day/year. In a few citations by other authors or compilers the order is made clear in the footnote; e.g., while Narayan generally cites by day/month/year, he gave the citations referred to in this book by month/day/year; the only citation from Bose is transcribed from his "5/11/31" to "5 Nov. 31". The fullest scholarly satisfaction would be gained by tracing these quotations in the Collected Works (now approaching 100 volumes), which are now beginning to become more generally accessible. But as this is intended to be an analytical/reconstructive and critical work, the *via media* of including statment and/or publication dates for each citation has been used.

CONTENTS

Preface   *xiii*
Acknowledgements   *xv*

Part I
SECTION ONE
AN EXPOSITION OF GANDHI'S CONCEPT, METAPHYSICS &
IDEOLOGY OF NON-VIOLENCE

Chapter 1.   **Ahimsa: Gandhi's Concept**   3

(1) A Positive Denotation, Not a Simple Negation; Denoted by a
Coined Term   3 / (2) Central Concept of a Moral Ideology
Defined by Gandhi's Views of God and of Good and Evil   4 /
(3) Exemplifies a Spiritual and Moral Metaphysics of Self,
Freedom, Bondage and Release   7 / (4) Non-violence as
Non-Retaliation   10 / (5) Not an Empirical
Denotation   11 / (6) As Non-Killing and Non-
Tearing   11 / (7) Defines a Moral Principle and a Social
Political Method   13 / (8) Law, Efficacy and Moral
Science   14 / (9) Denotes a Perfectly Non-Coercive
Force   16 / (10) Denotes a Wholly Non-Personal
Force   16 / (11) And the Conscious Discrimination of
"Doer" and "Deed"   16 / (12) Interpreted by Equating Non-
violence with Consciousness   17

SECTION TWO
SATYĀGRAHA: THE PRACTICAL APPLICATION OF NON-VIOLENCE
    Introduction   19

Chapter 2.   **The Spiritual Basis of Satyāgraha**   20

A. Gandhi's Aim   20
   Spiritual Realization   21 / Demonstration of Practical
   Claims: A Progressive Substitution   23

B. *Satyāgraha* in the Context of the Upaniṣads: Analysis from
   the Standpoint of Spiritual Knowledge   26
   Truth and Self   26 / Human Condition of
   Ignorance   31 / Experience and Experiments   33 /
   Need to Apply on Basis of a "Science" of Action   34

C. *Satyāgraha* in the Context of the Bhagavad Gītā: Spiritual
   Analysis from the Standpoint of Action   34
   Argument of the Gītā   36 / Battle Within: Origin of
   Conflict and the Means of Dissolving It   37 / Human
   Condition of Bondage   38 / *Anāsakti* and *Yajña*   44 /
   Need to Apply to Problems of the Age and Locale   49

Chapter 3. **Practical Application of Non-violence:**
           As a Sādhana, a Means of Spiritual Realization   53
           Introduction   53
           A. Gandhi's Aim   54
              Realization in an Age of Action by Service, Redress and
              Social Reform   54 / Resort Only to Non-violent Force in
              Furtherance of Realization and Reform against Resistance
              and Obstruction: Demonstration of a Complete Substitute
              for Methods of Violence   58 / The Final Criterion   59
           B. Principles of *Satyāgraha*   61
              Holding to Truth   62 / Human Predicament   65 /
              Self-Conversion and Substitution Ethics: Positive Material
              Effort   67 / Non-Retaliation and
              Self-Sacrifice: Non-Phenomenal
              Response   75 / . . . As the Final Criterion   76
           C. Methods of *Satyāgraha*: Tapaścārya   78
              Holding to Truth in Practical Action:
              Karmayoga   79 / Fit Principles to the Evil
              Challenged   81 / Tapaścaryā: Drawing Out the Power of
              the Soul by Self-Suffering   85 / Methods and
              Vows   86 / Method Types   88 / Vows   93

Chapter 4. **Criteria and Claims of *Satyāgraha***
           Introduction   95
           A. Equation of Criteria through "TRUTH": The Spiritual, the
              Moral and the Practical, Synonymous   95
              Truth and the Expedient   95 / The Moral and the
              Expedient   97
           B. Practical Efficacy of *Satyāgraha* Actions Achieving External
              Ends   98 / Achievement of Reform   98 / Non-violent
              Defense and Retaining Gains   99
           C. Moral Efficacy of *Satyāgraha* Actions: Having Intrinsic
              Worth   102
              Individual: Death at Duty Without
              Ill-Will   102 / Relations: Enmity Vanishes, Friendship
              Established   104 / Motives, Quality of Acts and Change
              of Self . 105
           D. Permanence   106
              Conversion, Not Suppression   106 /
              "Non-violence / Violence" as "Eternal/Ephemeral"   107
           E. Universality and Infallibility   108
              Basis of His Claims   108 / Mundane, Corporate and
              Political   111 / Dynamics of Suffering   112 / Contra-
              Mundane Additions of Strength   113 / Summary and
              Transition   115

Part II
SECTION THREE
GANDHI'S PRACTICAL CLAIM & THE JUSTIFIABILITY OF VIOLENCE
    Introduction   119

Chapter 5. Gandhi's Mission, and the Context of His Argument:
           A New Debate and the Problem of Justification   120
           Introduction   120
           A. Gandhi's Practical Claim and the Absolute Rightness of Non-violence: Its Objective Validity: Discounting the Ideological Basis   120
           B. Gandhi's Mission to Show the Unjustifiability of Violence, and His Argument to Defeat the Proposal of Violence as a Last Resort   121
              The Last Resort Argument   124 / A New Debate   125
           C. Concept, Context and Means:
              The Problem of Justification   125
              Not the *Prima Facie* Case   127 / Not a Naive
              Claim   128 / Justification   129 / Justifiability   129
           D. Two Arguments and a "Dependent" Absolute Claim   130
              Theoretical Inquiry (Examination of Spiritual Facts to Vindicate a Universal Claim and Prove the Absolute Rightness of Non-violence   131 / Practical Inquiry (Examination of the Justifiability of Violence by Practical Factors that Prove its Non-necessity   131 / Absolute "Dependent" Claim (Absolute Claim for Perfect Practical Efficacy, Non-Naive in Granting Its Conditional and Dependent Nature)   131 / Core of Non-Retaliation   132 / Science   133 / Ideology   133

Chapter 6. Standpoint of an Objective Evaluation: Scope and Limits of Gandhi's Non-Violence
           Introduction   135
           A. Problem of Evaluation   135
              1. Objective Standpoint   135
                 Internal Invulnerability of Ideology   135 / Necessity of Practical Criteria   136
              2. Criteria   136
                 Experience, Common Sense and the Test Case   136 / Universalizability, Heteronomy and Confusion   138
              3. Valid Core of Two Inquiries: Non-Retaliation   139
                 Correct Analysis of Violence as Retaliation   139 / Exploratory Instrument: The Last Resort Argument   140
           B. Rightness and Necessity   140
              1. Gandhi's Position: Defining Necessity by Dichotomy Confuses the Analysis of Violence   141
                 Necessity and Self-Deception   141 / Simplifying Moral Reality   142 / The Critical Standpoint: Defining Real Necessity   144 / Necessity of Fighting Evil   145

2. Commonsense Position: Defining Moral Necessity, A
   Real Need for Violence   146
   Violence Morally Required by Its Own Evil Nature: "A
   House Divided . . ."   147/ Required to Control Evil
   by Its Own Methods: How Evil Functions, A
   Rationale   148/ Gandhi's Rejoinder: Hate Not the
   Doer but the Deed   151/ Gandhi's Partial Validity,
   but Non-Necessity   153/ Failure of Gandhi's Position
   to Respect Categorical Truths   155 / Gandhi's
   Failure of Commonsense   155
3. Last Resort: Condition of Applying the
   Necessity Criterion   156
   Defining the Good Use of Violence: Preservation of
   Goodness   156/ Sincerity and Clarity   157/
   Patience, and Restraint on Use of Violence   158/
   Intelligence and Objectivity   158/ Peace, an End and
   Aim, Not a Means   159/ Sum   159

Chapter 7. Critical Examination of Gandhi's Views on War: The Limiting
            Case of Conflict, Violence and the Last-Resort Argument
            (Real Necessity: Application of the Objective Analysis
            of the Limiting Case, I)   161
            Introduction   161
            A. Non-Retaliation and the Ideological Interpretation of the
               Maxim "Two Wrongs Don't Make a Right"   161
            B. Gandhi's Analysis of War in the Gītā and Judgments of Its
               Justifiability   165
               1. Misuse of Logical Principles of the Identity of Micro-/ and
                  Macro-Cosmic Reality: Confusion of Basic
                  Distinctions   166
                  Real and Ideal: Appearance and Reality   166/
                  Confused Valuation of Life: Peace at Any Price   168
               2. Views on the Justifiability of War and Violence:
                  Analysis Vitiated by Ideological Homogeneity from Wrong
                  Use of Identity   168
                  Justifiability: War Is in No Way Justifiable   168/
                  Gandhi's Interpretation of the Gītā as a Pacifist
                  Document: Outer Form of the Moral Attack on Inner
                  Causes   174/ Confusion of Basic Categories: The
                  Logic of Gandhi's Over-Valuation of Life   177/
                  (1) Arjuna's Pacifist Arguments Universalized
                  1-6   177/ (2) Confusion of the Moral with the
                  Spiritual   178/ (3) Confusion of the Ideal with the
                  Phenomenal   179/ (4) Confusion of the Moral with
                  the Practical   182
               3. "Non-violence/Violence", Not an Absolute Distinction:
                  Right-Making Factors   183
                  Need for Accurate Analysis of the Action Situation:
                  Motive, Intention, Results   183/ Motive and Intent
                  Are Real Factors: Contradictory Criteria   185/ Non-
                  violence and Violence: Justification by Balance or
                  Results   186/ No Ideal War   188

4. *Svadharma* and *Anāsakti*: The Spiritual Content of
   Gandhi's Ideal   192
   Fundamental Heteronomy: Formal and Universal
   Standard of Self-Realization (*Svadharma*) / Ideological
   Standard of Practical Non-violence   192 / *Anāsakti*:
   Also Heteronomously Interpreted   194 / Moral
   Imagination: Cannot Solve Moral Dilemmas, But Only
   Reinforce Falsifying Dichotomous Views   195 /
   Confuses Outer and Inner Battles   196

Chapter 8.   **Critical Examination of Gandhi's *Satyāgraha*:
              Again, A Limiting Case in Conflict, Violence and the
              Last Resort Argument
              (Real Necessity: Application of the Objective Analysis
              of the Limiting Case, II)   199**

   A. *Satyāgraha*: Failure of Gandhi's Final Resort and
      Complete Substitution   199
      Gandhi's Moral Metaphysics Defeat His Practical Ethics:
      Reopens the Question of Balancing Good and Evil   199 /
      Protection of Life: Value Equals Potency, the Key Equation
      in Gandhi's Argument   199 / Life, the Chief Value:
      Wrong Aims and Methods, and False Views   200
      1. False Views and Values   200
         Assumes Equivalences of "Highest Value" and "Supreme
         Potency"   200 / Factual Reality, a Moral Mix; Not
         Determinable *a priori*   200 / Confusion of Material
         Destruction and Death of Body, with Killing and Loss of
         Life   201
      2. False Aims and Methods   202
         "Law of the Sword": Not a "Law"   202 / Non-
         Retaliation: Self-Defeating Principle at the Logical,
         Practical and Moral Limits   203 / Universalizability
         Criterion: Paradox of Highest Means Equated with
         Ultimate Ends (Fallacy of Assuming Their Ideal
         Identity)   203 / Ideological Axioms Cannot Replace
         Commonsense Assessment   204 / Textual Authority,
         Inadequate "Warrant": Assumes the Ideal It Is Intended
         to Validate as Universal   204
   B. Law of Being: Gandhi's Basic Argument Against Violence as
      a Last Resort   205
      Faulty Claim to Scientific Validity: *Satyāgraha*, a Tool of
      Ideological Inquiry; Non-violence, No "Law" of
      Being   205 / Parity of Reasoning: Counter Claims of
      Commonsense Faith   206 / Gandhi's Key Admission:
      Argument Invalid if "Law of Love" Not the "Law of Our
      Being"   206 / Gandhi's Basic Arguments 1-8: Specific
      Criticism   207 / *Satyāgraha* Argument Vitiated: Same
      Core of Categorical Confusions; Their Form in Practice and
      Method   211 / Non-Universality of *Satyāgraha*: Principal
      Criticism of Gandhi's "Law of Being" Argument as Basis of
      Practical Methods and Argument (His Mis-analysis of
      Human Rational and Moral Nature)   212 / Rational
      Nature   214 / Gandhi Acknowledges Human

Incorrigibility to Non-violence: Defeat of His "Law of Being" Argument and therewith His Total Practical Position   215

C. *Satyāgraha*: A Coercive Force   217
Need for Positive Criticism   217 / Methods, Claims and Facts   217 / Gandhi's Displaced Onus for Coercive Effects: Methods Coercive in Principal and in Fact   218 / Coercive in Effect; Coercive in Principle: Therefore, Coercive   219 / Insistence on Coercive Methods: Terrible Pressure of Reformist Ideology   220 / Sources of Coerciveness   221 / (1) Terrible Pressure of Reform   221 / (2) Radical Heteronomy   221 / (3) Intent to Influence   221 / (4) Ideological Posture   221 / (5) Moral Insistence   222 / (6) Conformism to Great Ideas and Great Actions   223 / (7) Social Norms   223 / (8) Public Opinion   224 / Ascetic Roots of *Satyāgraha* Coercion   224 / Gandhi's Definition of Coercion   225

Chapter 9. **Assessment, Summary and Application   228**
Introduction   228

A. Summary: Analysis, Assessment, Application   228
Objective Analysis and Assessment   228 / Justice and Truth in Today's World; Justice and Condition of Peace   229

B. Operative Core   234
Critique of Gandhi's Analysis of the Operative Core of All Struggle for Justice and Truth   234

C. Truth and Practice   236
Inadequacy of Ideology   237 / Limit of Gandhi's Self-Evaluations; Admission of Failure Also Needs Analysis and Qualification   237

D. New Debate   240
Nuclear Context   240 / Plural Nations and Histories   241 / Disarmament and Conversion of the Heart   243 / Adapting Non-violence   247 / Final Value and Critique   252

Notes   255
Bibliography   265
Index   277

Gandhi's work seems to put into a new context the perennial debate of whether non-violence is always right or whether violence might sometimes be justified, and if it is, how and when. Does Gandhi's concept inaugurate a new debate, the content and significance of which has not been captured by previous concepts? In the Christian peace witness and recent European and American social and political philosophies, "non-violence" denoted sometimes a very different concept from Gandhi's concept. In the Indic traditions, related concepts have not been applied in the absolute and universal way that Gandhi attempts. Gandhi in fact coined the term "non-violence", which now is used imprecisely to cover these other concepts as well.

Gandhi calls for a reasoned understanding of the moral ideal of non-violence and its application:

> The virtues of mercy, non-violence, and love in any man can be truly tested only when they are pitted against ruthlessness, violence, hate and untruth . . . it is incorrect to say that *Ahiṁsā* [Skt.-lit., non-killing, non-harming] is of no avail before a murderer . . . *Ahiṁsā* in the face of a murderer is to seek self-destruction. But this is the real test of *Ahiṁsā* . . . It is another matter that our non-violence has not reached such heights. It would be wholly wrong for us to lower the standard of *Ahiṁsā* by reason of our own frailty or lack of experience. Without true understanding of the ideal, we can never hope to reach it. It is necessary for us, therefore, to apply our reason to understand the power of non-violence.[1]

The purpose of this inquiry is the critical exposition and evaluation of Gandhi's philosophy of non-violence.

Gandhi's concept, metaphysics, principles of action, methods and criteria are, however, merely part of his mission to propagate non-violence as a practical rejoinder to the commonsense argument for the justified use of violence or force. An adequate study of his philosophy of non-violent action must examine his concept, metaphysics and methods in the context of the critical examination of his wider aims.

The book is divided into two parts and four sections. Part I is expository. Part II is critical. The first section gives an exposition of Gandhi's concept, ideology and metaphysics of *ahiṁsā*, or non-violence; and the second section examines the practical application of these in *satyāgraha* [lit.-insistence on Truth]. The third section critically examines Gandhi's radical normative and prescriptive claims that non-violence is always right and ought always to be applied. It focuses on Gandhi's radical practical claim that non-violence is universally applicable and has perfect practical efficacy. The fourth section summarizes the argument of the book and recommends a more moderate practical conclusion.

It should be noted that Gandhi's absolute practical claim does not translate consistently into the absolute proscription of violence that it logically ought to, and that most believe to be his ultimate value judgment on violence. Although this is part of the concluding critique in Section IV, it is important to keep the perspective of this acknowledgement throughout the book. This critical study attempts to construct Gandhi's "best case". It represents the fullest account of the position he fell back on as a reflective and self-critical ideologue. But, in fact, it is difficult to say he has the consistency claimed or imputed. Gandhi repeatedly and explicitly makes statements preferring violence to cowardice. He advises violence to his son, were that the only means by which he could protect his mother and sisters, in 1908 in South Africa. Again, he allowed violence to the Indian Government in 1947, in defense of Kashmir, as preferrable to injustice and cowardice.

That Gandhi does not in fact give violence an absolute negative value *corresponding* to the absolute positive value he ascribes to non-violence, reveals an ambivalence in his thought. The positive value he sees in violence must be born in mind throughout the argument. The argument must focus on Gandhi's ideology—but Gandhi the man is often inconsistent with Gandhi the ideologue and moralist.

ACKNOWLEDGEMENTS

I should like to acknowledge here the many debts I have incurred in producing this book. I thank Professor K.D. Irani, who, with great kindness, gave encouragement and specific philosophical and professional guidance in my early efforts, Professor Marshall Cohen, who was critical, forthright, patient and withal sympathetic and supportive during its long middle period, and Professor Virginia Held, who guided me to a concrete proposal and plan. Professor Gertrude Ezorsky gave me a crucial general framework and much needed guidance to bring the proposal to a complete study. I owe a great debt to Professor Dennis Dalton for his generous and ready help, and his steady encouragement from the inception of this work to his careful criticism of the final version. Thanks also to Professor Ainslie Embree who took valuable time from his very full schedule to read the completed manuscript and play the hard critic for me.

I acknowledge the generous permission of Navajivan Trust to "quote freely" from Gandhi's writings in various publications. Thanks also to the Government of India, and in particular to Mr. M.S. Mehta, Deputy Counsul General of the Indian Consulate in New York City, who was most helpful with my requests.

Thanks also to Bill Eastman, Director of SUNY Press, for his constant encouragement and accommodative advice and support for this book from the first query to its final printing. And I acknowledge with thanks Sushila Blackman, who smoothed out the manuscript in copy-editing and gave the book its beautifully appropriate design; and Peggy Gifford, the production manager at SUNY Press who coordinated the entire effort to have the book out for Gandhi's birth anniversary, as well as gave some critically sensitive help in completing the index.

I would like to acknowledge Sadhana Temple of New York, for use of the writings of Swami Ramanand—*Evolutionary Spiritualism, Evolutionary Outlook on Life, Gītā Vimarśa* and letters—which have provided the leading ideals and concepts of spiritualism and reason that have guided this study from its inception.

Finally, I am very grateful to Sydney Smith for the use of her thoughtful and specially expressive drawing of Gandhi that appears on the front cover.

Part One ━━━━━━━━━━━━━━━━━━━━━━ ₰

1.   Ahiṁsā: *Gandhi's Concept*

Non-violence denotes a spiritual force and connotes a related moral ideology. This chapter outlines how Gandhi's ideology is constructed to explain the working of that force in its practical application.

Though Gandhi's work is highly experimental and pragmatic, it is referred to as a "moral ideology" for reasons that are explained in this chapter. His concept of non-violence is situated in his wider philosophy and moral thought.

1. *A Positive Denotation, Not a Simple Negation; Denoted by a Coined Term.*   The exposition of Gandhi's concept must center on the fact that "non-violence" denotes a substantive moral and spiritual force—the soul's force. According to Gandhi, non-violence "is a force which is more positive than electricity . . . At the centre of non-violence is a force which is self-acting."[2]

Gandhi writes that just as the soul does not depend on the physical body for its existence, "similarly, non-violence, or soul-force, too, does not need physical aid for its propagation or effect. It acts independently of them. It transcends time and space."[3] His concept and methods are constructed on the basis of attributes and powers he believes to be inherent in that force, and he conceives his activities to be channels for it. Activities that Gandhi describes as "non-violent" are those whose effectiveness consists in displacing violence by means of soul-force, thus nullifying evil.

Gandhi coined the term "non-violence" to translate "*ahiṁsā*". He writes that non-violence ". . . is the greatest and the activist force in the world. One cannot be passively non-violent. In fact 'non-violence' is a term I had to coin in order to bring out the root meaning of *ahiṁsā*. In spite of the negative particle 'non', it is no negative force."[4]

The negative construction describes a restraint of expected violence.[5] Gandhi believes this restraint to be the chief and invariable effect of spiritual force. He contrasts this "non-violence" with "un-violence". "It should be remembered also that non-violence comes into play only when it comes in contact with violence. One who refrains from violence when there is no occasion for its exercise is simply un-violent and has no credit for his inaction."[6]

2. *Central Concept of a Moral Ideology Defined by Gandhi's Views of God and of Good and Evil.* Gandhi refers to Truth and non-violence as "'Gandhite' ideology and the means of propagating it . . . by actually living these principles."[7] His non-violence has specifically ideological characteristics.

These characteristics are: use of dichotomy, the equation of violence with evil, presumption of universal applicability, a moral definition of Truth, the equation of non-violence with Truth and justification by definition.

"Violence/non-violence" is the principle dichotomy of Gandhi's moral ideology, and he insists that all analysis proceed in terms of this dichotomy. This is the first characteristic.

The second characteristic is Gandhi's equation of "violence" with "evil". He writes that "in the sense in which I have defined violence its good use is inconceivable."[8] It is on the basis of this equation that Gandhi derives the normative claim that non-violence is always right and its obverse that violence is always wrong.

The third characteristic of Gandhi's ideology is the programmatic aim of demonstrating the universal applicability of non-violence. He claims that it is his "mission . . . to demonstrate that there is no remedy for the many ills of life save that of non-violence."[9]

The fourth characteristic of Gandhi's ideology is his definition of Truth as moral authenticity. Moral authenticity means the effort to bring inner states and outer conduct into congruence by speaking and acting on one's convictions. Gandhi believes that this effort brings into the world the moral quality denoted by "Truth", and this justifies his absolute prescription for moral authenticity and forthrightness.

The fifth characteristic of Gandhi's ideology of non-violence is the

equation of Truth with non-violence. He usually speaks of non-
violence as the means to realize Truth. But since he believes in the
convertibility of means and ends in every moral action, Gandhi
equates non-violence with the Truth that it serves to realize. Conversely, he believes that the Truth involved in moral authenticity will
surely lead to non-violence. "We have to live a life of *Ahimsā* in the
midst of a world of *himsā* and that is possible only if we cling to
Truth. That is how I deduce *Ahimsā* from Truth."[10] . . . "*Ahimsā* is
my God, and Truth is my God. When I look for *Ahimsā*, Truth says:
'Find it through me.' When I look for Truth, *Ahimsā* says: 'Find it
through me.' "[11]

Finally, Gandhi often defers to his definitions to answer arguments.[12] This is a chief characteristic of ideological justification.
However, Gandhi uses these definitions also to formulate a course of
experimental moral action. He constructs his experiments in terms of
the opposition of violence and non-violence (which by his ideological
equation are "evil" and "good", respectively). Conversely, he uses
the results of his experiments to justify his definitions. This circularity is the first critical point to note.

Gandhi gives his ideology a basis in classical Indic metaphysics.
He claims that "I am an *Advaitist* [believer in non-dual subsistent reality underlying all diversity] and yet I can support *Dvaitism* [dual-
ism]. The world is changing every moment and is, therefore, unreal;
it has no permanent existence. But though it is constantly changing,
it has something about it which persists and it is, therefore, to that
extent real. I have no objection to calling it real and unreal and being
called an *Anekāntavādi* [Jaina term for one who takes all logical conclusions to be non-final] or a *Syādvādi* [Jaina term for one who believes truth can be seen only through its many facets, and specifically
by synthesis of seven logical vantage points] . . . I very much like this
doctrine of the manyness of Reality."[13]

Thus Gandhi accepts "manyness of viewpoints" on a single impartible reality, but for him the dual viewpoint of the practical/spiri-
tual distinction has an inherent moral qualification, a tinge that
infects all action and activity (the indenumerable ever-changing Reality), as these stand in opposition to the One changeless Reality.
Gandhi writes, "I believe in *Advaita* (non-dualism). I believe in the
essential unity of man and for that matter of all that lives. . . . When

we *descend to the empirical level*,* [italics mine] we descend to the world of duality. In God there is no duality. But as soon as we descend to the empirical level, we get two forces — God and Satan . . ."[14]

Since "empirical" is a technical term, "empirical/spiritual", as an analytic distinction, will cause confusion if used in a general way in place of the more precise "practical/spiritual" or "material/spiritual" distinctions. This study will use "practical" and "material" to mark the contrast, as either is appropriate to the given analytic context.

Gandhi identifies God with "What *Is*", and calls this totality "Truth". This connects his metaphysics of Truth with his spiritual ideal, and these together give his religion-based moral ideology. He identifies the force of non-violence ultimately with God, or Truth, and he believes that since "man's ultimate aim is the realization of God . . . all his activities, social, political, religious, have to be guided by the ultimate aim . . ."[15]

Combining his metaphysics of existence and of God, Gandhi gives us his metaphysics of morals. The central aim of Gandhi's moral ideology and metaphysics of non-violence is the realization of God. But, as will be seen in Section II, below, Gandhi believes this realization to be fundamentally a matter of moral action.

---

*N.B. - For Gandhi, "empirical", "practical" and "material" refer to any phenomena that may stand as object to consciousness. Gandhi draws the line "empirical/spiritual" in terms of "duality/non-duality". In accord with the Indic spiritual epistemology and metaphysics, he postulates pure, self-absorbed, objectiveless consciousness, the ontological opposite of all objectively known phenomena. This is not entirely accurate because the non-dual Spirit, in itself ineffable, includes and supersedes both matter and consciousness, and as such is inexpressible in terms of either. Both "matter" and "consciousness" are abstractions. This is in contrast with a rationalist epistemology and metaphysics which draw the "spiritual" distinction between mind and body — mental phenomena are considered "spiritual" in contrast to physical phenomena, which alone are considered "material". Therefore, the spiritualist definition of the empirical, practical and material will include thoughts, beliefs, motives, intentions and emotions in its scope. The physical, emotional or mental phenomena are thought of as grosser or subtler material forms, and these all may be spoken of in terms of their qualities and activities. For purposes of our study, this broader spiritualist definition of the practical and the material will provide the primary analytic contrast to the spiritual.

Gandhi believes that though God is One, and though God is all Goodness, it is God who also creates in this world what we, as mental beings, would imagine as evil, and would, as moral beings, actively struggle against. Though the evil is ultimately imaginary, it is not unreal, because the moral imagination which creates it follows its own laws. Gandhi writes that "the distinction [between Good and Evil] is not unimportant. Nor do these thoughts come haphazard. They follow some law, which the scriptures have tried to enunciate . . . I say the distinction is imaginary. God is one, without a second. He alone is . . ." And he continues, "In reality, there is no God who is at war with Satan; but we have imagined that . . . war . . . It is we who entertain thoughts, and again it is we ourselves who repulse. We have thus to strive against ourselves . . . This duel is imaginary, not real. We can, however, sustain ourselves in the world only by assuming the existence of the imaginary duel to be real."[16] God creates this evil in mental consciousness to induce the activity, virtues and discrimination that are prerequisite to Self- or God-realization.

Finally, Gandhi offers his methods of non-violence as the "sovereign" means for the realization of Truth through this moral struggle.

Realization of this Truth involves various problems of the validity and status of reason, faith, and intuition.[17] But in brief, this realization means to Gandhi coming to a consciousness, a living awareness that one's soul is identical with God or Reality, and so with all men and creatures.

This realization is not possible through the five senses or the mind, and the content of this realization is more real than the consciousness given by these empirical faculties. The transformation called for by Gandhi's non-violence is such that it can "only be done through a definite realization more real than the five senses can ever produce."[18] If this realization is valid, it gives an experience of divine presence and power, in which it can be said as Gandhi does "I am surer of His existence than of the fact that you and I are sitting in this room."[19] "I feel this living presence in every fibre of my veins."[20]

3. *Exemplifies a Spiritual and Moral Metaphysics of Self, Freedom, Bondage and Release.* In fact, the chief originality of Gandhi's concept of non-violence is (1) its analysis of violence and non-violence in

terms of the reality of Spirit and the precedence of spiritual and moral considerations in the study of human action, and (2) its radical practical claim for universal applicability and perfect efficacy. No other conception takes into account this inner reality and its experience as factors in the analysis, method and strategy of non-violence.

The ideal of a moral philosophy gives its essence. Gandhi bases his concept of the ideal non-violent man (*sthitaprajña*—man of steady wisdom, or one whose "understanding is secure"[21]) on the model of the Bhagavad Gītā (Chap. II:54–72), the principal text used by Gandhi in his development of non-violence. The *sthitaprajña* is one whose consciousness is established in the Spirit above the mutual pulling and tearing of material forces.

This man "can speak from experience his innermost conviction that he is not this body but *Ātman* (soul) and that he may use the body only with a view to expressing *Ātman*, only with a view to self-realization. And from that experience he evolves the ethics of subduing desires, anger, ignorance, malice, and other passions."[22] This is the key to Gandhi's entire philosophy, ethics and practice of non-violence. The man of Spirit has no material interest in action and its consequences, and so he takes a non-attached view of them (*anā-sakti*). He does not "grasp" at results, and so he does not "tear" at reality (see point 6 below). By this exercise of restraint he progressively grows in the power to express non-violence even in his material make-up, physical and otherwise.

Gandhi's belief that this ideal is not attainable in outward life introduces an ambiguity in his concept. This is the second critical point to note.

Though Gandhi often identifies non-violence as an absolute state and equates it with perfection and Truth, he also replaces non-violence with the ideal of non-attachment (*anāsakti*), and relegates non-violence to the status of a comprehensive but still instrumental virtue.

In the latter case, non-violence and violence are opposed as material or practical conditions, while *anāsakti* is interpreted as a state of the Spirit, untouched by the opposition of these two.

This ambiguity points to a deep and crucial paradox in Gandhi's conception. This paradox, described below, will be examined for its full implications in Section III.

Gandhi offers a radical analysis of violence and non-violence in

terms of a metaphysics of freedom and action. Gandhi believes that
freedom is an attribute of the soul, a quality of consciousness that
the soul, when embodied, seems to lose. Subscribing to the Gītā's
analysis of action, Gandhi believes that "it is beyond dispute that all
action binds, . . . (that) all activity, whether mental or physical, is included in the term action,"[23] and further, that "all *karmas* [lit., actions, work], all activity, all occupation of space involves violence in
some form or other."[24] From this he concludes that since possession
and use of the body, "eating, drinking and moving about necessarily
involve some *himsā* [lit., killing, harming] he can never become entirely free from outward *himsā*."[25]

According to this statement, embodiment is itself fundamental violence, and the desire to maintain bodily existence results automatically in self-perpetuating bondage. Entanglement in violent action and
counteraction is inherent in phenomenal activity, and body and mind
can never for a moment be inactive. Gandhi believes the victory over
violence, even by the *anāsakti* of the *sthitaprajña*, cannot be complete so long as the desire for bodily existence (*abhiniveśa*) itself remains; but, that desire gone, the body must drop from the soul and
dissolve.

Strictly speaking, then, perfect release from the bondage of action,
in terms of violence and non-violence as Gandhi conceives them, is
possible only on dissolution of the body and the consequent deliver-
ance from *karmic* activity. God-realization or realization of Truth,
according to his concept, is possible only after this total release, inner
and outer.

It is the logic of this analysis of soul and action that forces Gandhi
to conceive of non-violence as an unattainable ideal which must be
constantly striven for as if achievable.

Gandhi's ideological concept of non-violence thus defines and limits his conception of the spiritual aim. According to Gandhi, "*Mokṣa*
[lit., release, liberation] is a bodiless super-physical state."[26] Gandhi
accepts the extreme logical conclusion implied in his ideological
dichotomies: "The fullest application of *Ahimsā* does make life impossible. Then let the truth remain though we may all perish."[27]
Perfect *ahimsā* is *mokṣa*, and both are possible only on dissolution of
the body.

For Gandhi there is no value in physical life per se. Soul is the life
of the body and Truth is the life of the soul itself. Without Truth life

is meaningless, and with Truth life is unnecessary. Gandhi's account cannot resolve this paradox.

4. *Non-violence as Non-retaliation.* "Non-retaliation" and "non-violence" denote the same spiritual force. However, non-retaliation describes a particular power of this force which, according to Gandhi, is always manifest since evil is ubiquitous and constantly fighting the good.

But just as "non-violence" is not so full a term for soul-force as "Love", so "non-retaliation" is not so full a term as "non-violence" is for denoting the same force. These distinctions have special practical significance. In social and political action true non-retaliation is possible only to the extent that one has disciplined himself in Love.

How to define this "Love" in terms of disciplined practical action and a beautifully ordered, efficient and wholesome life is the entire object of Gandhi's own lifelong inquiry into non-violence—even as he believed it was the sole inquiry of Socrates and of Jesus in their lifetime and for their historical circumstances.

Through the practical principle of non-retaliation, Gandhi connects non-violence as a moral force, method, state and attitude. By his moral ideology, developed in terms of non-retaliation, Gandhi attempts to demonstrate the practical viability of the seemingly impracticable ideal of total non-violence. He believes that the analysis of the operation of non-violent force, in terms of its property of non-retaliation, is fundamental in developing practical non-violent methods, and in developing a non-violent attitude and mental state.

Gandhi believes the soul's nature shows most clearly in this abstention from the return of violence for violence, and that therefore non-retaliation well represents his spiritual aim and ideal of self-realization within and without.

Though by non-violence and non-retaliation Gandhi primarily means a force, secondarily he means the method which uses that force to achieve practical ends. Gandhi's general term for these methods is "*satyāgraha*" which he uses also to connote the actual force of non-violence, the soul's force. His methods involve that mental state or attitude which can invoke and propagate this force.

Satyāgraha is based on this same metaphysics and moral ideology. It will be examined in detail in Section II.

5. *Not an Empirical Denotation.* It must be repeatedly stressed that for Gandhi mental and emotional movements are material. The quality of these indicates the presence or absence of non-violent force. Goodness, love and non-retaliation indicate its presence.

Gandhi believes that the quality of evil is a material quality which arises and resides in the mind, heart and senses. He believes that only a force whose origin is spiritual and whose power is greater than that of any material force can displace violence, the evil quality inherent in material existence.

Gandhi's methods do not work by rearrangement of material elements, but rather draw into action this spiritual force of the soul which alone, he claims, has the power to change the quality of human relations. He thinks of the non-violent struggle as taking place at the level of motives, intentions and beliefs. Because non-violent force is stronger and works at this level its use is Gandhi's solution to the perennial ethical problem of the inability of the human mind to curb its own passions (*akrasia*).

Gandhi believes his moral psychology studies the laws of invoking and directing the spiritual force of non-violence by means of practical activities. It studies the laws of transforming the subjective material elements and bringing them under direct command of the Spirit. Gandhi believes himself to have found in *satyāgraha* the beginnings of a science of this spiritual force. His program of experimental non-violent action was intended to systematically explore the application of soul-force to realize social and political ends.

6. *As Non-killing and Non-tearing.* For purposes of this study it is important to understand three senses Gandhi gives "*hiṁsā*": "killing", "killing by inches" and "tearing".

Though *ahiṁsā* translates literally as "non-killing", Gandhi explicitly denies that this means killing merely in the material sense of ending physical life, though it involves this as well. The life principle is Spirit, and "killing" or "injury" primarily refer to the soul, but the soul is imperishable so *ahiṁsā* cannot mean "non-killing". He defines *hiṁsā* as injury done or suffering caused, except if done for the wider benefit of the individual who would suffer the injury.

According to Gandhi's concept, severing the body from the soul, where no other remedy is available for ending that soul's suffering, is equivalent to amputation of a limb for the sake of the whole body. It is merely the extreme remedy for the soul's otherwise irremediable suffering. He also defines *himsā* as killing for the sake of the perishable body, which would include such activities as eating, breathing and occupying space, which he believes kills innumerable beings. He considers life to be a sacred principle, the reflection of the soul. He considers the life of all creatures to be of equal value.

Gandhi also speaks of "killing by inches", by which he means both obstruction of the soul's natural life and growth in the body and the resultant cumulative damage to the body. Terror, repression, humiliation, systematic false trade, starvation and chronic undernourishment constitute such "killing". These all involve tearing of the body and suffering of the soul since he believes that no matter is unendowed with soul, the life principle.

Essentially, whatever tears at one's material make-up, physical, emotional or mental, is "violence". Gandhi believes the soul has a total sensitivity and it will register even the least such tearing, which may be far below the threshold of empirical consciousness. The soul provides an absolute register and standard of violence and non-violence.

Gandhi believes that both a subtle grasping and an unconscious retaliatory will are intrinsic to even the slightest activity. Inherently restless material existence is characterized by tearing or violence.

Gandhi's view is tantamount to a doctrine of original sin since one is morally liable for the violent friction, tearing and killing involved in the very processes of life existence, viz. movement of air in the lungs, coursing of blood, sloughing of hair and nails, killing of cells.

According to Gandhi's view one is morally liable for the mere will to live (*abhiniveśa*), to have a body through which alone desires may be fulfilled. He is morally liable for all the killing and suffering that this desireful possession of the physical bodies entails. "Tearing" most clearly characterizes the quality of this embodied existence.

Though Gandhi uses "injury", "harm" and "suffering", rather than "tearing", this book will refer to *himsā* as tearing, an interpretation supported by Gandhi's usage and his texts.

By interpreting violence as a universal quality of material existence, by interpreting non-violence as an independent spiritual force and by conceiving the soul to be an "ideal observer" of these both, Gandhi makes of "violence" and "non-violence" ultimate moral categories. He believes that this ideal vantage point of his theory and

the categorical nature of his terms renders his moral ideology objectively valid.

Gandhi believes that though ultimately it is the quality of one's intentions that determines the quality and moral value of his actions, it
is only soul or God that can judge intentions accurately. According
to Gandhi's theory, purity of intention is determined by its non-
violence and its non-violence is known by the degree to which it pos-
sesses this non-tearing quality. Thus, ideally Gandhi's concepts are
defined by intentions and motives, but practically they are defined by
the quality of actions and results.

Gandhi's stated methods of action and thought are built on this
dual definition of non-violence. They are meant to minimize this
tearing quality in all material life by progressively purging it of violence. They are designed to induce this non-tearing quality of non-
violence into social relations and political institutions, as well as in
individual life. He believes this non-tearing quality will be conferred
on any material elements to the extent their activities are brought
about by soul-force.

7. *Defines a Moral Principle and a Social/Political Method.*   As a
moral principle, Gandhi's "non-violence" refers to the purification
and strengthening of the will by effort at non-retaliation and constructive work.

The flow of soul-force thus invoked cleanses and strengthens the
various elements of one's subtle material make-up. He believes that
this force uproots the violence-causing passions of self-interest, viz.
greed, anger, vengeance, malice, hate, lust, possessiveness, fear, despondency, etc. One is strengthened by the effort and exercise involved in the activities invoking this force.

Similarly, as a social/political means, "non-violence" refers to actions (usually corporate) intended to draw this force into interper-
sonal, intergroup and international relations. These relations are also
purged of the evils of self-interest as they appear corporately in communal intolerance, aggrandizement, exploitation, aggressiveness, imperialism, colonialism, hegemony, territorialism, expansionism, etc.
These relations are strengthened by building moral bonds of truth,
trust, non-violence, solidarity, loyalty, justice, respect, non-interfer-
ence, non-alignment, etc.

On the basis of his theory of Truth, Gandhi believes methods of corporate and international action should be modeled on individual and domestic ones.

In the social and political spheres non-violence involves the search for ways to bring about the "good of all" (*sarvodaya*) by means of corporate activity. He believes that since the principle of "the greatest good for the greatest number" stops short of "all", it necessarily entails violence to "some". On this conception a rigid application of the majority principle reduces to the principle of "might is right" which for Gandhi exemplifies the operation of brute force and violence in human affairs.

"The good of all", on the contrary, exemplifies the operation of soul-force. Gandhi thus contrasts the principle of utility with the principle of *sarvodaya* as moral criteria, and he proposes that "violent" and "non-violent" social methods be distinguished according to which of these two principles they draw upon to explain their operation or justify their use.

8. *Law, Efficacy and Moral Science.* Gandhi identifies "non-violence" as the "law of one's being" — or, the soul's natural action in oneself. It is a pervasive force which operates as the law describes, and its operation is describable by the same law throughout the field of material existence.

Gandhi equates this force with "God", "Life", "Goodness" and "Morals", claiming for this "Moral" law a conscious, self-active and intelligent quality (which he describes as a "conscious law") in which it seems the Law, the Lawgiver, and the Executive Power are "rolled into one". Thus according to Gandhi the entire universe is under moral government, and its law is not the narrow mechanical legislation of human concepts of justice but the expression of divine justice. The law of non-violence is the self-conscious and intelligent expression of the soul's omniscience and omnibenevolence. The force of non-violence is the expression of its omnipotence. These two cannot be separately understood.

Gandhi believes that morals without living faith in God are "lifeless" and that they cannot stand real tests. But true morals based on this living faith draw on the soul's force and so have an assured practical efficacy. He believes that knowledge of this law and its efficacy are matters for experimental verification and may thus serve as premises for developing a moral science. They are not products of mere speculative argument.

The moral law studied in this science simply describes the powers of the force of the soul, while the "law of non-violence" describes one of its powers as it pervades the material existence and governs all material activity. This power uniformly and invariably causes the existence to behave in the way the law describes. Gandhi formulates this law according to his metaphysics of action and his concepts of Truth and non-violence.

For Gandhi, the soul expresses its freedom through the moral law. Moral law overrides the operation of empirical law upon life and matter; the law of "return of good for evil" overrides the law of retaliation, viz. "an eye for an eye". If material reality were the only reality then all action could be made up of only retaliatory reactions to the other impinging material forces. But Gandhi conceives the soul to be a superior reality having the power to restrain these reactions by considering feelings and standpoints other than its own. It is this restraint that can be described in general terms as "moral law". As a practical doctrine Gandhi conceived non-violence as the law of the soul's freedom, acting in terms of which gives one power over practical reality. He calls this self-mastery or self-governance, "*swarāj*" (lit., self-rule).

According to the above arguments a component of practical efficacy is *logically* included in Gandhi's conception of non-violence as a spiritual and moral force. He claims that "superiority over physical strength, however overwhelming, is the core of *Ahimsā*,"[28] and that for any practical problem "if non-violence does not provide an effective antidote, it is not the active force of my conception," and he concludes, "non-violence is the supreme law."[29]

For Gandhi "law" connotes these characteristics of perfect objective validity, uniform operation and necessary efficacy of consciously applied soul-force. "Moral", for Gandhi, connotes this logical inclusion of a practical component. His non-violence is not merely the object of aesthetic or even ethical contemplation. The present attempt to gain a complete, clear and accurate depiction of his concept is thus essential for understanding Gandhi's practical methods, since, as will be seen in Section III, these derive from this practical component of his concept of non-violence.

9. *Denotes a Perfectly Non-coercive Force.* Gandhi's analysis is novel in collapsing the distinction between "violence" and "force" (he takes them as fundamentally the same phenomenon) while most accounts of violence and non-violence seek to consolidate it, emphasizing certain features exclusively specific to either term, the two terms denoting fundamentally different phenomena.

Gandhi conceives non-violence as absolute non-coercion because he defines "injury", and therefore "violence", in terms of the soul's inherent freedom and absolute sensitivity to the tearing inherent in pressures caused by the operation of material forces. He defines as "coercive" any pressures originating externally to the soul and operating against or in disregard to the soul's dignity, freedom and self-determination. "Coercion" is "violence to the soul".

Coercion is also invariably injury to the body, however subtle, since in Gandhi's conception of Truth it is axiomatic that the macrocosm without reflects the microcosm within. He therefore finds in coercion an inevitable tearing of the material being.

Finally, in coercion the material elements are forced from the activity and course of individual moral growth that would most naturally and harmoniously reflect and advance the spiritual development of the indwelling soul (*jīvātmā*).

10. *Denotes a Wholly Non-personal Force.* Gandhi believes that perfectly non-coercive action is possible only when one's activities have absolutely no personal end to gain. Personal interest contradicts the criterion of being motivated and guided only by the ideal of the "good of all", and so it is inherently "violent". According to Gandhi the "good of all" reflects the oneness of Truth, and personal interest reflects one's self-division from this moral unity.

Because non-violence is an inherently impersonal force, deriving as it does from the soul which is one and the same in all, it operates for the realization in all of this oneness of Truth. "Impersonal" in this context has no privative connotation.

11. *And the Conscious Discrimination of "Doer" and "Deed".* Gandhi believes that the force of non-violence is drawn into one's activities only where a constant discrimination between the "doer" and

his "deed", in all judgments and actions, has established in moral consciousness an active attitude of love and impersonal viewpoint of Truth.

The principles of action, non-retaliation, non-resistance and the "return of good for evil", that define *ahiṁsā* or Love, are not possible without this impersonal point of view and the active detachment that this discrimination makes possible. This discrimination is possible only as a result of a similar discrimination of "self" and "not-self" within one's own consciousness. The latter discrimination separates "cognition of self" from "identification with its temporary material vehicles".

In Gandhi's view, it is the realization of *ātman* (lit., self, soul) in oneself that alone enables one to effectively discriminate between the "doer" and "deed" in others. It is this discrimination which consequently gives the capability to non-violently engage the evil in the "deed" while loving and not-hurting the person, the "doer". Gandhi believes that this discrimination and attitude alone can enable one to maintain the poise and clarity that are necessary to see Truth and to persevere in the struggle to realize it in the midst of that engagement.

12. *Interpreted by Equating Non-violence with Consciousness.* Gandhi's "non-violence" may be defined as identical with "consciousness".

Carefulness, intensity of awareness and single-mindedness, are ordinarily equated with love. The expression "labor of love" evidences this connection of consciousness and love. The loving effort finds no work too great but seeks to give all the strength and attention the task demands.

The loving effort attends to the smallest detail of the task as to the largest. This effort at careful, non-injurious, quick, but firm action expands and sharpens consciousness, while conversely, the effort to expand and focus awareness automatically makes one more careful and less violent.

Gandhi believes that consciousness specially evolves by effort and attention put into active service of others. This type of activity particularly exercises the impersonal aspects of consciousness and brings into action the quality denoted by "love"—that quality of consciousness which Gandhi believes to be the result of the inundation of soul-force invoked by those activities of service of others.

This equation of consciousness with non-violence is a singular contribution by Gandhi to the theory of practical non-violence.

Gandhi is able, through his moral doctrine of the convertibility of ends and means, to discover in non-violence an active attribute of moral being which is also a moral quality of action. Because of the ends-means convertibility, this attribute and quality can be augmented by methods of practical action. The attempt to be more conscious in activity and relations automatically increases one's non-violence; one's efforts to be more non-violent, loving, careful and attentive in action automatically increase consciousness. These are two aspects of the same thing.

But even this equation must fail to capture the quality of love in its completeness.

Gandhi's theory collapses the distinction between "quality" and "quantity", but the identity of these two as one can only be acknowledged as the logical conclusion of theory and cannot be directly described. Gandhi believes that since love as non-violence is identical with Truth and God, it cannot be described by a language evolved only to explain things in relative terms, whereas these "qualities" of love and non-violence represent "absolute quantities".

In the next section, Gandhi's concept of non-violence as delineated above is examined from the standpoint of its practical application.

INTRODUCTION

For two reasons Gandhi's *satyāgraha* provides the necessary focus for examining his practical application of non-violence. First, *satyāgraha* is Gandhi's means of spiritual realization through practical activity. Second, as such it connects the material/practical and spiritual realities in terms of non-violence and soul-force.

Gandhi uses *satyāgraha* to achieve moral, social and political reform, which are all equally both religious reform and spiritual practice. His *satyāgraha* is distinguished from other methods of non-violence by its ideal of exact truthful and non-violent conduct, and by his radical practical claims for the universal applicability and perfect practical efficacy of that non-violent conduct.

This section has three chapters: Chapter 2 examines the spiritual basis of *satyāgraha*, its aims and principles, from the standpoints of the spiritual knowlege elaborated in the Upaniṣads, and of the theory of action presented in the Bhagavad Gītā. Chapter 3 examines the practical application of *satyāgraha*, first in terms of the general principles of its operation and its principles of action, and second, in terms of the ultimate translation of these principles to concrete methods and campaigns. Chapter 4 examines the components of Gandhi's practical claim in terms of the criteria by which he differentiates his from every other type of non-violence and by which he evaluates his own application of it in his *satyāgraha* actions.

2. *The Spiritual Basis of* Satyāgraha

This chapter has three sections: (A) Gandhi's aim, (B) *Satyāgraha* in the context of the Upaniṣads: Analysis from the standpoint of spiritual knowledge, and (C) *Satyāgraha* in the context of the Bhagavad Gītā: Spiritual analysis from the standpoint of action. The second and third sections are parallel in structure. First, they elaborate the aim from the standpoint of the Upaniṣads or the Gītā; second, they describe the condition to be overcome in the effort to realize that aim; third, they elaborate the principles of action that shape this effort; and fourth, they describe the problem of application that links that section with the development of the chapter as a whole.

Chapter 3 follows this same format and thus completes the exposition of *satyāgraha* from its most general basis, in a spiritual analysis of factual reality, to its final concrete expression in practical action.

A. GANDHI'S AIM

Gandhi's ultimate aim in all his activities is spiritual realization. *Satyāgraha* is the means by which he hoped ultimately to achieve that aim.

However, Gandhi's immediate aim was to establish an abiding thought current and disposition (*śraddhā*—lit., "faith"; what one holds onto; according to Gandhi, a vital faculty cleansing, whetting and informing disciplined reason from the supra-rational standpoint of the Spirit) which have the power to conduct one to this ultimate realization.

By "realization" Gandhi does not mean "knowledge" in the empirical or discursive sense. His aim is to come into possession of this spiritual awareness or thought current as a vital and permanent experience, not as a piece of information. This realization and faith are specific to the individual, and so essentially incommunicable. Gandhi believes that complete realization is in fact impossible in the embodied state. But since when Truth obtains means and ends are convertible, and inner and outer states reflect each other, therefore, the accurate and intelligent modeling of oneself and one's environs as an external counterpart of the spiritual reality within is a progressive means to the individual's spiritual self-realization. This produces in physical, emotional and mental life a progressive substitution of Truth for untruth and of soul-force for brute-force. The demonstration of superior moral and practical efficacy becomes for Gandhi a visible, measurable aim expressive of, and a means to, the primary inward spiritual realization, actually its exact outer counterpart.

The content and relation of these inner and outer aspects of Gandhi's spiritual aim are explained below.

Spiritual Realization: It is necessary first to understand the aim of spiritual realization that gives the content of Gandhi's entire work.

Gandhi describes the realization he seeks as self-realization, God-realization, realization of Truth and *mokṣa*. He says that such realization means essentially coming into a consciousness of reality which transcends that consciousness given by the five senses and the mind. It is therefore indescribable. This reality is recognized as permanent while all that the senses experience passes away. One who has this realization is more sure and more aware of that existence than of the contents of sensory experience. In contrast, sense experience seems an ephemeral, insubstantial and impotent superimposition on the surface of a changeless substantial potent reality.

Gandhi calls "faith" a faculty or "sixth sense" which can be progressively awakened into cognition of that reality by judicious training and purification.

Gandhi writes that this reality can be called "God" since it is self-active and all-pervading, more vital and more instinct with intelligence than the totality of sensory and mental life. It is possessed of an inborn bliss that is finer and superior to all sensory pleasure, or pleasure of the heart or intellect. It seems to be omnipresent, omniscient, omnipotent and omnibenevolent.

Gandhi ascribes to this Reality, known as God, the attributes of creator (*Brahmā*), and ruler (*Īśvara*). He describes It as a conscious law which combines in its operation intelligence, self-awareness and force, as if law, law-giver and executor were "rolled in one". He identifies this ruler with the sum of *karma* (action and consequences), creatures, or of life, immanent in all existence but also transcendent of it, and he describes It as a oneness or unity that subsists within and sustains all diversity, and that makes "kin" of all existences.

As law or supreme will, Gandhi calls this reality "Fate" that allows freedom of actions but reserves to itself power over results.

Gandhi sums up his conception as follows:

> This God whom we seek to realize is Truth. Or to put it another way Truth is God. This Truth is not merely the Truth we are expected to speak. It is that which alone is, which constitutes the stuff of which all things are made, which subsists by virtue of its own power, which is not supported by anything else but supports everything that exists. Truth alone is eternal, everything else is momentary. It need not assume shape or form. It is pure intelligence as well as pure bliss. We call it *Īśvara* because everything is regulated by Its will. It and the Law it promulgates are one. Therefore it is not a blind Law. It governs the entire universe.[30]

This Truth to be realized is also the God and the power that is the *satyāgrahī's* soul-force. Soul-force originates in that power. Its attributes define points of contact and linkage needed to bring that reality into practical relation with material life.

Each of these attributes is significant for *satyāgraha* because it inheres identically in soul-force which Gandhi asserts is the "decisive factor" in *satyāgraha*. Further, Gandhi structures the entire conception of *satyāgraha*, viz., doctrine, methods and application, on the notion of a living and potent link with this reality, either by direct realization or by cultivation of a vital faith that suppresses and surpasses the claims of sensory experience and mental dogma.

Gandhi believes that the only means to this realization is exact conduct based on the ideals of Truth and non-violence, progressively refined and strengthened by constant self-examination, application and correction in light of those ideals. For Gandhi this means is *satyāgraha*. "Satyāgraha" denotes an experimental inquiry into the form of non-violent exact conduct for solving every conceivable problem of human relations, and *satyāgraha* thus constitutes a *sādhanā* of *karma*, a means of spiritual realization through practical activity.

The non-violent, exact conduct of *satyāgraha* is physical activity the characteristics of which are ideally attributes of the state to be realized—qualities for which one is striving. According to Gandhi, the *sine qua non* of this realization is the establishment in consciousness of an equanimity (as is the *sthitaprajña*), peace and self-sustained joy.

Corresponding to this realization in consciousness is an accession to power and release of force that converts one's material make-up, influences the conduct of others and infects one's surroundings with the same qualities of equanimity, power and joy. This realizational and transformational capability of non-violent exact conduct is the potent core of *satyāgraha*.

"*Satyāgraha*" translates as "holding to Truth", to which Gandhi, as author of the term, adds, "in thought, word and deed" according to his concepts of Truth and non-violence. "Exact conduct" denotes the physical aspect of this "holding to Truth". As the focus of the entire concept and method, its practice changes one's attitude and outlook. The entire material existence and all practical activities become a vehicle both of the expression and the realization of God known as Truth.

Gandhi claims to see God face-to-face in the spinning wheel, service to the untouchables and the principle of Hindu-Muslim unity. Thus Gandhi believes that realization of Truth progresses in step with the widening scope of the practical application of non-violence through that exact non-violent conduct.

The form of this practical expression of realization is self-dedication in reform, redress and service, and in non-retaliation when these activities are resisted.

Demonstration of Practical Claims: A Progressive Substitution. Since for Gandhi the full realization of Truth is an eschatological problem, the focus for the study of *satyāgraha* must be on the means for its progressive approximation in material and practical life.

Because Gandhi's moral ideal of Truth requires that means and ends be convertible, the progressive effort to approximate the practical to the ideal by means of exact conduct will increasingly confer the ideal qualities of spiritual reality on the material elements and energies. Since spiritual Truth is all-inclusive, therefore its practical means should be universal and infallible. Thus an essential component of Gandhi's efforts for spiritual realization is the program to demonstrate that *only* the translation of non-violence to exact conduct and non-retaliation as *satyāgraha* is capable of the universal application and perfect practical efficacy implied in the progressive realization of Truth.

This radical practical claim constitutes the differentia between Gandhi's *satyāgraha* and all other methods of non-violent action. Non-retaliation as the chief expression and principal mechanism of soul-force applies without exception to all empirical dimensions of activity, so it provides the absolute core of exact conduct in *satyāgraha*. Physical non-retaliation is a visible *sine qua non*.

Gandhi stresses the difficulty of specifying this claim because of the number of unknown factors involved in any religious movement, the unanalyzable complexity of human action, the invisibility of the mass of spiritual effects and the lack of a defined means of measurement in spiritual matters. But Gandhi insists that *satyāgraha* holds true without exception or qualification, independent of any conceivable conditions of application.

Gandhi asserts that inapplicability is always the result of ignorance of the actual application conditions, and that faithful inspection of them and examination of oneself in terms of the ideals of Truth and non-violence will invariably reveal the true conditions. If these ideals are in fact the law of life as Gandhi believes, then he can know *a priori* that there will never be a set of material conditions, whether physical, psychological, social or political, for which exact conduct in terms of those ideals cannot be prescribed, and which would fulfill those conditions and bring the laws of Truth and non-violence into manifest practical operation.

Gandhi claimed that these principles are not his original discovery. The most ancient and time honored texts of all religions were based on the same laws. He only made new experiments with them on as vast a scale as possible. This effort merely constituted his mission to demonstrate their universal validity and thus to propagate their use. The critical debate over their validity centers on his extensions in the scope of the practical application of non-violence.

Gandhi believes that non-violence is a law not only for highly qualified spiritual practicants, but even more so for the common man. "Treat all as one's brother," could not be a command only for the specially qualified individual.

Gandhi extends this principle to include relations among groups and nations. He reasons that if it is the law of life, then it should be applicable everywhere and in any manner, towards anyone and through everyone.

Gandhi lists the fields of this extended experimentation as nonviolence against abuses by constituted authority, against dacoity and criminal culture, against communal conflicts and rioting and against invading armies. Self-defense, defense of one's ward or entrusted property and national defense are test cases since they involve direct jeopardy to one's own life, and since they imply the clearest and strongest opposition by overt violence.

Gandhi does not hesitate to claim that in these cases as well, nonviolent resistance is *more* efficient than the violent methods it replaces. Gandhi's claim is that *satyāgraha*, relying on soul-force, is a complete substitute for methods of violence relying on brute-force. To use these pure means for all practical needs is the simple way to progressively change the world by replacing untruth with Truth.

For Gandhi, this external aspect of spiritual realization, while no less important than its internal aspect, is subordinate to it as means to ends. The form of the means will change with circumstances and spiritual growth. Gandhi writes that his politics were a stage on his pilgrimage of spirit, and that his involvement in demonstrating the validity of non-violence in the political field was dictated by the fact that his work in social service and social reform involved him in politics and political reform. He states also that his politics were universal because they had to do with inner growth, and that being universal and operating at this fundamental level, they were naturally peculiarly effective. For purposes of the present study these external aspects are focal, though they can only be understood as an aspect of the wider spiritual realization and as means to the fulfillment of that spiritual aim.

To act effectively requires knowledge. In spiritual realization this knowledge must come from a knower who has realized that state to which the action is meant to bring one.

The basic sources for Gandhi's investigations were the Upaniṣads and the Bhagavad Gītā. According to Gandhi, the Upaniṣads provide a compendium of spiritual knowledge, and the Gītā elaborates the means by which that knowledge may be gained through practical ac-

26/ tion and daily activity. The Upaniṣads provide the root concepts of that elaboration.

B. SATYĀGRAHA IN THE CONTEXT OF THE UPANIṢADS:
ANALYSIS FROM THE STANDPOINT OF SPIRITUAL KNOWLEDGE

Gandhi viewed the Upaniṣadic texts as a record of their authors' experiments in the spiritual field. These are the oldest and most catholic such inquiries we have, and Gandhi considered their conclusions to be verified by the conforming experience of sixty years of his own research, and by the similar findings of numerous co-workers. Many by reason and experience have thought the Upaniṣads to report metaphysical investigations without equal, model philosophical and scientific treatises both in content and expression. Gandhi claimed that his *satyāgraha* merely continued the researches reported in those texts.

Gandhi speaks of his mission of non-violence and Truth as teaching the people to leave the ephemeral and seek the Real.

In these texts the distinction between the material and the spiritual translates as that of the ephemeral and the permanent or Real. The Upaniṣads teach what constitutes the Real, what constitutes the ephemeral and what is the relation between them.

This is the principal distinction for understanding Gandhi's metaphysical analysis of the realization of Truth and his metaphysical interpretation of logical principles that he uses to aid that realization through mental understanding.

Truth and Self: *Satyāgraha* is based on the Upaniṣadic analysis of reality as *ātmabrahma*, which Gandhi translates as *satya*, Truth.

There are two aspects of Reality: *ātman*, essential self-conscious reality, single but thought of as many from the point of view of the individuals who comprise its external but non-separate parts; and *brahman*, the "large" or "full" all-inclusive reality of the Absolute, also self-conscious but rather of itself as the Individual Whole, the Body composed of, and the materials composing, all the externalized *ātmans* (phenomenal individuals).

The key to the Upaniṣadic analysis of Reality is the identity of these two aspects and their total non-difference in ultimate reality, a transcendental identity undefinable except relatively through these two aspects. The key to Gandhi's *satyāgraha* is the set of logical principles that he derives from this identity, and the categorical difference between Truth and Reality thus realized and the finite truth and reality apprehended in empirical consciousness.

The basic features of Upaniṣadic reality as Gandhi perceives them are as follows: The eternality of the Absolute corresponds to the immortality of the soul; their realization as such is not the result of any *karma* (action) since the infinite and eternal reality cannot be seen by means of a finite and ephemeral body. They are therefore beyond good and evil (which are attributes of action), unless those actions are being judged good or evil relatively to realization of *ātmabrahma*.

The content of the realization of *ātmabrahma* is the consciousness of one's infinite self-existence as the Eternal, the Infinite, made of absolute power or existence, absolute intelligence or consciousness and absolute bliss, *sat-cit-ānanda*.

The Upaniṣads also analyze reality more abstractly as Being (*sat*) and not-being (*asat*), and as Truth (*satyam*) beyond these both. Gandhi considers Truth, *satyam*, to be the best designation of God or Reality. He finds *sat* the designation most useful for aiding his own realization, so far as this relies on preparation of consciousness by serious thought. To Gandhi, *satyam* comprehends all aspects of reality, i.e., spiritual, metaphysical, logical, psychological, scientific and ethical.

Gandhi derives his logico-metaphysical principles as follows: *ātmabrahma* can be pointed to only negatively as the complete or full Truth (*satya*) to which all contradictory predicates refer equally, but which is real beyond the grasp of any such dual notion (being and non-being), and so is essentially indescribable. Its unique logical status may be appreciated by the process of negating every possible predication by "*neti, neti . . .*" (not this, nor this . . .). His logical principles are derived from this inapplicability of any predicates because affirmation would exclude the predicates' opposite and inclusion of all contradictories is the logical property that is special and unique to *ātmabrahma*.

Through the Upaniṣadic equation of *ātmabrahma* the equation of the microcosm with the macrocosm becomes a fundamental principle of explanation and discovery. Gandhi takes the Upaniṣadic formula, *yathā piṇḍe tathā brahmāṇḍe*,—"as within, so without", "as the atom, so the universe", "as here, so there"—as the basic positive formula of Truth when Truth appears in dual or plural form, as it does to empirical observation.

From this principle the Upaniṣads derive the methods of scientific inference—knowing the large by examining the small, knowing the far by examining the near and knowing the unfamiliar by examining the known. They derive logical principles of analogy, negation, extrapolation and interpolation, and these become the central principles of spiritual investigation by reversing the direction of inquiry from outside to within.

Gandhi writes that all one needs to know is "as without, so within". The outer world may be known by looking within, since the same totality of Reality is comprehended in either direction.

Moreover, the totality is directly accessible only to consciousness within since only there is consciousness independent of the limiting adjuncts of the subtle material instruments of empirical knowledge and discursive understanding, viz., apperception and individuating ego-sense (*ahaṅkāra*), discriminating intelligence (*buddhi*), conceptualizing mind (*manas*), perceiving senses (*jñānendriya*), and motor senses (*karmendriya*).

Gandhi expressed his growing appreciation of the Upaniṣadic formula, *brahmasatyam jagan mithyā*, "Brahma, Spirit, alone is Real, True; all else, the World, is unreal, false". By affirming all value of Truth only to the Spirit and denying all value of Truth to the phenomenal reality, this formulation directly turns consciousness away from material limited reality towards the spiritual unlimited reality.

Since this equation is equivalent to the identity equation "as here, so there", one can substitute any empirical expression for world, and any attribute connoting changelessness or ultimacy or uniqueness or completeness, for *brahma*.

In each application of the formula, "*brahmasatyam . . .*" performs the function of "*neti, neti . . .*". Through any specific predication and knowledge content this formula annuls the entire empirical reality as essentially illusion while simultaneously affirming its substantial reality as no different from *brahma* known anywhere else through any other predicate and knowledge content.

By this process of logical substitution Gandhi translates the "material/spiritual" distinction to the "ephemeral/real" and "illusory/true" distinctions, and by the process of reversal and substitution, he constructs his concept of non-violence. These substitutions, positive and negative, are not merely abstract and logical, they are interpreted through the spiritual view of reality. In that view, the "violence" that is negated in the term "non-violence" refers to an entire category which includes all material existence, all phenomenal reality.

For Gandhi these logical principles provide a calculus for relating terms which are categorically distinct. The principles are useful for relating terms and for expressing and understanding metaphysical relations between different realities or modes of knowing. Analogy in this case is across categorical borders and the categorical nature of the negation is indicated by *all* logical procedures being reversed within the category. Substitution is of new *categorical* contents. The metaphysico-logical discovery or explanation then, is not between two contents of empirical consciousness but across categorical borders, between two entirely disparate modalities of consciousness; the new mode of comprehension established is one in which both categories are comprehended and the categorical difference is no longer fundamental.

Thus the Upaniṣadic logical principles Gandhi uses are metaphysically informative and create a potent current of faith, only when the primary term (the thing in its *brahmic* nature) is contemplated as unrealized by oneself though known by those who have realization, while the derivative term (the thing as empirically known), though familiar, is contemplated as essentially unknown.

Gandhi connects his aims of spiritual realization and the demonstration of his practical claim by a similar logico-metaphysical interpretation of the pragmatic distinction between ends and means. This interprets "*yathā piṇḍe* . . ." from the practical standpoint. From the standpoint of the ideal, all reality is one uniform, vital substance, and from that standpoint, whatever reality is comprehended as "means" will be found to be identical with whatever reality is comprehended as "ends". From the standpoint of Truth all predication, including "ends" and "means", is false.

According to Gandhi, if there is a Truth-relation between what is comprehended as "ends" and what is comprehended as "means", then these terms will by definition be convertible. We have discovered the self-same Truth under two translations related by practice and a pragmatic criterion.

Where "Truth" is the aim, what is "ends" and what is "means" will be merely a matter of orientation, and in a true "ends-means" relation both terms in fact designate the same ultimate reality, but through action-and-result considered as a term in the complete Truth-relation. Where there is no Truth-relation subtending the ends-means predication, the predication will merely be false and failure of convertibility will only indicate that one has not found a true ends-means relation but has imposed those terms without regard to Truth. The appropriate practical result cannot follow.

Gandhi's peculiar ideological interpretation adds to this spiritual pragmatism of the Upaniṣads the moral prescription of *satyāgraha* that one ought always to act so as to reveal in the "means" its intrinsic identity with the "ends", and so in every action to strive to manifest the truth of "*yathā piṇḍe . . .*", and "*brahmasatyam . . .*". This is the aim of his non-violent exact conduct.

Gandhi derives his program for the demonstration of his practical claims for non-violence from these considerations of the Upaniṣadic principles of Truth. By action in terms of true practical ends-means relations something of the Truth is manifested by success (*siddhi*), and in the theory of *satyāgraha*, this accumulating demonstration of practical success is inherent in the application of a pure spiritual principle. Truth is a force whose attributes include the power to unfailingly determine a true ends-means relation by action on true principles; this is the definition of Gandhi's morally exact conduct.

Thus Gandhi finds in the Upaniṣads a moral connection between one's orientation towards Truth and the means of spiritual realization. He writes that the materialist believes that desire makes one seek the knowledge which is necessary for its fulfillment; so the materialist believes that the multiplication of wants leads one progressively towards knowledge of the Infinite. The spiritualist believes just the opposite. He believes that no accumulation of finite empirical information can give realization of the Infinite. Reduction of wants, which by nature thrive on difference, is the correct preparation for realization of Truth. Truth reveals itself when there is not the empirical superimposition that desire inherently produces.

Although Gandhi derived the central means and core doctrines of *satyāgraha* primarily from the Gītā on the basis of logico-metaphysical analysis, he later believed that the first verse (*mantra*) of the Īśā Upaniṣad contains the essence of the Gītā and of all the Upaniṣads. He believed this single verse was the best means of teaching people Truth and non-violence. Gandhi interprets this verse as: "God has created out of himself all that there is and is himself its Ruler (*Īśvara*). Renounce it all, since it truly is not yours, and then you should enjoy what your Father will give you for your needs and duties. Do not covet the possessions of your brothers."

This interpretation of renunciation, and the logico-metaphysical extension of the spiritual fact that existing beings constitute a conscious family, are the two key bases of Gandhi's doctrine of realization and demonstration. Renunciation is prescribed as a means to a second birth into spiritual awareness inasmuch as it is intended to lead to a detachment from the entire empirical and illusory reality. To Gandhi the verse advises "trusteeship" of what is given, and its use in service of all as the means of this renunciation. The type of the renunciation is implied in the ideas of the brotherhood of man and the fatherhood of God, and in the principle of non-covetousness. The second birth attained by such renunciation is thus a birth into the one universal spiritual family.

In sum, the verse suggests a practical means to realize the Infinite. The means is renunciation based on an outlook that recognizes the facts of one's spiritual origins in Truth, or soul, and one's spiritual relation to all creation as one's family.

Human Condition of Ignorance: Without knowledge that there is a favorable state to be attained and that one is in a comparatively unfavorable state, no realization of a greater reality is possible.

Gandhi believes that the Upaniṣadic texts give the necessary impetus and direction. He believes that the arguments presented in those texts represent experienced, realized knowledge and have the flavor of reality. They bring one to conscious recognition of one's ignorance as a "plight", and they give faith in the possibility of a way of its amelioration. The texts give the assurance that "Truth (as the only reality) shall prevail" (*satyam eva jayate*).

Gandhi believes that serious and faithful study of the texts bring one to feel the need of disillusionment and transmit the triumphant quality of the declaration "*satyam eva jayate*"; this creates the current of faith that is the basis of *satyāgraha*. These all combine to create a real impetus and urge to reach those states and realize the Truth the Upaniṣads proclaim.

Besides knowledge of the state to be realized and recognition that one ought to realize it, the votary needs scientific knowledge of the condition he is in and what it is for that state to be negated.

The Upaniṣads describe the normal state of self-identity as the ego-complex of knowing, willing and feeling centered in the material elements of body, senses, mind and intellect. This ego state manifests as arrogation of individual existence and doership and as desire of possession.

Although the material elements of this complex successively dissolve at death, a subtle storage capability in the soul persists as the repository of experience (*karmasaṅskāra*) and qualities (*guṇas*) gained through these material vehicles. Experiences are assimilated and the "seed" of a new personality is put forth, suitable to the soul's further evolution. This causal structure creates a new ego structure (body-sense-mind-intellect-individuation complex). This structure connects up with a body appropriate to its *karmas* and continues its illusory experience as an ultimate separate entitative consciousness. The essence of this principle, is its creation of ignorance of the fundamental reality and identity as *ātmabrahma*.

Gandhi accepts this account of transmigration and the perpetuation of illusion. He defines *mokṣa*, liberation, as the culmination of realization of one's true status as soul. This recognition has the power to cut through the ego-centered illusion and annul the consciousness which identifies itself with the structures whose laws of transformation constitute the process of transmigration. The state of ignorance and illusion depends on maintaining and periodically reconstituting the provisional ego structure.

Gandhi notes that this recognition is essential to *satyāgraha* because one cannot have use of his own soul-force if he has no vital recognition of his spiritual status. He is like the "lion raised among lambs" and so cannot resort to his true lion-nature even for self-defense.

The primary illusion and cause of its continuation is the belief that one is himself the doer of action, and is therefore, by the law of *karma* (conservation of energy and quality), perpetually entangled in nature's reactions to his actions.

The law of *karma* says that for the entire category of material or phenomenal reality, characterized by constant motion of actions and qualities, every action has its opposite and equal reaction, all forces of any transaction are conserved in the resultant; and in any transaction, quality is preserved through the chain of actions and consequences.

The soul, by means of the ego-body structure, misidentifies itself with some point in the causal nexus and believes itself to be an originator of actions. This creates innumerable relative points of view and agency in the material field. They are sustained by that illusion in consciousness which causes the misidentification. This misidentification allows the flow of the soul's force, the power of reality, to repeatedly cause to coalesce an ego-agent structure. This structure in turn propagates actions that conserve its energies in binding reactions and transferences of qualities. Thus the soul continues in the illusion.

Gandhi believes that recognition of the nature of this moving and changing reality and especially of the triviality of its isolated passing events, is "more than half the battle" in re-identifying with one's true nature and escaping the illusion of separate mortal existence. Study of this knowledge given by the Upaniṣads accomplishes this change in both perception and outlook and thus gives new values and feelings, and, consequently, a new orientation towards reality and a new basis to action and practical life.

This dis-illusionment and reorientation based on the deeper facts of individuality, personality and evolving soul, is a significant second step in the process of spiritual realization.

Experience and Experiments: To Gandhi, *satyāgraha* is a continuation of the line of researches represented in the Upaniṣads so far as they are guides on a path of progressive realization that is essentially experimental and experiential in nature. The texts present a mounting awareness of more comprehensive, deeper and subtler realities, and a liberating culmination. They present a map of the progressive stages leading to that realization.

Gandhi considers these texts to be uniformly testable by reason and experience, since they are based on reason and experience, and to be scientific since they lead to uniform spiritual experience when similarly applied. He asserts that this general validity of the texts is demonstrated by the uniform transformation in the conduct of those who, with a critically reasoned faith, apply those texts to their daily lives.

Gandhi thus believes that without applying this knowledge to pursuit of Truth in activity, there is no occasion to pursue or to swerve from Truth, and so there is no occasion to test one's realization and apprehension.

Though what Gandhi calls Truth is by definition eternal and its laws uniform and unchanging, its correct application is always a matter for fresh experiment. Material reality is by nature constant activity, changing quality and ephemeral structure. Application conditions and the actual operation of Truth must be a matter of judgment and discovery so long as one is embodied and identified with the ego-agent complex as the doer of actions in such a material field.

Need to Apply on Basis of a "Science" of Action: Since *satyāgraha* assumes as its starting point the Upaniṣadic analysis of the condition of illusion and progressive disillusionment (and not the culminating [infinite] realization of *Satya* [Truth and *ātmabrahma*]), it is Gandhi's program for continuing the Upaniṣadic researches, specifically from the point of view of action used as the means to realization.

Gandhi considers the Bhagavad Gītā to be a commentary on the Īśā Upaniṣad, in that it shows how to give "eternal verities" active shape in practical actions that lead to spiritual realization. The problem in devising *satyāgraha*, defined from the Upaniṣadic point of view, is thus the metaphysical and scientific problem of substituting the real for the ephemeral by means of practical activity.

C. SATYĀGRAHA IN THE CONTEXT OF THE BHAGAVAD GĪTĀ:
SPIRITUAL ANALYSIS FROM THE STANDPOINT OF ACTION

Gandhi based his *satyāgraha* explicitly on the Gītā. He studied it daily for almost sixty years, and he considered the Gītā to be his "dictionary of conduct".

But Gandhi did not find in the Gītā a "code of conduct" to be

blindly applied. To him the Gītā gives the findings of an "experienced Krishna", both a king and as The Master of Yoga (union) of
the Vedic-Upaniṣadic tradition.

These findings take the form of an analysis of the state to be realized, the realities to be spanned, the human condition of bondage
and the universal principles of action, *anāsakti* (non-attached action)
and *yajña* (action of sacrifice).

Gandhi believes that this analysis, similarly to that of the Upaniṣads, is presented as universal and scientific findings based on realizable fact. They cannot be correctly interpreted aside from application
and experience in the medium of action. He believes that here, as in
any matter of Truth, experience is the final guide and criterion, and
he claims to cite only verses the Truth of which he himself had realized in experience.

Gandhi claims that his doctrines of *satyāgraha*, though originally
derived from the Gītā and the Upaniṣads, stand on their own, independently of the texts, as any reasoned and scientific knowledge
must do. He cites the canons of trained and sober reason, of disciplined and refined moral sense when reason can be applied (and he
notes that all practical action is such), and of faith in the uniform experience of trusted guides or companions where understanding involves states of awareness not accessible to mind and intellect in
their present state of evolution, or to senses where facts are not de-
ducible from phenomenal experience.

In applying the Gītā analysis for his *satyāgraha* investigations,
Gandhi gives a moral interpretation of the distinction between the
ephemeral and the real by equating evil with the ephemeral and material, and good with the real and spiritual.

The Gītā is a 700-verse text set in the 100,000-verse Mahābhārata
(Great War of the Bhāratas) epic.

Gandhi interprets this epic as an allegory of the ascent of the soul
through its history in human evolution. To him it represents the
battle between the forces of good and evil that incessantly goes on
within the individual.

This inner moral battle is the context in which *satyāgraha* must be
understood since it is from this battle of good with evil that Gandhi
evolved the doctrine and method of *satyāgraha* as a means to realize
the state beyond good and evil, beyond the life and state of alternat-
ing happiness and suffering. Since the battle is within and perpetual,

the Gītā's principles must apply to every act, and the exact conduct of *satyāgraha* must be based on these same principles.

Argument of the Gītā: The Gītā depicts the beginning of the great war to save justice and civilization, in which the protagonist, Arjuna, a prince and a chief warrior for the forces of justice, shrinks on seeing his nearest relations, teachers and friends in the opposing army. The Lord Kṛṣṇa is his charioteer and guide.

Arjuna is required by duty, as warrior in a righteous war (*dharmayuddha*), to kill these relatives, companions, teachers and elders.

Arjuna brings the arguments that those he would have to kill are those for whom alone he would want to win the kingdom. His victory would serve no purpose and lose all taste from his standpoint. Killing one's relatives is the worst of sins. Its consequences would be ruin of the family and destruction of custom, tradition and the total moral order that rests on the family structure and kin affinities. There could be no justification for this sin considering consequences both for himself and for the social order. Even if the enemy were guilty, it is out of ignorance. The wise, knowing better, should rather accept death without resistance as a nobler course. Arjuna appeals to Kṛṣṇa for guidance. But the bow slips from his hands and he says he cannot fight.

Kṛṣṇa upbraids him as a coward in order to bring him back to his real character and to awaken him to his duty as a warrior for the side of right, who must fight without regard to personal ties. Kṛṣṇa gives a short argument from the Upaniṣads to relieve Arjuna from guilt of sin that he believes would result from killing kin. The soul is immortal and untouched by any action while bodies are continually born and destroyed in the natural course of things. The knower neither slays nor is slain; only bodies kill and are killed. All embodied beings will die. Arjuna, performing his duty, fighting for justice at the threat of its annihilation from the world, will not only not sin and incur demerit in the present war, but he will have glory in heaven if he dies fighting, and victory and glory on earth if he wins.

Sin and ignominy lie rather in abandonment of duty and righteousness. The real moral order is sustained by duty and justice, not by institutions among bodies. Hence there is only the fight to be carried through. Arjuna should take pleasure and pain, loss and gain,

victory and defeat, as equal, and fight. These all belong to the body
and have no lasting value. They only cloud the apprehension of duty
and right.

Kṛṣṇa promises Arjuna also that this fight with the attitude of detachment in duty is not only not sin, but it is right action in this
world, and it is the means of realizing the supreme state beyond all
opposites, beyond all qualities and beyond all activity and bondage
of the three modes (*guṇas*) of phenomenal existence. These modes all
attach only to the body and not to the soul.

Kṛṣṇa enunciates the key principle of the *sādhanā* or *yoga* of
karma (means to realization by action): "Your right is to work only,
but never to the fruit thereof. Let not the fruit of action be your object, nor let your attachment be to inaction"[31] (Gītā II:47). Kṛṣṇa
tells Arjuna that equanimity, sameness towards all material concomitants and consequences of action, frees one from bondage and brings
him to the "blissful supreme state of *brahma*."

Battle Within: Origin of Conflict and the Means of Dissolving It:
On the basis of his logical principle "*yathā piṇḍe . . .*", Gandhi
equates the outer and inner moral battles. But on the basis of his
moral ideology, he gives the equation a bias and says that the "real"
battle is within, and that the Gītā does not teach fighting war as
such. It teaches self-examination and struggle with one's ego-desire
self.

Gandhi interprets the opening scene of the Gītā as depicting the
origin of conflict. Arjuna does not refuse to fight on principle but
from attachment to his relatives and friends. Gandhi writes in his
commentary on the Gītā that the root of evil is the ego-sense which
puts pride of self, "I", and pride of possession and power, "mine",
behind all acts.

The Gītā locates the seat of evil in the mind, intellect and senses.
Gandhi says that the root of sin is ignorance of one's true nature as
soul beyond sin. To be beyond sin is to be rooted in that true nature
and therefore to be unswayed by the activity of intellect, mind and
senses that are most often merely the vehicles for realizing the claims
of "I" and "mine". Gandhi finds these claims to be the cause of all
conflict. The empirical "I's" contend over ephemeral objects that by
nature cannot be possessed equally and simultaneously by two "I's"

who each wants to enjoy them exclusively. It is the ego-sense that imposes the distinction between "relatives" and "strangers" or the "enemy".

This corresponds to the tendency in the human mind to like or dislike, to be attracted or repulsed, on an arbitrary basis, due to the narrowed focus of consciousness and reason. Gandhi believes that the solution to this conflict is ridding the mind and senses of their in-born tendencies, thus removing the ego's imposition of "I" and "mine" that sustains and is sustained by those tendencies.

If the origin of conflict is this indiscriminate and arbitrary distinction and untruth, partiality and injustice, then the means of its resolution is the establishment of Truth wherein all interests are viewed and protected equally.

Gandhi finds in the Gītā's theory of action the science of materially accomplishing this substitution of Truth (Peace) for conflict.

Human Condition of Bondage: Arjuna's dejection and despondency are the result of a confusion about duty. It comes from ignorance. Duty as the Truth of action and relations is clear so long as there are no personal considerations. Duty is spontaneous. But when there is an upsurge of ego and desire which is not in accordance with Truth, confrontation and conflict result—usually bolstered and augmented on both sides by untruth and self-deception, as reason aligns with ego to justify desire.

Action is demanded by circumstances and by Arjuna's previous actions and commitments, but because of attachment his energies go out of balance with Truth, inner complexity is created, he is bound to the extent of paralysis and cannot act.

In such circumstances the human condition of bondage becomes evident. For Gandhi the importance of the Gītā is in its demonstration that the natural condition of *all* human action is perpetuation of bondage in ignorance born of ego and desire.

As in his interpretation of the Upaniṣads, Gandhi notes that the first condition of seeking knowledge is recognition of ignorance, of one's condition of bondage and of the need for liberation. The Gītā depicts this same state from the standpoint of action and of the common experience of conflict between duty and desire.

Fear and attachment predominate in this state of ignorance even

when there is no overt conflict between the demands of duty and desire. The elements of the ego-desire complex are never at rest; conflict is their nature, and visible violence is incipient, maintaining a
constant subliminal tension always on the verge of manifesting (Gītā
III:4–5).

The Gītā teaches the method of renunciation, as does the Īśā
Upaniṣad, for escaping bondage and realizing Truth.

Gandhi finds that, in both the Upaniṣads and the Gītā, knowledge
completes action and only action based on Truth can accomplish its
projected purposes. Likewise, the acts of renunciation of the Īśā
Upaniṣad and the Gītā are only effective when there is knowledge of
the deeper and wider factors involved in the action.

What is true of the physical aspects of action is true equally of the
spiritual aspects, as indicated by *"yathā piṇḍe . . ."*. Renunciation
can only be effective if there is knowledge of the state to be attained
by the renunciation, knowledge of the relation between that state
and the present one and conscious self-awareness of what constitutes
the renunciate or sacrificial character of one's action.

A fundamental fact for *satyāgraha* in the Gītā's science of action is
that not only the content of knowledge, but even more so the state
of the subjective material make-up of the knowing faculties is the
determining factor in the outcome of an action. The quality of the
knowledge-state, and its material activity, are the basis of the overt
physical movements.

In Gandhi's interpretation of Truth, if Truth obtains, the two are
actually aspects of the same reality; when the subjective material
state is not a knowledge-state, and more than an habitual response is
called for by circumstances, states of dejection and paralysis are the
natural result. The Gītā's purpose is to inculcate the knowledge and
wisdom needed to prevent this condition. This understanding functions in the process of realization itself and Gandhi notes that without practice and experience it does not become a part of the subjective make-up. A dogmatic understanding cannot make it a vital part
of the subtle subjective material state and therefore an effective
factor either in practical reason or in the action. Building of the
knowledge-state and the true knowledge content are one and the
same process.

The Gītā gives a categorical analysis of the phenomenal field in
which all activity has its origin and propagates its effects. Based on

this characterization of the whole field as a singular unit, the Gītā then gives an analysis of the state of non-doership and the detached mode of action that achieves it (Gītā XIII).

In the Gītā there are five main analyses of the condition of bondage that are important from the standpoint of *satyāgraha*. Each analysis presents a basic phenomenal distinction through which one is liable to attach himself in mind, senses and action to material formations or through material complexes.

Liberation is described for each distinction as non-attachment from that point of view through the two fundamental characteristics of *sthitaprajña*—evenness of temperament and equality of treatment, with regard to all that is described under that distinction.

The fundamental mechanism of bondage is always ignorance of the true nature of the binding elements and processes and of the way they are actually operating in the individual and the situation, and of the reactive mode of action that this ignorance sustains. The final means of release is always realization of the reality beyond this condition by detachment with knowledge and faith.

In *dvandvabandha* (bondage in dualities), emphasis is on the role of mental and sensory likes and dislikes as determinants in action. One is swayed by hot and cold, pleasure and pain, success and failure, virtue and sin, merit and demerit, honor and dishonor, etc. Truth cannot be known where these dualities pull the understanding in different directions. These are characteristics of merely individual states and actions and therefore create forces contrary to those of non-individuated reality. One who is established in *ātman*, in Truth, is *nirdvandva* (without dualities) and is called a *yogī* (one who is self-controlled and even-minded towards all dualities).

In *prakṛti/guṇabandha*, *prakṛti*, primal matter of which all phenomenal reality is made, binds one through the three exclusive and exhaustive qualitative energies (*guṇas*) which constitute it. The *guṇas* (*sattva*, knowledge, clarity, harmony, happiness; *rajas*, doubt, confusion, activity, passion; *tamas*, ignorance, darkness, inertia, sloth) give rise to desire and anger, which in turn give rise to actions (*karmas*) that involve one in endlessly ramifying reactions with material reality.

The Gītā gives general and complex analyses of action, conduct and knowledge in terms of the *guṇas*. It analyzes the empirical ego as a material formation sustained by a concatenation of forces which may be described in terms of the proportions of these *guṇas*. The ego and passions appear to be causes, but are themselves only limited movements (*vikāra*, modifications, evolutes) of the *guṇas* of *prakṛti*. These in turn are produced and controlled by the divine *māyā* (creative power and delusion, mystery).

The *puruṣa* (experiencing consciousness; soul) is bound in actions only by its ignorance of its own nature as separate from *guṇaprakṛti*, the medium in which actions take place. It is a part of the Supreme Reality who is the true cause behind the movement of the *guṇas*. One is free when one sees that the *guṇas* act out of their own nature as moved and directed by *Īśvara*. One whose consciousness is centered above the activities of the *guṇas*, (*guṇātīta*) (Gītā XIV:25), is free from the bondage of action, embodiment and birth.

Satyāgraha is based on the surrender and nullification of ego. This nullification, according to Gandhi, allows God's plan and power to work manifestly through the *satyāgrahī*. Gandhi derives this doctrine directly from the Gītā's analysis of action as the independent interplay of the *guṇas* and material forces. This analysis is repeated many times in the Gītā in order to make clear from many points of view, the principle of the non-doership of the soul.

This argument is summed up in the concluding chapter of the Gītā. Gandhi gives the core of the analysis as follows:

> There are three things that inspire action: knowledge, the object of knowledge, and the knower. And there are three constituents of action: the organ, the deed, and the doer. The thing to be done is the object of knowledge; the method of doing it is the knowledge; and he who knows is the knower. After he has thus received an impulse to action, he performs an action in which the senses serve as instruments. Thought is thus translated into action.[32]

The possible forms of interactions of these elements are described in terms of the three *guṇas*.

Thus if one is truly the soul, then he is free to separate himself from bondage in the circle of *karmas* by realizing that the ego really is no cause of results at all.

Gandhi completes his paraphrase of the argument in terms of the analysis of the causes of action and consequences:

> He who does not abandon the fruits of action, must enjoy or put up with the natural consequences of his own acts, and is thus a bond-

slave for ever. But he who gives up the fruits of action, achieves freedom.

And why should a man feel attachments for action? It is idle for anybody to imagine that he himself is a doer. There are five causes for the accomplishment of all actions, namely, this body, the doer, the various instruments, efforts, and, last but by no means the least, Providence.[33]

The last cause, Providence, is at the center of Gandhi's *anāsakti* and *satyāgraha*.

Gandhi writes repeatedly that no action is complete aside from God's completion of it. The activity of the ego-body complex is only a reflection of the divine will. The divine will, "the Inscrutable One" here called "Fate", is the sum of incalculable other factors that conspire to produce any given resultant of action.

Gandhi concludes:

Realizing this, a man should give up pride. He who does something without egoism, may be said to be not doing it in spite of his doing it, for he is not bound by his action . . . a humble man, has reduced himself to zero.[34]

Gandhi describes the full state as spontaneity in which all action is natural, egoless and un-self-conscious, like the blink of the eye, or better, like digestion.

God alone is the cause of all action and producer of all results (only the omniscient and omnipotent could balance the totality of effects to the "good of all" through the actions of each, and thus manifest His omnibenevolence).

The soul can realize this by contemplating the Truth and giving himself in service as God's instrument, acting selflessly for the needs of all.

This contemplation replaces all ego-originated inspiration and impetus to action. Its complete form is realization of identity in and with the Divine, for whom this is the natural mode of action.

The analysis and contemplation of the field of bondage, the relation of causes of *karmas* to results, and the awareness of God's doership, give the knowledge and perspective that are a potent aid for realizing the state of non-doership, viz., self-realization.

Gandhi puts this analysis of non-doership in terms of the Gītā's analysis of reality as the Field, or body, and its Knower (*kṣetra-*

kṣetrajña) (Gītā XIII). The field, *kṣetra*, is the material body, subjective and objective. It is the form that the *guṇas* and the pairs of opposites, *dvandva*, take when considered from the standpoints of cosmology and psychology. *Kṣetra* is comprised of the elements, senses, mind, intellect, ego, undifferentiated material substratum (*avyakta*), and empirical and discursive consciousness with its modifications, viz., desire, dislike, pleasure, pain, coordination of functions, cohesion of elements. These structures and phases of the phenomenal field are analyzed in terms of the *guṇas* and the pairs of opposites. The field, the *guṇas*, the *dvandvas* and *karmas* are all *vikāras* (modifications) of *prakṛti* (undifferentiated material stuff).

The "knower of the field" is the *jīvātmā* or individuated embodied soul. The Supreme Reality is the knower in all the fields, *Paramātman*; the highest soul or state, *Puruṣottama*.

This is the Knower who ought to be known. Knowledge is constituted of those "states of character" which lead to recognition of the changeful and painful nature of the field, dampen reactions from without, and produce steadiness in the material make-up within (*sthitaprajña*). These states are virtues, attitudes and disposition which have, as an actively motivating component, knowledge of the comparative nature of the knower and the field—freedom from pride, non-violence, forgiveness, uprightness, steadfastness, self-restraint, aversion to sense objects, absence of attachment, unwavering devotion to *Īśvara*, etc. These are all forms of renunciation of the field.

A further analysis to which Gandhi attaches special significance is the Gītā's description of the field of bondage as the *aśvattha* tree of sense objects rooted in *brahma* above, but nourished by the *guṇas* and endlessly ramifying in the form of the worlds below, sustained by the same attachment, desire and actions (Gītā XV).

The Gītā advises that this tree is to be cut down by the "weapon of detachment". Gandhi translates this as the "weapon of non-cooperation," the principle method of his *satyāgraha*.

Lastly, the sense of dependence on God's power that is basic to *satyāgraha* is given form by several enumerations of all the things (*vibhūti*) in these worlds that the Lord has become and that specially manifest His creative power, *māyā*. Without knowledge of the superintending Deity, all the *vibhūtis* are thought themselves to constitute the field. But contemplating the fact that all things as *vibhūti* are expressions of divine power, the ego-sense and doership are extirpated (Gītā VII, IX, X, XV).

The Gītā defines the mechanism of bondage in moral terms of the form of sin as that which causes the ignorance which allows material reality to bind. Attachment (*rāga*), aversion (*dveśa*), desire (*kāma*), anger (*krodha*) (Gītā III:37), lust, greed and ego cause action to be based on false views and thus lead to binding actions. In this view, sin really reduces to ignorance; nevertheless, Gandhi maintains the contemning moral force of the word "sin".

According to Gandhi, the Gītā represents the human condition as one of struggle. But the struggle outside, in which Arjuna represents the cause of justice, only mirrors the struggle inside, in which Arjuna is the soul failing to stick to the duty of defending justice because of personal partiality.

The analysis of the field and release applies equally to both aspects, inner and outer. The path of realization in the Gītā is the way of struggle in human action, and Gandhi believes there is a law of struggle in the spiritual world just as there is in the physical. But the spiritual struggle is with one's own nature, by the soul on the path of its ascent.

The Gītā teaches progressive *abhyāsa* and *vairāgya* (devoted practice and dispassion) (Gītā VI), based on *ātmānātma-viveka* (Gītā II) (discrimination of soul/not-soul), and *mārga-viveka* (Gītā VIII) (discrimination between the paths of liberation and bondage, good and evil). The human struggle, therefore, is to attain an even temperament, a steady mind, as the condition of realization and of practical mastery, and of the success which follows and reflects it.

Understanding Gandhi's method of the struggle requires the preceding analysis of this condition of struggle and bondage in terms of the field. Gandhi constantly writes in these terms.

Anāsakti and Yajña: The ideal *satyāgrahī* is the Gītā's ideal of the *sthitaprajña*, "man of steady wisdom". Gandhi finds the means to attain this state in the practice of sense control.

But according to Gandhi's true ends-means relation, *sthitaprajña* must refer to both an end state and a means. As a state it represents realization of Truth itself, the ideal state of detachment from all material evolutes, energies and activities, *anāsakti*. As a means it is the struggle for sense-control based on the moral analysis of bondage through the senses. Fundamental to the analysis of *satyāgraha* as a weapon of self-purification is the Gītā's analysis of the moral psychology of desire and sense-life, detailed above.

In the Gītā's analysis of the attached state there is an escalation of self-tearing which leads to self-destruction (Gītā II:62–63).

By brooding on objects of sense, attachment is born. This special contact repeats itself as there is occasion and becomes desire, an active seeking. This desire, inevitably and invariably frustrated, turns back on itself to become anger. Anger clouds the mind and leads to stupefication, which leads to loss of memory. Loss of memory disables reason, and with destruction of reason, the individual is destroyed (Gītā II:62–63).

The point at which to break the chain is at the level of the senses before attachment develops. Control of the senses is the recommended practice to break the chain and make reason steady. But this self-control is known to be a very difficult and dubious process. The Gītā says even the wise are swept away by the sense currents. We are born with and develop sensory and mental tendencies or habits before the process of self-control can begin.

It was previously noted that desire and anger are the causes of sin, even for one who knows their nature. They are constituted of the *guṇas* and reside in the organs of knowledge which are also constituted of *guṇas*. The goal is to reach beyond the *guṇas*, but the organs of knowledge and of action are constitutionally incapable of this emancipation.

The Gītā solves the dilemma by pointing out the paths of knowledge and devotion. If one constantly turns the mind to remembrance of *Īśvara*, it cannot get stuck in the objects of sense. By the law of *puruṣakāra-karma*—you become what you do, believe, or yearn after—whose exercise is *abhyāsa*, devoted practice, this remembrance would bring vision of that Divine Reality. That realization has the power to burn up the ego structure and the lower tendencies that it supports.

Further, the Gītā ranges the subjective organs strategically in an ascending order and advises their progressive enlistment in the fight against sin. The senses (*indriyas*) are more subtle and powerful than sense objects; the mind (*manas*) more subtle and powerful than the senses; the intellect (*buddhi*) more subtle and powerful than the mind; desire, the enemy, is subtler and more powerful even than this *buddhi*. But the soul is the "subtlemost" and most powerful reality, and by confidence, or faith in oneself, the force of the soul can be drawn down and used to attack the enemy, desire and anger, in his camp, the mind, intellect and senses, and to destroy the subjective convolutions and complexes in which those tendencies and qualities inhere (Gītā III:42–43).

But one who is constantly called upon to act in daily life may not be able to develop this practice. Gandhi says that the Gītā prescribes renunciation of the fruits of action as a universal duty, and as the means to achieve the state of detachment. He claims that this striving is man's sole obligation. It is in this state that soul-force becomes the natural instrument of action and of spiritual realization and a part of one's constant consciousness as such.

Anāsaktiyoga: The Gospel of Selfless Action, is Gandhi's interpretation of the Gītā's doctrine of renunciation. The votary renounces the fruit of his actions and thus exhausts the externally binding, material interests since their continued strength requires the exercise of pursuing those fruits. The votary completes the external renunciation by dedicating the actions to *Īśvara*. He renounces his internal makeup as well by the attitude of surrender of mind and soul to *brahma* (*brahmasamārpaṇa*).

In its positive form, detached action consists of *yajña*, sacrifice. This is the principal concept in the Gītā's analysis of nonbinding action, or action that leads to realization. The Gītā states that *only* action for sacrifice does not bind (Gītā III:9). The ego-sense limits interest to satisfaction of material inclinations of the individual structure. This is a denial of Truth.

The Gītā's analysis of the field, *kṣetra*, includes the fact that with creation of material existence sacrifice was born as the inherent tendency and urge to interdependence. The movement of *prakṛti* is a reflection of the total benevolence of its creator. Every movement is geared to the benefit of all. The laws by which actions bear fruit and bring knowledge inhere in nature and consciousness. According to Gandhi, action that accords with that law and will is service to the entire creation. Action prompted by the ego-sense is necessarily in conflict with the law of sacrifice and operates to favor only the individual.

Only action devoid of ego-sense will exhaust its energies in the act

since such action will address the fullest reality of its field and objective. When ego interferes, most of the energy of the action will be
only incidental to the ego's intentions, and its actions will so far
draw reactions, not foreseen nor prepared for, and these will necessarily bind the doer in externality. This is the self-bondage of attachment to material consequences of action for which one has to remain
embodied or take up new bodies that can receive these consequences
and exhaust the potentialities created by earlier actions.

Gandhi finds in the Gītā the *satyāgraha* doctrine of self-purification by which the votary seeks to reduce the ego-sense to zero and
become an instrument of the divine will.

This requires the intelligent renunciation and the obedience to divine law that lifts consciousness to the realized state of *anāsaktiyoga*,
the detached soul. This state makes action the spontaneous response
of the subjective organs and body to the divine will which is presiding over every force that impinges on them. Gandhi considers the
process of conscious sacrifice, the balanced use of mental, physical
and spiritual faculties in service of all, to be the *sine qua non* of the
path of self-purification, the ascent to knowledge and the final realization. He finds here the practical means to realize the first verse of
the Īśā Upaniṣad.

Anāsakti and *yajña* form the inner and outer conditions of unerr-
ingly perceiving and following duty. Action stemming from duty is
action that reflects the Truth. One follows the method of renunciation of fruits by assuming the attitude of detachment and sacrifice in
which there is no scope for personal consideration of consequences
and concomitants. Duty or Truth become the natural mode of one's
activity.

Yajña has value because in it means and ends are convertible. It is
self-sustained and self-contained action. The key is renunciation of
fruits (*Anāsaktiyoga* No. 14 & 15). Sacrifice is both a means to realization and the reflection of that realization when it is achieved as
the end. If there is desire for fruit, e.g., reward for virtue of sacrifice
or duty, then the action loses the quality it was valued for—convert-
ibly both means and end of realization, Truth—there is now an extraneous end involved. Such an action does not fulfill the definition
of Gandhi and the Gītā as inspired by modes of knowledge able to
purify action of its binding capabilities.

It is significant for Gandhi's ideology and *satyāgraha* that in the

Gītā's analysis of action as sacrifice, sacrifice is continued after realization of the end (Gītā III:20–26). Sacrifice is thereafter purely a means for corporate realization, while it had been only partially so on the way to the individual's realization. Realization is not the end as such. A basic principle of *satyāgraha* is propagation of Truth, directly via the inner state of the realized actor, and indirectly via external apprehension by the unrealized votary and opponent. The Gītā teaches the propriety of continuing to act on the means even when the ends seemed to have been realized. Similarly, according to Gandhi's ideology, since detachment and duty are part of the means of sacrifice and devotion, conversely they aid in establishing detachment and duty. Achievement of a perpetual dynamic state and activity of pure sacrifice is the end, not any static achievement, or objective.

Related to the problem of action in the realized state, it is important to note the Gītā's resolution of the debate between knowledge votaries and votaries of devoted action (Gītā III:1–7; V:1–7; XII: 1–8).

First, *satyāgraha* is a method of devoted action *par excellence*, though Gandhi is a votary of knowledge also and preeminently. This is evident from his preference for the maxim "Truth is God", and by the dependence of his methods on this impersonal designation, *satya-āgraha*.

Second, in answer to the classical debate over liability to action in the state of realization, the Gītā notes that for the contemplative votary who has burned up his experience impressions (*karma-sanskāra*), by knowledge of *ātman*, the means to spiritual realization of *brahman* is contentment, waiting, without activity and with attention centered in *ātman* (Gītā VI:3). For the votary still bound in tendencies to action, and who has no experience of his *ātmic* identity, the means is action while giving up the fruits which Gandhi interprets as self-dedicated service in constant devotion or remembrance of *Īśvara*.

The result of each means is the same state of *parabrahman*. However, action in devotion is a means all by itself and does not require a stage of inactivity. In fact, the Lord of the Gītā, Yogeśvara Kṛṣṇa, gives preference to the path of devoted action (Gītā XII:6–7).

The path of contemplation of the formless, attributeless reality is nearly impossible for embodied beings; this path of devotional action is more reliable since it is personally presided over and protected by the omniscient, omnipotent and omnibenevolent Lord.

The final consideration for both the Upaniṣads and the Gītā, and the keystone of *satyāgraha*, is grace (Gītā X:10–11, XV, XVIII:56–62). The final realization and external success are ultimately determined only by the will of *Maheśvara*—the superintendent creating, protecting and destroying conscious power which is itself the object of realization.

The contemplative may pass to the imperishable and merge in the attributeless reality, having completed his spiritual course, and remain inactive or give up the body. But he may also continue to act as a perfectly tuned instrument with no personal motive, having no ego structure left intact. On Gandhi's reading, this is not "acting" at all.

Those who follow the path of action and devotion, having abolished the ego-sense, having burnt up all impelling sense and mental impressions, and feeling no lack since fulfilled by the source of bliss from within, remain active in activities of sacrifice, totally detached. They serve as an exemplar to others of the means by which their own spiritual realization may be furthered and completed. Gandhi adds that such a life exhibits also the highest beauty—the special beauty of Truth itself. We may know it, in part, as "moral beauty" of *satyāgraha*. *Satyāgraha* postulates that the actions of a realized being have the power to reveal that Truth into which he has merged himself.

Need to Apply to Problems of the Age and Locale: In an "age of action", eternal principles must meet the problems of action and the active modern life.

Gandhi considers the purpose of religion to be the spiritualizing of the mundane; to him this is equivalent to "true Happiness" and "true Beauty". But with the Gītā he believes that no other action than sacrificial (sacred) action can free one from bondage and painful qualities; sacrifice is the core of religion.

Gandhi considers the principles of detachment and sacrifice to be eternal laws of conscious being, but the form of action through which these self-modifying attitudes may express and increase themselves is determined by the age, social customs, traditions, family and body into which the soul has been born. Gandhi takes the Gītā as a timeless teacher, an allegory of the inner battle that characterizes the embodied condition, viz. whenever *kṣetra* and *kṣetrajña, prakṛti* and *puruṣa*, matter and soul are connected.

According to Gandhi, the Gītā, as a scientific treatise on spiritual realization and its means, cannot answer questions of conduct in terms of a code or casuistry. The problems of freedom and bondage are related to specific practical problems of the material life and environment. The problem of release is how to relate the facts of the soul's existence and the unity of all existence to daily action and life that seem to deny those facts.

This is an eternal problem which is implied in the apparent "co-eternality" of both primal undifferentiated stuff (*avyakta*) and pristine, objectiveless self-awareness (*puruṣa*). But its solution is ever-fresh as each soul (*jīva*) passes through this stage of its spiritual evolution.

Gandhi writes that the world will eternally be an alien place for the soul; although existence in it is essentially evil (*hiṁsic*), it also provides the vehicle (body and mind) and occasion (the environment differentiated as good and evil) for action by which that evolution can be self-consciously aided.

Satyāgraha seeks practical means. Besides knowing the relation of consciousness or spirit to matter in general, the universal principle must meet specific problems having a definite material form and locale. Gandhi writes that though the Gītā represents perfect knowledge of these eternal relations,

> . . . (this) should not mean that we can obtain from the Gītā direct answers to all the questions that arise from day to day, just as we find the meaning of words by looking up in the dictionary. This would not be desirable even if it were possible, for, in that case, there would be nothing like progress or discovery for mankind. Human intelligence would then simply atrophy from disuse. Therefore, questions that arise in each age must be solved by the people of that age through their own effort. Our difficulties at present, such as world war, must be met by applying the general principles derived from the Gītā and similar books which can only be of help to a limited extent. Real help can come only from our endeavours and struggles.[35]

Gandhi explains by his principle of analogy: "In books on medicine, we find various virtues attributed to a number of drugs. But their descriptions can serve only as guides. So long as these drugs have not been tested in actual practice, our theoretical knowledge of them not only serves no useful purpose, but is even burdensome. The same is true of the questions in life that clamour for solution."[36]

Gandhi believes that though there are various religions and codes of conduct, they have only a few immutable principles at their bases, and that these are common to all true religions and moralities. But the form of the code will change with the conditions of application in the given age. They may change with each generation according to the customs and needs of the times.

Anāsakti, yajña, and *brahmasamārpaṇa* are immutable principles invariant with respect to the problems they confront, and the ideal of *sthitaprajña* is a timeless ideal. Gandhi deduces *satyāgraha* mainly from these principles as the form that the Gītā and Upaniṣads should take in this age.

Again, Truth and non-violence are basic principles unchanging from age to age. But as Gandhi considers *satyāgraha* to be a practical corollary of these two, as such it becomes an object of research and experiment to find specific remedies for evils of the particular age and locale.

As Truth and *ahiṃsā* take on the form of *anāsakti, yajña* and *brahmasamārpaṇa* considered under the distinction between material and spiritual, so these take on the form of *satyāgraha* when applied under the distinction between good and evil. This gives the one un-differentiated reality a specific form in terms of which it can be acted upon and struggled against for the purpose of spiritual realization, *karmayoga.*

Gandhi's *satyāgraha* is his attempt to define and find a type of action which effectively connects the spiritual and empirical wills in order to extirpate the seeming difference between the material and the spiritual. Gandhi believes that to suit this "democratic" age, such a means must fit the average: It must be suitable for man ignorant of self and caught in consciousness of agency. And it must itself manifest visibly that Truth—a means impossible but for an extraordinary supernatural force such as Gandhi claims soul-force to be.

Gandhi often writes from the point of view of an anonymous sage in order to give his deduction a sense of historical validity and timelessness. Though his writings may not be historically accurate, they represent his deepest conviction as to the authenticity and validity of his principles and interpretations as in fact deriving from established traditions. They give insight into his concepts and methods. Gandhi is that sage and scientist.

But when Gandhi says that sages have taught the means of realization from the Truth of their own realization, it is not a scholar's or scientist's study he is reporting but that of an ideologist. Behind his views can be found the ardent religious and social reformer. This caution should accompany the study of his deduction of *satyāgraha* doctrines and methods from their classical sources.

3. Practical Application of Non-Violence: As A Sādhana, A Means of Spiritual Realization

The new factor in Gandhi's adaptation of the Gītā's ideal of *anāsakti* is the prominence of the practical.

Gandhi equates "purest religion" with "highest expediency". According to Gandhi, annulling the illusion that these two are different requires power aside from that ascribed by the Gītā to soul-force and God's *vibhūti* and *māyā*.

The three new elements in Gandhi's interpretation of the Gītā as a treatise on practical non-violence are non-violence as (1) detachment and self-control, (2) soul-force, and (3) self-sacrifice in the form of self-suffering.

Self-suffering is further interpreted as *tapas* (an external means of penance or self-purification; invoking and accumulating energy); detachment and *tapas* become specifications of *anāsakti* and *yajña*, respectively. Soul-force, the element essential for realizing the practical aim of *satyāgraha* and for carrying out Gandhi's particular form of *tapas,* is his own contribution to interpreting the classical texts.

In a political age, Gandhi postulates *satyāgraha* for bringing soul-force to bear in practical relations. This is done by reducing self to nil and making oneself its conduit and by discovering actions and attitudes that will invoke the activity of soul-force, allowing it to work in the given conditions of ignorance and bondage that face the votary of reform.

Thus, this chapter will develop the link between the spiritual reality, ideals and principles and the practical sphere of human relations. *Satyāgraha* denotes this link.

This link, a compression of Gandhi's three new elements in the analysis of *ahiṁsā*, has two sides. The ideal half is the eternal and immutable principles as Gandhi has interpreted them; the empirical half is his findings in their application to practical problems.

This chapter follows the same progression as Chapter 2, elaborating the aim of *satyāgraha,* conditions of its obstruction, means of release and relation to the whole scheme of application as it moves from the most abstract principles to concrete action. The analysis, however, is from a new standpoint—the practical side of the spiritual aim.

This chapter does not depict Gandhi's methods and actions in detail. It completes the exposition of his principles of non-violent action, bringing the analysis just to the point of concrete application. It brings to bear at that point the viewpoint developed through the progressive elaboration of the entire section.

At this point Gandhi's claims for the universal applicability and perfect practical efficacy of his principles come into question. The exposition of these claims is the topic of Chapter 4, and their critical examination is the problem of Section III.

A. GANDHI'S AIM

Realization in an Age of Action by Service, Redress and Social Reform: Gandhi believes that spiritual realization is an inherent urge of man, and in whatever age or circumstance he finds himself, the same duty of self-restraint and desireless action is there as his means of realization. The effort toward realization is of course obligatory. Gandhi writes that, as its means, desirelessness alone is universally obligatory; the soul-force of the Gītā is the only means of restraining desires.

Since Gandhi characterizes this age as the age of action, reason and democracy, his general *sādhana* should reflect those temporal conditions by some adaptation of *anāsakti*. Gandhi enumerates the conditions of this age as follows:

Ignorance of spiritual reality is basic. The urge and need to act— industry—are basic. The corporate aspect of life is pervasive; it is the age of the masses. Social identity and self-purification through a sense of interdependence and mutual responsibility have the greatest scope for development. Public life is an inevitable feature, and self-conscious allegiances and identities are expanded and intensified. The necessity of greatest individual growth and responsibility in the widest social and political contexts give rise to the ideals of Equality, Fraternity and Liberty.

But, also, modern technology has produced, according to Gandhi, a world moving at a pace unnatural to it, creating pressures and a sense of compression that he classifies as violence. It produces an ease and unreality that dulls sensitivities, ingenuity, balance, rhythm and the sense of proportion that daily untechnologized necessity, the "daily rounds", sustains. Gandhi considers this unnatural state a breeding ground of desire and ignorance. Thus competitiveness is characteristic of the age. Greed is intensified in both the mass and individualized setting.

The large forms of this greed are world colonization by worldly strong powers over worldly weak ones, and world wars between competing colonial powers.

Mass inequality, exploitation and oppression are the natural results of this greed. Arrogation of status, injustice and humiliation are ubiquitous evils in these socio-economic contexts. They appear as economic class conflict and suppression, as conflict and suppression between agricultural and industrial sectors, between village and city life, between rich landowner and *kisan* (peasant, tenant), and between industrialist and laborer, as suppression by class differentiation and status, and as oppression and conflict between power haves and have-nots, and between one religious group and another.

For Gandhi, in India, these conditions took the specific forms of foreign rule and colonial exploitation, untouchability and caste arrogation, Hindu-Muslim intolerance and terrorism. The corollary of the colonial usurpation and the have/have-not disparity is social disease that stems from demoralization and abject poverty, viz. malaise, epidemic insanitation, entrenched social ignorance and illiteracy, disease, a growing social criminal element and tendency to infighting, preying on each other through pandering, exhorbitant pricing, account book justice and foreclosure, and alcohol and drug propagation.

For the exploiting power—authorities and wealthholders—these conditions meant growing insensitivity and brutalization, calculating misuse of reason, emasculation and cowardice.

Gandhi perceives the world as abundantly exhibiting all of these evils which in India were brought to a specially intense focus. Their elimination there would mean a moral advance for the whole world emerging from feudal and colonial conditions and mentalities.

Thus Gandhi believes that the ideal of *yajña,* implicit in the conditions of this age, is universal social service to redress injustices, rectify inequalities, restore dignity, health and strength and to reconstruct domestic, social, political and economic life on spiritual lines, viz. on the basis of the ideals of Truth and non-violence.

These problems are obviously too large for mere human and moral solution. The material resources and powers needed to begin the reforms are already usurped by the forces of evil to maintain the present conditions to their own advantage.

Solution of these problems would require power and ability greater than even evil could marshal. However, evil seems to have a monopoly of these material energies and resources, or at least a far surpassing interest in their use.

Gandhi identified exploitation as the essence of violence.

For Gandhi, the ideal is not merely social but spiritual. This implies attaining the utmost humility—where self vanishes and one becomes the non-doer, the instrument of the divine will. Non-doership is the prerequisite for enlisting this power and capability greater than evil's.

Gandhi believes that non-doership (the essence of non-violence) for this age implies not only identification with the lowest and poorest classes—as implied in his ideal of "Unto this last. . . ." (Ruskin's principle interpreted by Gandhi as a principle of non-violence in political economy)—but also with the least creatures, herbage and "particles of dust".

It is the need to rectify and balance these various aspects of the modern society in its state of social sickness that led Gandhi to seek to evolve *satyāgraha* as his *sādhana*.

Gandhi considered his political and social work to be stages on his path of God-realization. He said that his politics had to do with inner growth and as such were universal; they therefore had a marked external effect also. He believes all power such as he displayed in his political work was derived from his efforts in the spiritual sphere and the political work was only the very least part of that primary obligation.

The vastness of this reform would call for the new emphasis on power and force that is central to Gandhi's conception and methods of *satyāgraha*. But in fact it was the incorrigibility of the human materials and the entrenched nature of the problems, rather than their scope and size, which led Gandhi to seek a new practical force—

transformation of the "human stuff" in even the individual, in oneself, already a formidable objective.

For Gandhi, the possibility of reforming a large mass or segment
of society is a multiplication of the problem of converting one prejudiced community, one prejudiced man, one orthodox, one "legitimately" wealthy man, one indigent, one disabled, or one criminal —
and again, firstly, these characters actually or potentially in one's
self.

Gandhi began his active inquiry in South Africa. There he was
confronted with individual class and race prejudice, the exploiting
landlord and the insolent local authority or petty official. Gandhi
wanted to follow the Gītā and New Testament, treating all equally as
his nearest friend and family. It was his motivating concern to discover how to "return good for evil" under these circumstances and
how to maintain this equal good treatment of all with inner equanimity (samabhāva of the Gītā).

Gandhi writes that the precept of returning good for evil was
learned by him at the age of twelve from a "Gujarati didactic
stanza":

The truly noble know all men as one,
And return with gladness good for evil done.[37]

He writes that he immediately translated this precept into a widening
series of moral "experiments with Truth" which had by then become
his ideal.

Gandhi also writes that his resistance to social inequality and
arrogation began with his childlike but firm insistence on not recognizing the inferior status or supposed impurity and social infectious-
ness of an untouchable boy, Uka, who cleaned the household's privy.
Although his reservations and insistence were overt, in deference to
family opinion, he did not violate the domestic order.

Though the consciously deductive basis of his satyāgraha is the
Gītā and Upaniṣads, Gandhi considers his domestic experience and
its universality to be the origin, natural basis and verification of his
non-violent resistance; he considers the discovery and development
of soul-force to be the direct result of the realization that no amount
of brute-force or violence could remove evil at its root from the individual, much less from the corporate and mass realities. Brute-force
could only amplify and multiply evil by natural reaction.

*Resort Only to Non-violent Force in Furtherance of
Realization and Reform against Resistance and Obstruction:
Demonstration of a Complete Substitute for Methods of Violence.*

The natural concomitant of adopting reformist programs as a *sā-dhana* in an age of active social and political evil is resistance to that reform and obstruction to that means of realization. The corollary of these programs is the radical dimension of the second part of Gandhi's spiritual aim, viz. the demonstration of his practical claim.

There is both an inner and an outer aspect of the non-violent reformist's situation: inwardly, it seems to the reformist that evil is intrinsically incorrigible to ordinary force; outwardly, he is faced with the advent of the atom-bomb as the *reductio ad absurdum* of confronting violence with violence. All the aspects of recalcitrant lower human nature and un-reason are brought to a single undeniable focus here. No moral value seems to have the power to stop this escalation of violence, though use of atom-bomb against atom-bomb seems so obviously to mean only mutual self-obliteration.

Gandhi believes the categorical nature of the problem requires a categorical solution. If good and evil are comprehensive and exclusive categories in assessing human moral consciousness and consequent action, and if evil is incorrigible to force or violence, then the solution must involve a categorically opposite and yet practically superior force capable of completing the substitution for violence where that would normally be the chosen means. Knowing where such choice would lead, no choice must be left—the question is categorically foreclosed.

Given the amplified dimensions of modern individual life and the immediate international responsiveness to local events on the one hand, and threat of escalation to nuclear self-destruction on the other, mere practical considerations seem to rule out stopgap and partial solutions that do not resolve but only shift conflict and delay the conflagration.

Gandhi's final Truth substitution formula for practical application through *satyāgraha* is "Violence is unreal; Non-violence is Real".[38]

Non-violence is therefore equated with Truth or soul, or with eternal spiritual Reality which alone has power since it alone exists; violence is equated with illusion or material formation, the ephemeral, superimposed reality which is inert, formless (but for the divi-

sions and activity made to appear in it by the creative power of the
Spirit, *māyā)* and powerless.

"Non-violence" is whatever removes obstruction to Truth. The means of removing obstruction to Truth is imitation of Truth in the practical realm by the substitution of the unifying force of *ahiṁsā* for the divisive principle of violence.

Since Gandhi's *"ahiṁsā"* includes the component of visible non-violence, the truth formula is completed—microcosm and macrocosm, inner and outer, exactly mirror one another and reality *appears* as well as *is* again a seamless whole. All is full and beautiful; no negativity, privation or lack is left where the substitution of *ahiṁsā* for *hiṁsā,* real for unreal, is completed.

Gandhi writes,

> Truth—*Sat*—is positive; Non-violence is negative. Truth stands for the fact, the highest religion. Truth is self-evident; non-violence is its maturest fruit. It is contained in Truth . . . renunciation of the flesh is essential for realizing Truth. The sage who realized Truth found Non-violence out of violence raging all about him and said: 'Violence is unreal; Non-violence is Real.' Realization of Truth is impossible without Non-violence. *Ahiṁsā* is the soul of Truth. Man is an animal without it. The seeker will realize all this in his quest for Truth.[39]

The Final Criterion

Here, as in Chapter 1, it is shown how Gandhi equates non-violence, non-retaliation and love as denoting the same force, though he distinguishes them on practical grounds.

Though Gandhi ideologically equates Truth and non-violence as identifying the same reality, he maintains the practical distinction between ends and means.

Non-violence denotes soul-force through its attribute of love. Love connotes the power to annul all distinction in consciousness, to infect surroundings with the same recognition and to elicit the appropriate response in behavior. Gandhi therefore chooses as his fullest and final criterion of *ahiṁsā* Patañjali's aphorism (*Yogasūtra),* "The greatest enmity dissolves before *ahiṁsā."* Gandhi notes that this is the common experience of votaries of *ahiṁsā,* from Mahātmā Buddha to St. Francis. Naturally antagonistic animals and warring armies ceased conflict under the influence of purest soul-force.

According to Gandhi the universality of the principle is thus attested to and implies in human relations the criterion of love for the enemy. This fulfills the precept "return good for evil" and demonstrates the validity and completeness of the line of substitutions. The criterion thus implies the requisite superior practical efficacy.

On the use of *satyāgraha* against gross injustice in the principality of Rajkot, 1939, Gandhi wrote that his own development and technique of non-violence must be faulty because otherwise he would be able to see clearly how, with a few co-workers or even alone, he could face such festering, large-scale violence.

In Noakhali, 1946–47, against Hindu-Muslim mutual slaughter, Gandhi was making a similar attempt to test his principle and demonstrate the perfect efficacy of soul-force. It was a test-case of confronting insuperable material forces of violence and untruth with only a small band of votaries of *ahiṁsā*.

In his final fast to bring about conciliation between Hindu and Muslim factions warring in Delhi after Independence, Gandhi made a similar effort and reiterated the necessity of demonstrating the universal practical applicability of *satyāgraha* against whatever evils the age and locale presented. He advised courses of non-violent action against possible Japanese aggression in World War II and finally as the only antidote against atomic warfare.

Gandhi believes reason alone cannot suffice to bring about any amelioration of the conditions of the age. Extensive practical demonstration is required where there is no previous experience of universal *ahiṁsā* from which to draw the premises of arguments or to justify practical imperatives of non-violence.

Gandhi notes, too, that the human mind is remarkable for its insularity where belief is age-old or deep-seated. The inadequacy of language to express Reality is also a liability. He believed that the only way to propagate Truth in its fullness and to communicate its superior efficacy was to produce a series of demonstrations of its practical success and to create in himself and his co-workers a model of the transforming and empowering capabilities of that force.

In sum, Gandhi believed that resort to non-violence as the only means of realizing and propagating Truth in the face of opposition to reform is the *sine qua non* of non-violence in this age, and he made his mission research into the possibilities of this universal moral means.

Gandhi evolved *satyāgraha* as a religious principle. He equates religion with two factors: one, a recognition of or belief in the permanence of the soul and, two, a fundamental morality. Since *satyāgraha*
postulates the equation of purest religion and greatest expedience, so
he equates the ultimate practical power with God, Truth and soul.

Gandhi writes that "Truth and *Ahiṁsā* must incarnate in socialism" (of his conception). This becomes an epitome and test case of
his practical non-violence in the social sphere:

> In order that it can [incarnate socialism], the votary must have a liv-
> ing faith in God. Mere mechanical adherence to Truth and *Ahiṁsā* is
> likely to break down at the critical moment. Hence have I said that
> Truth is God. This God is a living Force. Our life is of that Force. That
> Force resides in, but is not the body. He who denies the existence of
> that great Force, denies to himself the use of that inexhaustible Power
> and thus remains impotent . . . The fact is it has always been a matter
> of strenuous research to know this great Force and its hidden possibili-
> ties.
>
> My claim is that in pursuit of that search lies the discovery of *satyā-
> graha* . . . (and) that every worthy object can be achieved by the use of
> *satyāgraha*. It is the highest infallible means, the greatest force. Social-
> ism will not be reached by any other means. *Satyāgraha* can rid society
> of all evils, political, economic, and moral.[40]

Gandhi does not require that one's definition of God be the same
as his. Only that it be a power one relies upon when all other recourse has failed and be capable of sustaining one through any pain
or suffering, including death. This constitutes for Gandhi a functional definition of "God" in the context of *satyāgraha*. *Satyāgraha*
designates Truth as "God" and its radical practical claim provides a
pragmatic criterion and definition of Truth.

Gandhi takes it as a fundamental practical proposition that that
power works (responds) only at moral and spiritual extremity, viz.
when one has exhausted all other means and resources and sus-
pended the claims of ego-sense. It in fact comes into play just at that
point where violence seems often legitimate as the last resort. But violence is chosen when the ego's claims are not given up. *Satyāgraha*
postulates rather the condition of self-nullity at this point—

recognition of helplessness, and call in faith for the power of God. Thus the grace, power and intelligence of that force, and faith in recourse to it, give the basis of a method of soul-force as both the moral and practical last resort.

In the context of the unrealized state of ignorant action, Gandhi's problem in *satyāgraha* is to find principles for devising actions that will invoke and propagate soul-force by propagating themselves visibly, manifestly as its exclusive means, as self-evidently an instrument of the divine agency.

Holding to Truth: The literal translation of "*satyāgraha*" is "holding to Truth". Gandhi intends this literal meaning. The above depiction of *satyāgraha* as Gandhi's inquiry for a complete substitute for violence is based on his interpretation of the logic of moral substitution as a method of discovery by logico-metaphysical reversal or negation. "Holding to Truth", as a substitute for using violence, means acting on what one believes to be Truth. But Truth must be the reverse of the reality "held to" by the advocate of violence, who holds to what is unreal. By belief in unreality as Truth, one holds to the material or practical reality as exhaustive, and to differentiation and distinction as fundamental. This is patent un-Truth. One holds to the belief that sensory objects are the only source of enjoyment.

The moral result of holding to un-Truth is clash from unmoderated interest in ephemeral objects of sensory enjoyment. Attached interest leads to dissatisfaction in all sensory situations and failure to find any principle to regulate desire or to moderate the means of fulfilling it in the face of mounting insatiety and growing insensitivity and malaise, weakness and vulnerability.

Gandhi, following the Gītā (Chap. XVI), finds that acting on the materialist metaphysic and empiricist moral ideology necessarily results in a consolidation of the ego-sense and sense of possession and in a burgeoning of greed, lust and anger. Gandhi finds that acting on these tendencies is the primary cause of bondage; the natural result of holding to untruth is its corollary of violence resorted to as the basic means for achieving one's ends. One is thereby bound in the habit of escalating violent pursuit of desire's objects.

"Holding to Truth" of *satyāgraha* is based on spiritual realization and so implies action based on the factual reality recognized by those

who have realized the spiritual Truth of reality, viz. faith in soul,
family relation of all created beings, oneness, unison and stability of
reality underlying all diversity, conflict and change, the inexorable
sway of moral law and the perfect practical efficacy of the "three-
fourths invisible" soul-force.

Since violence and untruth imply action that does not accord with
inner intention, with an ideal, or with the will of other material creation, such action seeks only to maintain one's own existence and
fails to call upon any forces but those constituting familiar material
structure. Truth and non-violence should imply action that exemplifies the opposite, viz. integrity of intention, act and ideal, respect and
protection of the body and rights of other fellow creation and dependence on a force guaranteeing this authenticity, idealism and protection.

The principle of "holding to Truth" is an explicit translation of
the principle of the Īśā Upaniṣad and the domestic principle which,
together with his logical principle of *"yathā piṇḍe . . ."*, lead Gandhi
to deduce the principle of exact conduct on the family model.

How to invoke soul-force and to manifest Truth as Love becomes
most simply, and immediately and urgently, the question of how to
treat the "near and dear".

Universality of a code of conduct requires that it apply equally to
near and dear relations and the stranger or the adversary. The code
must be in accordance with the spiritual fact that in reality all are
near and dear. This universality further implies infallibility since all
have the same soul and are fathered by the same Divine, *Īśvara*. The
same law must work for all.

Application of principle to family and enemy alike establishes for
Gandhi the equation of Truth and non-violence. This turns his moral
ideology into an instrument of moral discovery. Gandhi claims that
he evolved his principles and methods by rehearsing to himself various reforms and resistances in terms of his domestic model. *Satyāgraha* would be as valid against an unjust landlord as against a foreign power, as against one's child or as against one's parent.

Gandhi writes,

> This doctrine of *satyāgraha* is not new, it is merely an extension of
> the rule of domestic life to the political. Family disputes and differ-
> ences are generally settled according to the Law of Love. The injured
> member has so much regard for the others that he suffers injury for

the sake of his principles without retaliating and without being angry with those who differ from him. And as repression of anger, self-suffering are difficult processes, he does not dignify trifles into principles; but, in all non-essentials, readily agrees with the rest of the family and thus contrives to gain the maximum of peace for himself without disturbing that of others. Thus, his action, whether he resists or resigns, is always calculated to promote the common welfare of the family. It is this Law of Love which, silently but surely, governs the family. . . .[41] *Satyāgraha* is a law of universal application. Beginning with the family, its use can be extended to every other circle.[42]

Gandhi believes that since he can derive this rule from empirical facts he has further support for his claim that Truth may be known equally by its recognition from without as from within; the universal domestic experience and the claim of the Īśā Upaniṣad actually only mirror the same Truth from two viewpoints. The reality of Truth and Love is in itself inexpressible and we cannot define the quality of Love. The family experience only gives us some idea of its extent and effect. The Īśā Upaniṣad confirms that this same quality, content and effect are universally the ruling fact or law.

Gandhi finds also that the law of Love may dictate that one disassociate from the family member in order to wean him from wrong. But the domestic model equally requires immediate embrace of the loved member when he has left his evil action. This exemplifies practical application of the distinction noted in Chapter 1 between the doer and the deed. The doer remains loved and protected even if disassociation is necessary for helping him to give up the wrong and self-harmful deed.

Practical application based on the family model yields a new principle of non-violence, viz. self-suffering.

The requirement of universal applicability to satisfy the ideal of Truth yields the new principle of non-violence conceived as an ultimate force. But Gandhi believes that soul-force as Love understood in terms of the family model must omit physical force if the family unit is to be maintained. The incompatibility of soul-force and brute-force is basic to Gandhi's ideology. Therefore, the family law of Love rules out physical force just as soul-force rules out brute-force. Coercion is also ruled out since the purpose is to manifest the Truth, and he believes that one cannot be forced to become good (truthful and non-violent) by compulsion. Mere outward compliance would al-

ways harbor inner contradiction, injury and resentment, and ultimately the will to retaliate.

In accord with the Gītā and the Upaniṣads, Gandhi states the doctrine of *satyāgraha* in a "nutshell": since Truth, *sat,* is what is, and
untruth, *asat,* is what is not, Truth can never be destroyed and is itself the only power. Untruth, *asat,* has no existence and hence no
power. Gandhi translates the Upaniṣadic declaration "*Satyam eva
jayate*", "Truth alone prevails", as the Buddhistic "Conquer with
Truth". On the basis of the principle of "*yathā piṇḍe . . .*", this
translates to "Combat evil with exact conduct" of *satyāgraha*. *Satyāgraha* seeks to discover means of action, exact conduct, that make
Truth manifest by according exactly with the principle of truthfulness and non-violence, in thought, word and deed, to achieve the literal substitution for untruthfulness and violence implied in "holding
to Truth".

Human Predicament: In *satyāgraha*, Gandhi analyzes the human
condition of bondage and ignorance in terms of violence and non-
violence on the model of the Gītā (II: 62–63, etc.).

Ignorant of his true self-nature, being of the same soul as his opponent, and ignorant of the inevitable return of energies of action to
himself as their point of origin, man thinks only about the material
world, and only in terms of fear and sense enjoyment. He is attached
to his actions and their objects through attraction and aversion of the
sense organs and by the desire created in the mind. He follows his
desires, disregards others and becomes angry when they resist or obstruct. This leads to violence and counterviolence where the common
principle of conduct is return of "eye for eye".

Gandhi writes that "We want our opponent to do by force that
which we desire but he does not. And, if such a use of force is justifiable, surely he is entitled to do likewise. And so, we should never
come to an agreement. We simply fancy like the blind horse moving
in a circle round the mill, that we are making progress."[43]

If violence is justifiable by one's own desire, and, if material desire
and its objects present the only reality, then all are equally justified
by desire, the "I" sense is bolstered and incorrigible conflict is inevitable. Each side appears equally justified from the standpoint of the
ego-desire complex.

Gandhi believes that violence is a vicious and escalating circle with reason at its service, in which exhaustion and defeat, and co-brutalization and self-destruction, are the ultimate inevitable outcomes. The circle of retaliation and reprisal exemplifies the daily truth that "two wrongs do not make a right," and justification in terms of desire and asserted rights must be self-deception.

Gandhi believes that escape from this escalating self-destructive involvement, whether individual or international, is possible only if objectivity and reason replace reaction. Emancipation from the bondage of violence is possible where one partner recognizes the Truth of soul, *Brahman,* and *karma* as such objective realities.

Gandhi postulates that only from this vantage point is unilateral dissent, which can transform the relationship and cut through the binding interaction, possible.

Applying this analysis to political aspirations and ambitions, Gandhi writes that non-violence implies not a means of seizing power but of transforming relationships so that power would naturally and peacefully be transferred to its rightful representative and protector. The general question becomes one of how to transform relations when forceful insistence on one's own views and rights can only intensify the binding interaction. "Don't try to change the world, you will only make matters worse," is a folk wisdom that is demonstrated daily.

One bound in age-old beliefs, strong sympathy, antipathy and desire, cannot be changed by brute-force. Brute-force, or violence, could only elicit a further binding reaction and keep the opponent from seeing the wrongness of his position. Gandhi thus believes that the way to change relationships must be to change beliefs and motives.

The question in part is one of education, but can education per se ever be enough? How does one change another's beliefs and motives where violence admittedly cannot do this, where reason itself is based on false beliefs and perceptions, and is therefore incapable of producing the transformation?

Arguments are not a spontaneous production but have a deep and extensive basis in understanding. Their appreciation and evaluation cannot be immediate but require deep examination and serious reflection. Abstract argument to convince, without relevant experience and without the preparation of understanding, constitutes an external force and hence coercion. Violence is the characteristic form of daily un-self-conscious relationships in which this careful regard for the material requirements of transforming understanding is lacking.

Applied and multiplied through the principle of *"yathā piṇḍe . . ."*, the result is social transaction vitiated at every level regardless of the rational "form" of the interaction. In corporate, as in individual human relations, negotiation is also binding, self-defeating escalation if not founded in the fundamental truths of Spirit and field of bondage (*kṣetra*). Such negotiation must result in duplication of the evil rather than neutralization of the original wrong.

Gandhi applies the analysis of the retaliatory nature of the human predicament to every dimension of the interaction, even to education and to innocent-looking "rational" transactions that in fact neglect the Truth as it is.

Self-conversion and Substitution Ethics: Positive Material Effort. Most fundamentally, Gandhi believes the only way to break the circle and transform the relationship is to change oneself.

One must first stop the escalation in oneself. Gandhi, we have seen, follows the Gītā and says that this is possible only by turning the mind away from the sense objects and thinking about God and Truth. This is wholly an internal attack on the spiral of violence.

Gandhi believed that ultimately energy is a continuum and the more subtle the energy, the more powerful it is. The power for turning thought away from the senses and sense objects can therefore only come from soul-force as an energy not already involved in the closed circuit of material transactions (Gītā III:42–43). Only soul-force, drawn from the non-material Self and transmitting the characteristics of its origin, is subtler and more powerful than any forces of the senses, mind and intellect. Soul-force alone is beyond influence of desire inherent in these material faculties.

According to Gandhi, it is this *turning of thought* to remembrance of God that constitutes prayer.

Gandhi insists that *satyāgraha* is not possible without prayer and the action of this prayer-force and the soul-force it draws upon, can alone sustain one in resisting the material being's natural responses to violence—retaliation and vengeance.

But *satyāgraha* connotes external activity, and Gandhi believes equally that no reform is possible without direct action. Prayer and soul-force are the new powers that alone make this self-conversion and transformation of relations possible.

Corporate interaction also involves a material continuum. The physical level must also be converted; we call it social and political action when it is tied to tangible corporate results. Gandhi postulates a direct transmittal of soul-force capable of converting the opponent's material make-up just as, in the first instance, it converts the *satyāgrahī*'s.

The activity of soul-force is in fact ultimately independent of physical action, but Gandhi finds that wrong action interferes with or impedes for the moment its working through that particular instrument or in that particular locale.

Exact conduct of *satyāgraha* is his solution to the problem of finding modes of conduct and inner material states which lie on the same continuum of non-violent energy and which thus fit his concept of Truth and his moral ideology. Gandhi claims that from his concepts of Truth and non-violence directly derive the notion of exact conduct, its requirement of transparency of intent and action, and the depth of sincerity and good will required to invoke and transmit the power of Truth to infuse the surroundings with these qualities by means of that conduct. To uphold such a practical form of Truth is Gandhi's practical ideal of Love, and this visible concordance of ideal and practical forms in exact conduct Gandhi calls "non-violence".

At the heart of *satyāgraha* is the substitution ethics elaborated through the Gītā, Upaniṣads and Patañjali's *Yoga sūtra*. Its basic expression is the Buddhistic injunction "Conquer untruth with Truth, anger with non-anger, and hate with Love." Gandhi adds "Conquer violence with Non-violence." He uses "Return good for evil", "Leave the ephemeral for the real", and "Lead me from the unreal to the Real" (Upaniṣads), to express the same principles.

The logical substitution is simple and direct, but the question for *satyāgraha,* as a moral and spiritual *science,* is the metaphysical and practical question of substitutional ethics—how to materially accomplish this substitution of tendencies in actual practice.

On the external side Gandhi interprets this substitution literally as replacing discourtesy with courtesy, bullying with calm courage, violence with patient suffering and arrogance with humility. This follows the Buddhistic moral psychology and fulfills Gandhi's principles of *"yathā piṇḍe . . ."*. This literal interpretation in terms of conduct is merely the external counterpart of an internal substitution.

On the basis of the Gītā theory of *karma* and the Jaina metaphysics, Gandhi's problem involves displacing the material elements and formations that incline one to the first set of qualities and actions with material elements and formations that incline one to the second. (But it should be noted that the standard is a behavioral, an external norm.)

Gandhi believes that the conversion does not occur spontaneously, or with the immediacy of intellectual understanding or assent. It is a material process involving real energies, forces and formations. *Satyāgraha* elaborates the science of it based on the classical Indic moral texts.

However, we have noted that the basis of *satyāgraha* is the grace, guidance and power of God, and that Gandhi gives fundamental importance to prayer, which seems to leave science and practice out of account.

In an exchange with B. Tilak, in 1920, about the necessity of using pure means in politics, Gandhi wrote that "Conquer untruth with Truth" enunciates an eternal principle which the Gītā's "God metes to us as we mete to others"[44] applies. Gandhi interpreted this as the practical meaning of following "return good for evil", instead of "return eye for eye". If one is to escape punishment from God, then one should not mete out punishment to others.

Gandhi takes this as a variation of the fundamental law of *karma,* the law of life, that we reap only the consequences of what we sow. Only if one uses pure means alone, even returning good for evil, Truth for untruth, and non-violence for violence, will God mete out to him good, in spite of the evil that always is in one. Gandhi deduces that permanent success in terms of Truth is possible only upon this dispensation of God which overrides all material obstructions. Gandhi adds that this is an injunction essentially for the common man and not for the saint. It implies *puruṣakāra,* which Gandhi defines as the religious effort to become, in terms of the Jaina ideal, "a perfect gentleman." This effort, *puruṣakāra,* provides the measure that God metes out accordingly.

The basic proposition of Gandhi's *satyāgraha* ethics and principles of material and moral substitution is that ego and evil are not self-sustained. They cannot be said to exist since they are in the category of the violent (self-destructive), the false and untrue, the material, the ephemeral and the unreal. *Ego and evil have only a temporary existence through energy provided by the good.*

In political terms, Gandhi derives the principles of *satyāgraha* from the individual's inalienable right and inexpungible capability to say "no". Government has no authority or power except that given by voluntary submission of the citizen or submission extracted through fear or desire. Recognition of one's status as soul makes such extortion impossible since only brute-force is available to the abstract entity of evil government.

In social terms, Gandhi's observation is that the good-doer is usually not actively good, in the sense of a social reformer out to root out and defeat evil. His daily actions are usually a mixture of good and evil. Even when his motives and intentions are good, his actions involve many unconscious intentions and alliances; or if consequences are unexamined, even his mostly good actions may inadvertently support a wholly evil system. The ramifications of *karma,* of actions and their consequences, are cumulative and massive. They mostly do not come within the scope of conscious intention.

Non-violence, as shown in Chapter 1, is not a constructed moral concept but refers to avoidance of real injury at whatever the level of phenomenal activity. The real moral implications are thus subtle and extensive, and they usually are not consciously worked out in their full material form. Where desire is the inspiration, the consequences are calculated for only the very narrow and immediate range compassed by the desire. The most innocent intention guided by desire may have disastrous and harmful consequences by its mere blindness and inadvertence. A small desire pursued with great intensity, or several similar desires working together, may support a large structure of consequences never considered in the active intent.

Thus Gandhi's analysis of relations to the state leads to a highly personal political ethics. Responsibility for the extensive consequences of state policies devolves directly on the citizens by their failing to resist, or by unintended consequences of their otherwise unobjectionable acts. This may give evil policy active life. Therefore Gandhi believed that effective substitution of good for evil at every level begins with the individual. And further, his own conversion, reconstitution and emancipation imply the simultaneous conversion, reconstitution and emancipation in all relations at every social level of his *karmic* transactions.

Thus, according to Gandhi, the process of self-purification is the basis of his substitution ethics. It begins with becoming aware of the extensive moral and material consequences of one's actions and of the true condition of one's inner material make-up, the actions it prompts, and the qualities it propagates. He considers *self-examination the keystone* of self-purification, since recognizing the triviality of all passing material interests constitutes more than half the moral battle.

The process of substitution aims at the complete renunciation denoted by *anāsaktiyoga*. But full effort at renunciation is enough to constitute a spiritual rebirth, according to Gandhi. It hits at the ego-body complex when it is accompanied by knowledge of what this renunciation means in terms of violence and non-violence. Gandhi believes that though the full state is not attainable in the body, knowledge of the ideal state could displace all conscious evil intent, and a good deal of injurious inadvertence, if the will were brought to an intensity nullifying the "conscious" or empirical ego.

Effort sufficient to bring one asymptotically towards realization of the ideal is possible, though the ideal must by definition be that which ever recedes from its own realization in material terms. The idealism of full effort is all that Gandhi requires for his practical translation of spiritual non-violence. The conscious and knowing effort at renunciation is sufficient to further this process of self-purification. The complete purification is a long process, but each single moral effort undertaken with this knowledge component as an integral part of it leaves no room for conscious desire-constituted intent, and this constitutes free action while also keeping sustaining energies from reaching the ego complex.

Thus, according to Gandhi, though substituting modes of conduct is a necessary factor in the complete substitution of non-violence for violence, the fundamental work is on the material structure within. In fact, though the simple logical form of the substitution ethics *appears* to mislead because of the real dimensions of the task, the basic procedure *is* that simple. In this simplicity lies the material possibility and power of the process.

At the root of all action is thought, and Gandhi repeatedly notes that the quality of the act comes only from the quality of the thought inspiring or prompting it. If the thought is purified, evil action cannot follow. Again Gandhi postulates that if the individual cases are multiplied the result is corporate and mass non-violence as projected by the logical principle of *"yathā piṇḍe. . ."*

Gandhi writes that, *"Mokṣa* is liberation from impure thoughts. Complete extinction of impure thought is impossible without ceaseless penance. There is only one way to achieve this. The moment an impure thought arises confront it with a pure one."[45] This process would gradually transform the moral being by materially dismantling the ego-complex and changing the quality of the subjective elements and energies (the material counterparts of the thought contents).

A corollary to the theory of *karma,* the theory of *puruṣakāra* says that by repeated effort a tendency is strengthened and by disuse a tendency becomes impotent. Gandhi subscribes to this view and applies it to moral and spiritual tendencies in accordance with the theory of *karma.* He cites also the Gītā's practices of *abhyāsa* and *vairāgya* (see *supra,* Chapt. 2C.), and its principle of the conservation of right effort.

On this basis *satyāgraha* postulates the necessary victory of Truth in one who faithfully continues in the small efforts that are possible to him at this basic level; he needs only to conscientiously direct thought and conduct from the viewpoint of Truth and non-violence as these appear in his immediate thought contents and action possibilities. The continued confrontation of evil thought with good thus constitutes the basis of the moral conquest of evil by good through the universal substitution of Truth for untruth, and the substitution of infallible non-violence for self-defeating violence.

However, Gandhi believes that this process of penance, this ceaseless confrontation of evil thought and sense desires ("ceaseless prayer" by Gandhi's definition), is not possible by individual effort alone since the ego-complex, in its condition of bondage and ignorance, is tied up in its own complexities. The required opposition, whether of conduct or thought, is possible only by the power and omniscience of God. Again, the problem is not merely logical but scientific and practical.

Thus, according to Gandhi, more basic even than the substitution of thoughts is the Remembrance and repetition of "Rāma", the Name of God. Gandhi learned this Remembrance as a child. It was to become the mass congregational devotional song or chant (*bha-*

Hindu-Muslim terror of Noakhali and Delhi. Gandhi said repetition of this one Name was the final solution to his problem of finding true non-violence of the strong so far as he could discover it—its essence, sum and foundation—because it is the only universally practicable key to that divine grace and power on which *satyāgraha,* individual or mass, is founded. The science of practical substitution ethics in the moral psychology of non-violence requires a metaphysics of practical prayer in the spiritual substitutions that empower *satyāgraha.*

Gandhi continues the above instruction about ceaselessly confronting each evil thought: "This is possible only with God's grace, and God's grace comes through ceaseless communion with Him and complete self-surrender. This communion may in the beginning be just lip repetition of his name even disturbed by impure thoughts. But ultimately what is on the lips will possess the heart. . . . Impure thoughts need not dismay you. We are monarchs in the Domain of Effort. God is the sole Monarch in the Domain of Results."[46]

Gandhi wrote that though to require faith in God and active resort and practice of prayer for *satyāgraha* might exclude sincere workers, *satyāgraha* in fact relied completely on power and guidance given by God. Passive resistance or non-cooperation without that faith, prayer and power could not be called *"satyāgraha"*, nor be expected to yield the results he claimed were intrinsic to it. Without that power of Truth, non-violence must be only a passive material stance without the perfect practical efficacy he conceived and believed he experienced in practice. Gandhi's requirement of active faith and prayer, the basis of both the process of self-purification and invocation of power, is not an *optional* feature of his method.

In the same way that Gandhi believed that one may have any conception of God that would function as *satyāgraha* required, so he believed that prayer and remembrance of any Name would be effective. But he also states that *Rāmanāma* (the Name "Rāma") is found to have a special efficacy.[47]

Gandhi asserts that *Rāmanāma* sums up almost as a "mathematical formula" the research of ages. He found from experience that it has a special potency with respect to the moral substitution and spiritual conversion that *satyāgraha* requires. He also notes that when the subtle material structure of mind is filled with the energy and presence that remembrance of this Name brings, there is a reciprocal shedding of impurities in the surroundings. This is the realization of Patañjali's criterion of nonviolence.

Because of this direct spiritual, moral and practical potency, he also equates the Name "Rāma" with Truth as God, and he writes that it is hard to distinguish between the ends and means, the Divine and the Divine Name.

For practical purposes and for purposes of realization, repetition of the Name of Rāma becomes the principal means. And since it is identical with Truth, Gandhi recommends its use even when there is other sectarian preference. Thus, while fully respecting religious sentiments, he nevertheless maintains the scientific attitude and makes remembrance and repetition of the name "Rāma" not only his recommended practice for individuals but also the central prayer of his method of congregational worship. On this basis Gandhi connects the individual substitution ethics with the substitution ethics on the mass scale. It is on this basis that Gandhi made mass congregational prayer the main means in his program for creating effective non-violence in his effort to defuse the post-independence Hindu-Muslim conflict and terrorism in Noakhali, Bihar, Calcutta and Delhi referred to above.

As a mass means, Gandhi claimed for this congregational remembrance, or mass *bhajan,* a "unique" efficacy for transforming the moral atmosphere and for infusing votaries with "non-violence of the strong". Its general propagation and acceptance was then his basic mission. He believed that the simplicity and beauty of this repetition and remembrance gave it the potentiality of universal mass appeal and practice. He also believed that since any action possible on a mass scale automatically produced a special power, the mass congregational prayer of the Name of Rāma would accomplish the required substitution of non-violence for violence on the national corporate level.

Though it is evident how according to Gandhi corporate human action and growth and substitution of good for evil are too complex and subtle for any but divine power and guidance to accomplish, it is essential to see behind his corporate program and actions his insistence on individual practice, both in personal prayer and in reconstituting daily activity, thought and relationships.

In his last years, Gandhi told a friend that though he still had not

found the proper technique for evolving corporate and mass non-
violence of the strong, he felt the solution had to lie with the individual: "Of course there must be organized resistance to organized evil.
The difficulty arises when the organizers of *satyāgraha* try to imitate
the organizers of evil. I tried and failed hopelessly. The way of organ-
izing forces of good must be opposite to the evil way. What it exactly
is I do not yet know fully. I feel that it lies, as far as may be, through
perfection of individuals. It then acts as the leaven raising the whole
mass. But I am still groping."[48]

Only if this effort became the constant habit in small things where
one had some possibility of consciously affecting action could there
be the larger, cumulative purification and accumulation of non-
violent energy. He believed this accumulation necessary to fulfill the
practical requirements of mass non-violence in consciously confronting the evil of large social or political systems that had almost
an autonomous life. Without *satyāgraha,* in the full and basic sense
of self-purification and strengthening by reliance on, and infusion of,
the power of God, individuals could not hope to stand apart from
the system; by participating in the system they would lose the goodness they already possessed, falling to the level of the evil in which
they had participated.

Gandhi's final judgment was that he had in fact found the adequate means to instill mass non-violence of the strong through the
program of mass congregational prayer of the Name of Rāma and by
participation in the social reconstruction program and basic moral
reconstitution that this form of worship implied and empowered.

In sum to this point, the process of self-conversion by substitution
ethics and prayer is the basis of Gandhi's "holding to Truth" by
means of non-violent exact conduct. This process of substitution is
calculated to unilaterally break the circle of violence and its escalation to self-destruction that constitutes the human predicament.
Breaking this circle of violence constitutes both the means and end
of spiritual realization.

Non-retaliation and Self-sacrifice: Non-phenomenal Response.   Non-
retaliation is the basic form of restraint in the process of self-purification and in effectively breaking the circle of escalating violence.

Non-retaliation is Gandhi's moral prescription for the practical application of non-violence through his substitution ethics. The attack on and isolation of evil called for in non-violent redress and reform, necessarily bring material reaction; non-retaliation is meant to neutralize this reaction. It fulfills Gandhi's moral criteria being both means and end. The perfect state is non-reaction to any evil or violence. The process of conscious non-retaliation at all material levels draws soul-force, gradually building the tendency of non-retaliation into the subjective material make-up. Like the confrontation by good thoughts and remembrance of the Name of Rāma, the process of building a character-state of non-retaliation is one of *puruṣakāra*.

Non-retaliation is the basic *tapas* of *satyāgraha* and is therefore its fundamental means of purification and invocation of power for directly transforming relations and influencing conduct at the physical level. *It implies suffering the consequences of "holding onto Truth" by exact conduct.* Nevertheless, the power to do this again implies the operation of spiritual force since the material component of the *tapas* by itself could only duplicate the original violence and bind one further into its escalation. *Non-retaliation again constitutes the self-suffering, self-sacrifice and self-nullification that are integral to the self-purification presupposed in successful practical* satyāgraha.

Gandhi makes a fundamental distinction between "non-violence of the weak" and "non-violence of the strong", which the theory of *satyāgraha* elaborates for practice.

Passive resistance and non-cooperation, as material activities, can only be holding actions and a prelude to violence that will be resorted to as soon as there is material strength or strategic advantage. But Gandhi's primary position is that *satyāgraha* is a positive spiritual force more potent than any brute-force that violence can effectively combine.

The Gītā, after enumerating for an entire chapter the greatest manifestations of divine power (*vibhūti-māyā*) (Gītā X:7, 40–41), says that all of this is sustained by only the smallest particle of that power on which Gandhi bases *satyāgraha* (Gītā X:42).

. . . *As the Final Criterion*:   Gandhi believes that the earlier campaigns of his career in Bihar and Gujarat, and the success of the campaign for Independence, were failures judged by the criterion of non-violence of the strong. He states that though they achieved their

practical objectives this was only a strategic accomplishment of physical non-retaliation dependent on material conditions and processes.
If success had been the result of soul-force actively transforming all
given conditions and forces, it would have accomplished also the
moral conversion of the population and the transformation of relations to the active non-violence of Love. There could not then have
been, as there was, a later resurgence of corporate violence on both
sides.

The later Hindu-Muslim conflict proved that little of the practical
success was the result of non-violence of the strong. He defines non-
violence of the strong in pragmatic terms having both practical and
moral components constituting its criterion of success.

Principally, Gandhi deduces the criterion of non-retaliation from
Patañjali's criterion of non-violence. He writes, " 'Enmity vanishes
before *Ahiṁsā*', is a great aphorism. It means that the greatest enmity requires an equal measure of *ahiṁsā* for its abatement."[49]

Gandhi gives the following axioms of true non-violence:

(a) Non-violence implies a complete self-purification as is humanly
possible.

(b) Man for man the strength of non-violence is in exact proportion
to the ability, not the will, of the non-violent person to inflict violence.

(c) Non-violence is without exception superior to violence, as the
power at the disposal of a non-violent person is always greater than he
would have if he was violent.

(d) There is no such thing as defeat in non-violence. The end of violence is surest defeat.

(e) The ultimate end of non-violence is surest victory—if such a
term may be used in non-violence. In reality where there is no sense of
defeat, there is no sense of victory.[50]

These axioms are extremely important for the analysis of
Gandhi's work. They almost define non-violence by a pragmatic criterion. Thus Gandhi believes that true non-violence must meet any
type and any degree of violence with non-retaliation.

The failure of the Bihar Hindu masses to refrain from retaliating
for Muslim brutality in Noakhali proved that they had not previously exercised and evolved non-violence of the strong based on self-
purification and self-restraint by means of soul-force. Their earlier
non-violence had not followed 'sacrifice of self', and had contributed
only nominally if at all to the mass program towards spiritual real-

ization that Gandhi intended by the use of *satyāgraha,* and to the
spiritual method of substituting non-retaliation for the mechanical
return of violence for violence. That they could not practice non-
retaliation on this occasion proved to him that they had not exercised it earlier, for otherwise they would now be strong in it. That
they had not exercised it showed Gandhi that they had not practiced
true non-violence because true non-violence of whatever degree has
its own immediate moral effect, describable in terms of sweetness
and strength, which irresistibly invite further practice. There had
been no such change of taste and so no conversion as true non-
violence implied and true non-retaliation must manifest.

C. METHODS OF SATYĀGRAHA: TAPAŚCARYĀ

The methods of *satyāgraha* involve the third new element of
Gandhi's spiritual non-violence, viz. *tapaścaryā* of self-suffering.

The application of soul-force by means of exact conduct is a
method of *tapas* or penance. *Tapas* is a material means of invoking
and accumulating spiritual power. Gandhi defines *tapas* as "the steps
which one has to practice to reach an ideal."[51] *Tapas* in *satyāgraha*
is effort of the spiritual will to maintain exact conduct of Truth and
non-violence by acceptance of the suffering that adherence to these
ideals involves.

In *satyāgraha* the form of *tapas* is determined by specific physical
conditions of this effort to hold to the ideal. *Tapas* means literally
"what heats". Phenomenal structures and qualities are always disin-
tegrating, and "holding to the ideal" therefore always means resistance to the dissipation and resultant friction in the material elements. Thus an internal heat is created that is capable of materially
burning the ego-desire complex. The form of the heating resistance is
determined by the form of the dissipation to be countered, i.e. the
evil to be overcome.

Since *satyāgraha* is essentially a practical doctrine, material application conditions constitute half the final shape; the spiritual and the
practical requirements for the physical aspect of the *tapas* of *satyāgraha* thus coincide.

Ideally, each *satyāgraha* application would be a *deduction* from

the analysis of the spiritual aim and the practical aspect, the field, the
attributes of soul-force activated by resistance of that medium, the
particular evil to be undone or conquered within the individual or in
the group or society; these together determine the form of the action
as a means of non-violent resistance.

Because coercion in its subtler forms depends largely on the opponent's particular beliefs and attitudes and on the actual relationship
between *satyāgrahī* and opponent, Gandhi gave careful attention to
the material application conditions of particular methods of *satyāgraha*. This is clearly seen in his many detailed analyses of fasting as
a non-violent, non-coercive method. Gandhi considered this to be the
most powerful method at his disposal. But he also saw that since
fasting was the most likely method to inadvertently trade on the sus-
ceptibilities and weakness of opponent and co-worker, it was the
most in need of safeguarding regulation to prevent it from becoming
a form of coercion and violence.

Holding to Truth in Practical Action: Karmayoga.   For *satyāgraha,*
the body and the entire phenomenal field constitute only a means of
spiritual realization.

The votary is an individual bound in an active body and a web of
social relations. Gandhi believes that the humility and self-purification required to invoke and sustain the action of soul-force in one
are possible only through the medium of social life.

Self-reliance is the basis of soul-force in its individual aspect. Its
ultimate meaning is finding all contentment in the *ātman,* as defined
by the Gītā (II:55). Body is a means of self-realization, but the maintenance of body is not independent of the society; recognition of this
interdependence leads to the ideals of mutual regard and service by
which self-purification can be advanced and tested. Gandhi believes
that action in society rubs on the ego-sense most effectively and that
responsible social life constitutes the *sādhana* of *satyāgraha.*

Gandhi believes that a perfect being might remain apart and act
on society by means of pure thought. That perfectly pure thought
would have a self-acting power all its own and in fact would be the
material counterpart to self-active soul-force. But he is ambiguous as
to the real possibility of realizing this purely self-active thought
power. For imperfect beings the direct action of social service and

protection is the means of purification as also the means of drawing out soul-force in its practical expression.

Again, Gandhi's principle of *"yathā piṇḍe . . ."* requires a visible substitution. He finds this substitution for violence in voluntary self-suffering, since following duty imposed by the ideal of exact conduct necessarily involves a counter-provoking resistance from the self-interests that have so far maintained the unjust or socially malignant conditions.

Gandhi calls this social aspect the "Gospel of Service". It involves a constructive program that actively pursues general social reforms such as anti-untouchability, Hindu-Muslim unity, village industrial development and village sanitation, prohibition, agricultural research, nature cure research, etc. on non-violent lines.

Gandhi derives this program from the ideal of service referred to in the Gītā. Again, such sacrificial activity is not only a means to realization but also the expression of it. This ideal picture of sacrificial activity provides the model for the practical discipline of the "constructive program" of social service, and Gandhi believes that such "service" is the form of *yajña* for this age. Thus he believes that such service is also a form of *tapas* and *sādhana* as it is applied in *satyāgraha* as a non-violent means to external practical ends that are also a means to spiritual realization. The *satyāgrahī,* by his exact conduct, makes himself an exemplar of detached action in order to serve society and thereby to propagate the Truth that he has fully realized or towards which he has gained inexpungable experience of progress, viz. the simple, strong, healthy beauty of the life of divine love.

Non-violent resistance to obstruction of this positive service of redress and reform is accomplished by quietly suffering the reaction to the *satyāgrahī*'s continued insistence on the exact conduct of the reform and redress. Gandhi holds axiomatically that this non-retaliation and voluntary suffering of the innocent will inevitably melt the heart of the opponent and transform his understanding. It will give the opponent the depth of experience and the moral sensitivity required to support in his own empirical consciousness the propositions of Truth or justice which the *satyāgrahī*'s cause of reform or redress are intended to convey.

This is the educative basis of Gandhi's method, cutting evil at its roots by changing the beliefs, motives and perceptions of the opponent so he will no longer want to act in the untrue, unjust and injurious way to which he is blindly habituated. The opponent simply needs a basis and motivation for building new habits. This again is accomplished by a material conversion of the opponent's material make-up and not by a mere perceptual change gained from his viewing the novel, direct action of the *satyāgrahī* (as most theories of non-violence believe).

Gandhi adds that there is a safeguard built into the method. There is no guarantee that one's own views are the Truth. The *satyāgrahī* is an imperfect being striving for purification and perfection through empirical judgments about the Truth of a situation or the truly non-violent means of realizing, expressing and propagating it. If the *satyāgrahī* is wrong, only he will have suffered and there will be no irreparable injury or death to regret. Gandhi derives this from the moral proposition that God alone can destroy who alone can create.

Fit Principles to the Evil Challenged: Gandhi calls the Gītā a gospel of non-cooperation with evil.

Non-cooperation with evil is the moral interpretation of *anāsakti,* the ideal state of detached selfless action. Since Gandhi equates the entire phenomenal field with violence or evil, non-cooperation with and isolation of evil as methods to achieve *anāsakti* must take the form of the particular circle of violence that one must break out of. This circle is half constituted by inclinations rooted in one's particular ego-complex and half by those external material forces which constitute objects of or obstructions to enjoyment through that particular sense-mind-ego complex.

If the phenomenal form of the ego is greed, the confronting thought will be non-greed and the non-cooperation tactic will be a form of exact conduct that cuts the connection either between the desire and its object or the intermediary means to its fulfillment. For example, in resurgent India this meant boycott of foreign cloth by which she had been conquered and her people emasculated.

Satyāgraha seeks to find modes of thought and action which, in the individual's given embodiment and social position, will effectively isolate evil from the material resources that sustain it and will channel soul-force to hit at the ego-complex and evil means directly, while sustaining one against retaliation by those material elements and their inner and outer allies in evil. *The active quality of the soul-*

force invoked dismantles the evil and enlists the soul in the opponent to aid against the evil in himself. Those interactions are described from the empirical point of view as the "melting of the heart" that *seems* to be caused by seeing the voluntary suffering of the *satyāgrahī*. But it is common experience that seeing voluntary suffering may increase the brutality of resisted authorities.

Though the phenomenal conditions and reactions determine half the form of the method, Gandhi's analysis of method is *never based on the empirical vantage point only*. This physical analysis also refers always to transactions of energy that may not yield visible results until the subliminal results of many repeated non-violent actions accumulate to give the empirically calculable or visible resultant.

Gandhi believes that the speed of this visible efficacy depends on the purity of the *satyāgrahī* and his suffering and on the wisdom of his method. But he believes that any "truly" non-violent effort has its *immediate* result whether immediately visible or not. If the objective accords with Truth and the *satyāgrahī* has made the adequate self-sacrifice, God will produce the result using the *satyāgrahī*'s activities as an instrument. Some truly non-violent effect upon the world is guaranteed whether the action and consequence is looked at from the standpoint of Truth as God, or Truth as Law; this accords with Gandhi's equation of true religion, true science and true expedience or practical efficacy. So acting, the *satyāgrahī* participates in Truth and partakes of its nature.

The equation in practical reality cannot immediately manifest. In accordance with the Gītā's analysis of action and agency, Gandhi recognizes *no necessary connection* between fulfillment of the goal, as the practicant may envision it, and the final material result that God will bring about. The *satyāgrahī*'s activity, while authentic, is only one factor, and far from the decisive one (Gītā XVIII: 13–15).

Phenomenal conditions and belief may dictate that physical death of the *satyāgrahī* be the principle means for bringing about the larger resultant. In the extreme, Gandhi's method postulates voluntary immolation and death as the last weapon in his battle to displace in the opponent the untrue belief in materialism and ignorance of the soul that are at the root of and sustain the evil, the violence, in him and his actions. Gandhi believes that such a voluntary self-sacrifice would also replace the discredited belief with belief in soul and Truth, the

first condition of the opponent's release from his opposition viz. his
ignorance and bondage to evil.

Gandhi wrote that *satyāgraha:*

. . . is called soul-force, because a definite recognition of the soul
within is a necessity, if a *satyāgrahī* is to believe that death does not
mean cessation of the struggle, but a culmination. The body is merely
a vehicle for self expression; and he gladly gives up the body when its
existence is an obstruction in the way of the opponent seeing the Truth
for which the *satyāgrahī* stands. He gives up the body in the certain
faith that if anything would change his opponent's view, a willing sacrifice of the body must do so. And with the knowledge that the soul
survives the body, he is not impatient to see the triumph of Truth in
the present body. Indeed, victory lies in the ability to die in the attempt
to make the opponent see the Truth, which the *satyāgrahī* for the time
being expresses.[52]

If the *satyāgrahīs* are thus yet striving for perfection through *satyāgraha,* they are to that degree impure and therefore involved in
various manifestations of the ego-desire complex. A large cause may
require a large number of self-sacrificial deaths to finally achieve the
conversion of opponents and the practical translation of that conversion to a reform in consonance with the original cause.

The *satyāgrahīs* will play different roles in the total campaign as
they face different phenomenal aspects of the evil to be surmounted
and replaced. About the Vykom campaign to open a road to untouchables that passed by an orthodox caste temple, Gandhi writes
that the silent work at the spinning wheel or scavenging duty at the
satyāgraha camp was as important and effective in the campaign as
the non-resistance the *satyāgrahī's* offered at the barricades in the
form of silent vigil and peaceful picketing. He writes that the social
exclusion, disinheritance and intimidation suffered by the *satyāgrahīs*
at the hands of family and castemen was in fact more effective in the
total resultant than the direct actions of vigil and picketing; *that, "It
is not any single isolated act which can be called* satyāgraha *apart
from the spirit behind it."*[53]

The phenomenal conditions determine the shape of non-violent
acts that effectively allow soul-force to act on evil through the material medium, but no phenomenal act in and of itself accomplishes the
end in view or the evoking of soul-force. The physical aspect of exact

conduct is thus a condition of success but not its cause. Any causal function it could be said to have would be wholly secondary and made possible as a causal activity only as the result of a catalytic action by soul-force. But this secondary causal shape would be wholly determined by the material conditions it was invoked to ameliorate or counter.

It is important to remember that the physical component is *not* a product of empirical calculations, though there is in Gandhi's method an interplay of spiritual and rational faculties. Direct inspiration by God, awakened and purified conscience and disinterested analysis and reflection by sober trained reason all come into play. It is *axiomatic* for Gandhi that the human mind cannot handle the massive empirical problem even in its physical aspect.

Gandhi believes that the physical actions of *satyāgraha* must be the *spontaneous* expression of Love. But Love is another name for Truth and non-violence as these denote the power of soul-force by which it extinguishes distinctions and unifies material forces. Actions without the inspiration of soul-force, Love, can only further divide material reality against itself. It is the spirit of *anāsakti* alone that can invoke soul-force and give rise to effective, spontaneous non-violent action without the ego interposing its halting, diluting, vitiating empirical calculations based ultimately on desire and ignorance.

Nevertheless, properly guided use of reason is an essential component in *satyāgraha* action, and by the exercise of exact conduct the *satyāgrahī* incorporates into himself the materials that soul-force can spontaneously draw upon when needed. Gandhi intended his constant writings on the practice of *satyāgraha* to be a record of such experiments and to provide reflections for study by those interested in the same *sādhana*.

This spontaneity provides a touchstone for true *satyāgraha*. The ideal is spontaneous individual action prompted by the voice of conscience and spontaneous mass action prompted by the Truth of the cause itself, but there is no independent criterion assuring that the inner voice or the mass spontaneity are the genuine article. Usually, however, the response is out of all proportion to evident material incitements and this disproportion is enough to infer the operation of extraordinary causes, i.e., spiritual forces.

But Gandhi's aim was to introduce the method of conscience into public life. Before action, these claims are always suspect. He be-

lieved that claims for infallibility are possible only to consciousness
centered beyond the sway of phenomenal oppositions that are never
absent in sense and mental consciousness. For embodied beings there
is no infallible criterion for having reached this state. Assessments
about mass movements will always be relative judgments if not sta-
tistical inferences. Gandhi writes that time alone will tell and the acts
will indicate the validity of the claim as arising from the inner voice
only as consequences continue to accumulate and register.

Gandhi did give the immediate and necessary but not sufficient
criteria that claims of conscience or of the inner voice must be supported by long training and purification, and they should not oppose
trained, sober, disinterested reason or fundamental moral sense.
Where the claim is not supported by independent reason one may be
compelled to follow it, but does so at risk, relying only on the inner
criterion of past experience with the voice and reflection on acts and
results which inevitably reveal the voice's true character ("Know
them by their fruits").

Nevertheless, Gandhi's final criterion of Truth and non-violence is
what the purified heart grasps at the moment. Any external criterion
taken as more authoritative than the inner criterion would constitute
conformism and coercion. This would interfere with moral growth of
the individual and the society, both of which require the freedom to
err and correct themselves.

Lastly, the process of such analysis, reflection and self-examination is itself a means to attune conscience and reason and to better
prepare them for spontaneously molding action to the material application conditions when the need for non-violent direct action occurs.

Tapaścaryā: Drawing Out the Power of the Soul by Self-suffering.
Gandhi says that the universality and perfect practical efficacy of
non-violence *follow from the fact* that the soul is the same in all and
is the power of non-violence latent in all; *tapaścaryā* refers to the
path of self-suffering used to draw out that power.

Gandhi's third original element in non-violence is the ideological
requirement that *tapas* takes on a specific external form—a physical
activity and result; non-retaliation extended to the physical makes it
an absolute moral precept and gives an absolute practical dimension
that defines *satyāgraha* non-violence; the self-suffering involved in

trying to uphold this standard of non-retaliation constitutes the means of *satyāgraha*.

Gandhi writes that physical methods of *tapas* were discovered by sages who practiced austerities to inure themselves against the threats of tyrants. He claims only to have adapted these practices for the present age.

The Gītā and Upaniṣads restrict austerities to a means of self-purification and do not extend their use to accomplishing specific practical results. Certain classical Indic practices, e.g., fasting, social boycott, civil disobedience and *hijrat* (migration), do appear similar to Gandhi's methods from the physical standpoint. They lack, however, the moral and spiritual ideology of *satyāgraha*.

Gandhi found it necessary throughout his career to draw and re-draw carefully the distinction between his methods and similar-looking physical ones. He also needed to draw the distinction with traditional spiritual disciplines to which he added pragmatic criteria and his practical program of reform as integral components of a spiritual aim and *sādhana*. He called the individual and congregational prayer elaborated above *tapas,* but contrasted them with other methods of *satyāgraha* as purely inward acts whose penitential aspects are not peculiar to *satyāgraha*. Both the outward special *tapas* of self-suffering from holding to Truth and the usual *tapas* of prayer, worship, fasting, etc. function to invoke the spiritual power and increase purity by helping materially to dismantle the ego-desire complex and its passion-producing material adjuncts.

Methods and Vows: Gandhi's methods of non-violence are the general types of physical action that may on the one hand accord with the principles of *satyāgraha,* and on the other with the prevalent evils under which one can choose to suffer. As methods of *satyāgraha* they are methods of *tapas* meant to have a particular kind of material reaction on both the *satyāgrahī* and his surroundings.

The two basic forms of *tapas* are duty and love.

Holding to the requirements of either will necessarily bring resistance from the material elements whose ordinary reactions are not mediated by ideals. Demands of duty and love cannot coincide with the empirically self-centered sense elements.

The general functions of *satyāgraha* methods are to purify empiri-

cal consciousness, invoke soul-force, propagate ideals, awaken conscience to the inner voice, isolate and starve evil and substitute its
opposite, good. The basis of fulfilling all of these functions is the *law*
of suffering and innocence.

According to Gandhi, both the Gītā and experience teach that
the law of sacrifice is uniform throughout creation, but man is unique
in that he can follow this law consciously, deliberately and intelli-
gently, and further, that as the "law of suffering" he can apply it to
the solution of practical problems. *Satyāgraha* requires this suffering
to be the purest and most innocent. It thus entails the absolute non-
retaliation that would cheerfully suffer death without defense or ill-
will, a gift to the opponent as to a beloved.

Gandhi believes that though all reform and pursuit of right involve suffering, *satyāgraha* seeks to improve the efficiency and speed
by adding the innocence defined by his absolute standard of non-
retaliation. The greater the purity, the greater one's strength and the
faster the success because the greater the channeling of soul-force.

The chief meaning of "purity" in terms of non-violence and soul-
force is the innocence of non-retaliation, including no thought and
no feeling of hate while being killed in the line of duty and out of
love. But this suffering must be chosen deliberately, in recognition of
the principles of *satyāgraha* and with full awareness of their implications for suffering as a method. Knowledge and faith in the means
make this suffering immediately constitute an attack on the ego-
mind-body complex. It is insistence to suffer by holding to Truth and
right when the ego-mind-and-body insist on not suffering. Gandhi
describes it as a crucifixion of the flesh. This deliberate recognition is
satyāgraha's practical application of the knowledge component in
true renunciation, and thus constitutes the operative factor and effectiveness of the law of suffering innocence, the temporal adaptation
of eternal principle.

Whether or not there is a visible non-violent transaction and psychological interaction in the particular act of the *satyāgrahī*, the
progress takes place at the level of energy exchange. The innocence
of *satyāgraha* suffering is not a mere moral ascription or judgment
but a material condition and energetic state which will, with scientific precision, have its definite and inevitable effects on the environment and the opponent. Reasoned faith in these usually invisible effects and in his methods sustain the *satyāgrahī* in cheerful suffering,

even in the face of long-continued apparent failure of his actions to touch the opponent's heart and to visibly achieve redress or ameliorate conditions.

Gandhi claims that ideally the innocent suffering of one pure *satyāgrahī* could bring down an empire and lay the foundation for its reclamation. He often wrote that the death of one innocent *satyāgrahī* dying at duty without malice or retaliation was equivalent to "1,000,000" dying while in the act of killing. From near axioms such as these, Gandhi supported his practical claim. Gandhi acknowledged that since the ideal could not be reached in the body, soul-force could not act purely. It might in fact take thousands of such relatively pure deaths to accomplish a great reform, redress a long-standing injustice or avert a war. But he believed that the final accounting of suffering, violence and loss of life, would be far less than the traditional methods of killing while being killed.

Method Types: Gandhi evolved five types of method of purificatory suffering as means of substituting non-violence for violence, self-suffering for causing suffering, in *satyāgraha*:

(1) In *civil disobedience* one accepts the penalty of law, usually imprisonment, possibly attachment of property. (2) In *civil resistance* and *non-cooperation* one refuses the benefits of cooperation with the evil person or system. A type of non-cooperation involves giving more than is unjustly demanded. (3) In *hijrat* one gives up home and land. (4) In *fasting* one denies the flesh, senses and mind. (5) In *non-violent resistance* or *defense* unto death without retaliation, one gives life.

There is no end to means of suffering but these are generic types that Gandhi emphasized; each is meant to neutralize evil by reducing the sustaining energies that are given it by inadvertently supportive or ignorantly cooperative action by the good or neutral. The chief condition is the same throughout: i.e. non-retaliation in thought, word and deed, and the active loving quality of soul-force which communicates itself as an operative factor (but also which alone can sustain this non-retaliation past the endurance of the ego-mind-body complex).

Gandhi interprets these methods to bring about this condition in which alone non-violence of the strong begins to be effective. With-

out this degree of material purification and innocence there can only
be a change of form in the present interactions of material factors
that are already locked into mutually violent chain reactions.

The triggering degree of purity cannot be given by a rule and
therefore methods cannot be further defined. The first axiom of non-
violence (see p. 77) registers this requirement. No single standard
can be set because it depends on the actual constitution of the individual's ego-desire complex and on what activities and spiritual discipline are carried out with how intense and vital a faith.

Gandhi specifies the condition of effective *satyāgraha* as the extremity of helplessness. He writes that *satyāgraha* evolved from his
recognition of the fact stated in the Tamil verse, "God is the help of
the helpless". *Satyāgraha* presupposes non-violence of the strong, a
non-violence sustained by the power of God in the form of soul-
force, divine guidance and inner joy and force. This force is created
by divine dispensation of inner states and external circumstances.

The condition of receiving God's grace, support and power is an
invocation that exceeds the inertia or obstruction by the ego-desire
center of empirical consciousness, and which links this awakened
empirical consciousness with the spiritual states that are directly receptive to divine inspiration and energy. As God is omnipresent, so
His grace is always there, but the *satyāgrahī* will be a possible conscious recipient and participant only after he has materially cleared
himself of the stuff to which evil adheres, and at least momentarily
surpassed his own ego-state in which the infusion of subtler and
more potent energy is impossible.

According to Gandhi, the suffering of the *satyāgrahī* must therefore be a form of prayer in order for it to be effective for practical
purposes in a way which material suffering, with no basis beyond itself, cannot. In accordance with the above analysis, "prayer" simply
means that effort at inner communion or opening to one's higher nature which naturally subordinates the lower empirical, self-centered
will and allows spontaneous action in response to the larger reality.
In this case, both from inner and outer resources, more energy is operative in the individual in the prayer state than was in the ego state,
and Gandhi's third axiom of practical non-violence is fulfilled.

Finally, spiritual suffering as *tapas* in *satyāgraha* is an end in itself.
Gandhi writes that the exultation of truly giving oneself to a larger
cause transforms that material suffering into a type of joy superior to

and more powerful than the material suffering it is founded on. In this state the ideal of the Gītā is realized wherein pleasure and pain of sensory experiences, and success and failure and merit and demerit of mental and moral experience, become one and the same to the experiencing *ātman;* the ideal of *sthitaprajña* is attained in which there is no modification of consciousness, and it remains unaffected by any phenomenal movement whether of changing inner or outer states.

The principles of non-violent campaigning also are not important in their specific material adaptation. They will vary almost completely from campaign to campaign. Large-scale unique events or movements necessarily present novel problems with numerous combinations of component actions and movements existing within the larger campaign which may extend for months, years or even decades.

There are no generic techniques of campaigning or generic strategies as there are basic types of method. Given the complexity of human affairs, each application of these method types has a unique total makeup and will likely reveal new aspects of non-violence of general interest to the *satyāgrahī,* as a moral and spiritual scientist.

Each of Gandhi's campaigns was in fact novel and unique. He claims each was prompted by the inner voice and each seemed also to meet with spontaneous response from the masses. This confirmed him in the belief that they satisfied the basic criteria of *satyāgraha,* whatever the limitations of their successes. He considered his campaigns very imperfect specimens of *satyāgraha* and himself a very imperfect *satyāgraha* general.

The central point is that the non-violent general does not calculate strategy on the basis of empirical information and assessments of material power relations and resources. He is guided directly by the inner voice that he knows as God. His corporate actions are geared to be ends in themselves, i.e. to display his ideals of Truth and non-violence and to result in self-purification and invocation of soul-force regardless of falling short in terms of the visibly evident, pragmatic criterion of immediate practical success. Their aim is moral uplift and ennoblement, and spiritual advance and realization by the *satyāgrahī's* mere participation.

It may be noted that the day-to-day continuance of the action does have what might be referred to as negative tactical conditions that function as rules of thumb in campaigning. These merely express the attitudes of respect and non-compulsion that must underlie all non-violent action. Their content is not a matter of rote and they cannot be applied as "moral rules for winning a practical victory."

For example, that *satyāgraha* campaigns are never calculated to obstruct or to embarrass the opponent is such a general rule. This would constitute a form of violence as coercion. But what must be avoided in *satyāgraha* is the *motive* of embarrassment or obstruction. These may in fact be the unavoidable result of gearing action to a more fundamental demand of non-violence. Gandhi argues that the compromise cannot be justified in terms of non-violence, but it must be worked out to give the most protection possible to the ideal. Such compromise does eventually have the effect of propagating the ideal. Gandhi holds that one cannot be held responsible for all of the unintended consequences of his acts and that there is obviously no liability where the principle motive and constant effort has been on behalf of the ideal.

In South Africa in 1913–14, Gandhi's eight-year campaign against the color bar, unjust indenture laws and registration taxes seemed to gain its final victory by a striking example of the principle of non-embarrassment when every usual tactical consideration would have required taking advantage of the opponent's disability and moment of weakness. In 1940, Gandhi deferred to these principles when he pledged not to launch civil disobedience against the British during World War II. But when the British sought to silence his advocacy of non-violence as an ultimate moral principle and his absolute judgment that war is an immoral and ultimately impractical method of adjustment in human relations, he felt compelled to begin individual *satyāgraha* for freedom of speech to preach immutable moral principles. This freedom itself was an immutable moral principle to be protected even at the cost of unintended embarrassment or violence.

The duty of the *satyāgrahī* to propagate the ideals of Truth and non-violence surpasses any principle of non-violent campaigning for more specific practical goals or even less basic moral ones. Equally fundamentally, Gandhi believed that this *satyāgraha* was required by his love for Britain as well, and was intended as much for her good as for India's and that of humanity. His claim was that he would show the same "terrible" aspect of *satyāgraha* to a member of his family whose wrong behavior must cause harm to himself as well as to others, and moral harm was the worst that could be perpetrated.

The allies could not have India's moral support, which Gandhi believed they needed for material victory, without themselves making the effort for moral rectitude with regard to the colonized world and the ideals of Equality, Fraternity and Liberty that defined the democracy they claimed to be fighting to protect. Major moral issues were involved *on all sides*. In accordance with his ideology of non-violence, Gandhi considers surgical incision out of love to be non-violence in fact, and his civil disobedience, though embarrassing the opponent, constituted moral surgery.

Since the guiding principles behind all *satyāgraha* action are *anāsakti, yajña* and *brahmasamarpaṇa,* as means of detachment from all fruits of action (materialism), Gandhi's concept of *satyāgraha must* rule out tactical or strategic principles. Rather there is the moral preemptive effort and duties of love to always know, in terms of Truth and non-violence, the present needs and conditions and available resources; and to habitually engage in preventative and uplifting programs of construction and corporate cleansing that constitute the purity of waiting on God while working away at the necessities that would, if these lacks were unameliorated or necessities unmet, sooner or later call a non-violent army to service.

Lastly, Gandhi believes public opinion to be the most potent instrument of the *satyāgrahī.* All his methods are intended to awaken and educate it and to enlist its active support for the espoused cause. The empirical analysis of the phases and processes of this mass awakening and education is not important. It must only be recognized that public opinion is not mere weight of numbers. Gandhi looks to "weight of numbers" in public opinion only in terms of the majority that is neutral with regard to one's cause, or which favors the cause but is not awake to its own possible role in supporting and propagating that cause—numbers that once awakened by *satyāgraha* would be on the side of right and for true reasons. If the public opinion is the product of hysteria or misinformation, or if it is from a population that is itself actively involved in evil, it is not a vehicle of non-violence but a means of coercion, oppression or exploitation.

Public opinion as a weapon of non-violence must be the result of reason and moral appeal and it must act on principles of Truth and non-violence if it is to become involved in the campaign as more than a moral force.

Gandhi also restricts the type of support that may be given ac-

cording to the *karmic* and material analysis of the situation and the
cause. Thus a general principle is that an outsider may not offer the
penitential self-suffering of *satyāgraha*. Gandhi writes that the Christian, Mr. Joseph, could not represent the penitent Hindus in the
Vykom struggle against orthodox upholding of untouchability. The
orthodox would view it as outside interference and coercion rather
than as penance for a wrong in which one feels himself implicated
equally with his opponent. This rule also is complex and admits
qualification.

Again, as a weapon of *satyāgraha,* true and effective public opinion must be the result of the working of soul-force. This force of
opinion would result in proportion as one's suffering is pure and purifying, and so become a material vehicle for soul-force.

Vows: Vows are the general *tapas* of *satyāgraha*. They categorize
the moral efforts that uphold and propagate its fundamental ideals.

Gandhi lists eleven vows. The first five are the universal vows
of classical Indic moral discipline: Truth (*satya*), non-violence
(*ahiṁsā*), continence (*brahmacarya*), non-stealing (*asteya*) and non-possession (*aparigraha*).

Gandhi gives his own definitions of these. Briefly, Truth is accordance in thought, word and deed, with Truth of soul, unison of
life, law of *karma,* authenticity and conscience and sanctity of agreement; non-violence is avoidance of injury to all life by thought, word
and deed, and active non-violent protection of any creature under
attack; continence is control of all the senses and mind (celibacy
is a strategic but not exclusive component of this moral self-control);
non-stealing is not claiming what is not yours even if it comes to you
by accident; non-possession is not holding to what is not needed for
duty, and holding the body itself as only a trust for the duties of realization and service of God.

According to Gandhi, the essence of vow-taking is self-restraint.
Vows thus provide the basis of self-protection and self-purification in
both spiritual realization and non-violent campaigning. Gandhi derives all morals from Truth, non-violence and continence, and he derives non-violence and continence from Truth—they are based on
the distinction between soul and not-soul, the unity of all life and the
need to subordinate sense and mental life in order to realize the spiritual life.

These vows are not practiced for their difficulty, but for building the virtue of sticking to Truth regardless of difficulty. One should not take a vow beyond one's capacity but should vow to keep one's self-regulations even at the cost of life. This alone can prove their derivation from Truth of soul and give the required purifying potency.

By his logical principle of *"yathā piṇḍe . . ."*, Gandhi makes the practice of vow-taking subserve the Gītā ideal of non-doership or nullification of the ego. Just as the planets and all of nature work with unerring regularity, so the *satyāgrahī* should lead a life of self-imposed lawful regularity. Vows give the reliability and perseverance necessary for realizing spontaneous action, for making a habit or second nature of exact conduct—for observing Truth and non-violence in all the smallest details of life, easily and equally.

Gandhi adds six vows derived from Truth, non-violence and self-control, specially adapting them to the material needs of the age: (1) bread labor (physical labor each day, sufficient to pay for one's own "daily bread".), (2) control of the palate, (3) fearlessness, (4) equal regard for all religions, (5) *swadeśī* (patronage first of one's neighborhood, then district, province and nation for physical needs and services), and (6) removal of untouchability (in one's own conduct and in one's family and community).

These eleven vows taken together were the basis of self-discipline in Gandhi's *āśrama* (place where a group lives together for guidance, training, discipline, and mutual support in a common *sādhanā* and way of life) and campaigns.

Introduction: The criteria for the working of *satyāgraha*, and the practical claims underlying them, derive directly from Gandhi's concept of Truth and his moral ideology of non-violence. They have therefore been intimately involved in the elaboration of his principles and methods of *satyāgraha*.

The basic criterion of perfect moral and practical efficacy is really identical with his radical practical claim for the universal applicability of non-violence. These together form a basic component of the single aim of spiritual realization, as was introduced in Chapters 2 and 3.

The different components of the criterion are: the equation of the spiritual, the moral and the practical Truth; perfect practical efficacy; perfect moral efficacy; and the permanence of these as spiritual results.

The practical claim is composed of claims for the universal applicability and practicability of *satyāgraha*, and for its practical infallibility.

The bases and experience of these components of his criteria and claims have been developed in Chapters 2 and 3 as part of the elaboration of his concept, principles and methods. In this chapter these elements will be summarized and related to each other as evaluational categories in order to complete the exposition of Gandhi's non-violence.

A. EQUATION OF CRITERIA THROUGH "TRUTH":
THE SPIRITUAL, THE MORAL AND THE PRACTICAL—SYNONYMOUS

Truth and the Expedient: Since Gandhi refers to religion, ethics and expedience as synonyms, and says that purest religion is also the highest expedience, his chief criterion and claim is the spiritual one of permanence of result.

Gandhi's "Truth" is fundamentally a spiritual concept to which he assimilates the religious, moral and practical. It is set off from the phenomenal and material by the component of eternality as indicated by Gandhi's substitution formula of the ephemeral and real. All but Truth, the permanent element, undoes itself in time.

The possibility of *satyāgraha* as a practical method with self-suffering as its chief spiritual means is based on the permanence and changelessness of the soul's bliss and power. The "holding to Truth" of *satyāgraha* represents this permanence in physical terms.

For Gandhi, though the problem of full spiritual realization is eschatological, its active evolving counterpart, soul-force, may be made seeable through its effects as it interacts with the material field. It does what brute-force could not and its properties are thus deduced from contrast with the ordinary.

Gandhi acknowledges that the practical power of soul-force cannot be known by argument but only by demonstration, but also that "demonstration" as such can only convince one that some extraordinary factor has been introduced.

Gandhi agrees with the spiritualist's claim that one meaningful measure by which these dissimilar factors can be counterposed in a single experience is the distinction between the ephemeral and the changeless. They claim that properties ascribed to soul-force in contrast with brute-force, as these are seen in contradictory effects on the material medium, are understandable and demonstrable on this basis, if not provable.

Gandhi points to the transformation in conduct of the votary of Truth as he gains access to states inaccessible to senses and mind, as his subjective makeup is purified of ego-sense formations and as soul-force becomes active in him.

There is a corresponding transformation of values and outlook. The materially trivial becomes equal with the materially monumental. For Gandhi the consciousness and care with which the spinning wheel is plied becomes the direct monitor of the inner state of spiritual evolution and non-violence. He writes that the external efficiency in mundane duties becomes a direct indicator of the inner approach to Truth in which there is no distinction and differentiation. He claims even that were the means of independence, namely the constructive program of spinning, village industry, *khaddar* (homespun and home-woven cloth) manufacture, etc. fully implemented, the end could already have been achieved.

This is Gandhi's application of his ends/means criterion of Truth; Truth admits of no material difference between means and ends. If the ends are true, the immediate whole-hearted grasp and effort in the means, expunging the ego-self from the action, must be equivalent to the ends, requiring only a widening of its scope. Gandhi believed that only on the spiritual view of reality can this equation of means and ends be given this practical content, and that, therefore, even a limited approximation to this convertibility of truthful ends and successful means would justify his preliminary practical claims and his continued experiments in Truth and non-violence in the practical sphere.

The Moral and the Expedient: Gandhi's equation of the moral and the expedient is another aspect of his concept of Truth.

Gandhi believed that moral nature is fundamental to humanity and therefore a pragmatic criterion of action must be an abstraction. Empirical ideology of materialism makes moral nature look like a superimposition on pure fact, while Gandhi sees empiricism as an unjustified reductionism. Human relations cannot be understood on simply pragmatic lines. All practical problems of human relations have a moral component which marks them as "human problems"; "moral" refers to the permanent element or spirit in man, in terms of which all aspects of human activity and relations must be understood.

Action without regard to the inviolable individuality and inherent kinship of all man (sic) is demoralizing and its effects on the subjective make-up are patent. Gandhi's entire public effort was the infusion of moral values into the "practical" affairs of political, economic and social life where the spiritual element and propriety of means had been discounted as unrealistic. He advocated Ruskin's moral analysis which restored spiritual facts to the calculus of cause and effect in human affairs. Thus for Gandhi the moral realm is the realm of practical effort, and he believed that no ennobling or lasting results are possible in human transactions which ignore relations of rights and duties derived in terms of the spiritual facts of Truth, soul and human moral and spiritual growth through the laws of detachment, duty and sacrifice.

Achievement of Reform: Gandhi's "infallible" practical efficacy presupposes a "worthy result". A worthy result is one which injures none and lifts and advances the spiritual realization of all. It is not a product of the temporary ego-desire complex.

For Gandhi the "worthy result" is the only truly "practical" result. Attached to the spirit it will be sustained indefinitely, but what is brought about by force or fraud will last only until the supporting attention and forces are removed. If the inspiration to action is Truth and its mechanism is non-violence and soul-force, its result will be substantial and permanent compared to aims calculated on the basis of desire and material resources, which have self-destruction and ephemerality built into their conception and materials.

A "reform" is the practical solution of a moral problem in society or political life. A reform which replaced conditions that stultify spiritual growth with those which foster and inspire it would be a worthy result and a truly practical achievement. As material needs and desires shift, resources would be reclaimed and reallocated. The spirit requires stable conditions (virtues) for its refinement, growth and fuller expression and would therefore sustain these conditions, in order to fulfill a purpose outlasting any merely passing material purpose or interest attached to material structures as ends in themselves, that is, desires.

"Redress of wrong" is an aspect of practical efficacy understood in terms of reform. According to Gandhi, "wrong" is what hurts the moral being and disables it by damaging its sense of individual worth and capability, by obstructing growth of its individuality or by isolating it from the social interdependence which alone can refine that individuality and purify its ego-sense, strengthening and weakening it as the larger spiritual growth requires.

Gandhi's methods showed significant success in South Africa, Virangam, Champaran and Bardoli in the redress of injustice; and in temple entry and anti-untouchability campaigns in Vykom and Tamilnad. The independence of India, and settlements along the way, are in some measure the practical effects of Gandhi's *satyāgraha*. Gandhi also directed many successful labor strikes and picket-

ing campaigns, as well as his large non-cooperation movement and
Dandi Salt March and campaign.

Gandhi did not, however, consider these cases to be demonstrations of pure *satyāgraha*, or non-violence of the strong. They did not leave lasting moral conversion and in most cases it can be seen that the practical results were not sustained. He believed, nevertheless, these were significant results showing that some force was indeed operating and sufficiently so to justify further experiments.

Non-violent Defense and Retaining Gains: Gandhi considered the criterion of the practical validity of a certain force to be that the same force used to gain the result should suffice to retain the gains.

Wresting independence from Britain should be a more difficult task than defending it once attained; and if soul-force were the active factor in the gaining of it from a weak position, it should more easily accomplish the protection and defense of this gain from a position of strength.

Gandhi said the criterion of non-violence of the strong was that one felt stronger upon renouncing his arms and use of brute-force that he had previously depended on for all his sense of strength. *If fearlessness and strength were not the result then one's renunciation was not true and did not constitute an abdication of the ego-sense and accession to the soul's power.*

The votary should take up the violent means that he believes strengthen him rather than resort to demoralizing untruth of hypocrisy and behave non-violently out of cowardice only.

Gandhi believed that where the renunciation was true, the ensuing process of purification and the evolution of conscious force would result in an active quality of love and purity that would confer its own strength in practical terms, not only on oneself but on one's associates also.

Gandhi gave repeated rehearsals in his writings of how one should non-violently respond to armed robbery, or assault or ravage. True non-violence of the strong would be characterized by loving rebuke, calm reasoning and acceptance of the person of the criminal. If necessary, the votary would throw his body between the thief and the property entrusted to his care, or between the assailant and his victim, between a kidnapper and the ward under protection, or between the ravager and his intended victim. If the purity were sufficient this action would not be necessary. Soul-force alone would disarm the opponent, neutralize his violence and make him penitent. If one's purity or innocence and non-violent strength were not so evolved then the non-violent act of self-immolation would bring the assailant to his senses, satisfy his passion or frighten him away. Gandhi admits one might still fail, but failure was even more likely when return of violence adds incitement and stimulus.

The criterion as Gandhi conceives it is the necessary practical efficacy given adequate purity or innocence. This proviso of purity is not a loophole. It is implied in the total analysis of the phenomenal field as an entirety; where there is not the required material non-egoity, Truth cannot show through the material medium and soul-force cannot operate in the catalytic way of which it is otherwise capable.

Gandhi intends precisely that the purity of a woman would protect her against ravage, not by an abstract moral presumption but by the working of energies below the threshold of the empirically sensible. This depends on her having undergone a deliberate discipline and training in the requisite course of self-purification of *satyāgraha*.

In the absence of this training and purification, though her immediate and conscious response may be fright and repulsion, the organic and mental elements in an unreconstituted subjective makeup must react without regard to personal and social distinction. This would draw a response from the assailant and strengthen it. On the other hand, a material makeup purified by the course of non-violence, Truth and self-control, would neither respond nor retaliate, but would actively go out to meet, neutralize and disengage the opposing energies from the opponent's person, rendering the evil impotent.

The same analysis applies to the murderer. The non-retaliation of the trained *satyāgrahī* is an organic response and constitutes a protecting shield and a disarming, loving embrace to the opposing energies while disassembling their root structures. Regardless of the ferocious appearance of such energies on the visible level, they are really disordered and at odds amongst themselves having as their origin and aim only desire. They have not the power of disciplined love or even the relatively small degree of purification and training of a novice but sincere *satyāgrahī*.

These principles appear simple and almost moral truisms, but

Gandhi judged their discovery to be of far greater difficulty than faced Newton or Galileo, since what is involved is translation to an entirely other category of reality. To the votary they mean a wholly novel mode of apprehension and vantage point for viewing as only one aspect of reality what to him previously had constituted its whole.

Empirical science accomplishes its objective discovery by withdrawal of judging consciousness to the mental level, making all phenomenal movement objective and wholly opposed to the abstracted intellective faculties. Spiritual science must withdraw consciousness into fundamental self-awareness, *ātman,* making the whole category of the phenomenal (subjective as well) objective to it.

Gandhi expresses his highest admiration for the sage who was able to rise above the whole category of phenomenal reality, including his own ego-desire complex constituted in and by it, and from there to observe that all phenomenal activity is violence, that only spirit is *not*-violent, that only non-violence is lasting and real and therefore, only non-violence, soul-force, can solve the problem of violence and self-destruction. The principles are simple, but immediate threat to life and sway of *abhiniveśa* (will to survive) over fundamental moral consciousness vitiate theoretical understanding when this is unawake to ultimate spiritual basis and identity.

Difficult as it is to apply these principles to individual self-defense, Gandhi applies the same analysis to the problems of meeting an aggressor army in war as to quelling domestic rioting.

His plan for thousands to offer themselves as non-retaliating cannon-fodder to sicken and disarm the invading army appeals to moral sense and dramatic imagination. But the effective factor for Gandhi would still be the purity of the participants and the innocence of their dying. To the extent they die with retaliation or hate in thought, feeling or act, they would only excite and feed the lower nature of the invading army, justifying their violence, instead of neutralizing it, suffocating their lower nature and awakening their higher nature.

It might be conjectured that 1,000 incorrigible convicted murderers coerced into immolating themselves this way in preference to being slowly tortured to death would have little or no non-violent effect at all. Or again, the *satyāgrahī* needn't be far advanced in discipline or self-purification to effectively stem invasion if the invaders were relatively innocent and only performing action on pure ideal-istic but misinformed motives.

The central point is that Gandhi's claim of practical efficacy against most extensive violence may be qualified according to mate-rial conditions, but the principle of its spiritually necessary practical applicability is not thereby modified.

C. MORAL EFFICACY OF SATYĀGRAHA ACTIONS:
HAVING INTRINSIC WORTH

Moral efficacy is not an internal criterion opposed to the external one of practical efficacy. It refers to the subjective component of mo-tives and intentions, but in relation first to the character of the ac-tion, second, to the reaction upon the agent's moral consciousness and spiritual growth, and third, to its external consequences mea-sured in terms of the fundamental moral ideals of Truth and non-vio-lence.

The central principles are *anāsakti* and *brahmasamarpaṇa*, which inspire actions of *yajña*. Such actions have intrinsic worth, not need-ing to be justified by external practical results. Where these princi-ples are active, material or practical results are renounced, the ego-desire complex is weakened and non-tearing is a real moral result. But these are not extraneous effects. They are intrinsic aspects of the action, spontaneously produced, qualitative material counterparts of the active spiritual qualities of soul-force.

Individual: Death at Duty without Ill-will.   Gandhi considers this to be the ultimate *yajña*.

Gandhi cites Tulsīdās, summing up Hinduism in the verse, "The root of religion is embedded in mercy, whereas egotism is rooted in love of the body. Tulsī says that mercy should never be abandoned, even though the body perish."[54]

Gandhi wrote that the core of *satyāgraha* is giving up the body while holding to duty or insisting on Truth.

The ultimate moral value is renunciation of the ego-sense for real-ization of the Spirit and in deference to the Spirit's activity through oneself as its instrument. The physical body is the central plank in maintaining the ego-desire complex since through its senses and actions all material desires are fulfilled.

The fulfillment of *anāsakti* is the renunciation of fruits or denial of inspiration by hoped-for or expected results. The fullest renunciation of objective empirical inspiration to action, according to Gandhi, would be the voluntary renunciation of the entire instrumental means by which ego and desire fulfill themselves and by means of which they fight and cause injury when that fulfillment is obstructed and they turn into anger (Gītā II:62–63).

Though Gandhi is ambiguous as to the real possibility of ideal purity and so of the ideal efficacy it could engender, and he admits it will ordinarily take many *satyāgrahic* deaths to accomplish a practical result, he considered the moral results immediate and infectious. It is the infectious character of the working of non-violent forces and quality that gathers momentum and finally achieves the practical result. Gandhi claims that the immediate material effect on the quality of the atmosphere and the quality of human relations (e.g. a lessening of tensions, a sweetness in the atmosphere, softening of individuals and conversion in the opponent) is not unnotable. He ascribes this potency even to the physical aspect of the *satyāgrahī*'s exact conduct.

Gandhi claims that a general moral ennoblement and upliftment must occur in the society in which such voluntary sacrifice is the means of combat or reform. Suffering of a lesser degree has the same effect, in a proportionally lesser degree, with slower practical development.

But Gandhi allows to the sacrifice of self a special moral and spiritual efficacy aside from the acceleration towards the specific practical aim. He says that without this degree of readiness to sacrifice there is no non-violence of the strong and no claim can be made for the special efficacy he assigns to *satyāgraha*.

In accord with the Gītā, Gandhi claims that the quality of the soul at death is the test of its quality in life and that the state at the moment of death determines the spiritual course of the soul in the next embodiment and in the intervening non-physical states (Gītā VIII: 5–7). To die in the state of elevation produced by loving forgiveness, even under threat of death, is to release to the entire physical and spiritual world a moral potency whose effects cannot be calculated.

Its effect in terms of the immediate objective would metaphorically be "1,000,000" times more than what could be accomplished by death in the act of killing, whose only moral effect would be amplification of the original violence and so multiplication of evil in the world.

Gandhi believes that this is the law of retaliation, and by his logical principles, he claims that it must have exactly the opposite effect of non-retaliation while facing death. This is therefore the standard of the moral criterion not derived from merely ethical ideals but from an analysis of material and moral effects in terms of real operative energies and qualities.

Relations: Enmity Vanishes, Friendship Established.   The moral effect of *satyāgraha* on human relations is a further criterion.

Gandhi ascribes directly to soul-force the property of defusing the ego-desire complex and eliciting a response from the opponent's soul and moral consciousness. These two combine to weaken the negative interactions that supported the enmity relationship and to establish a true friendship with mutual respect and mutual concern. *The transformation of relations is the result of a reconstitution of the material being and material atmosphere and of its irradiation by the active quality of non-violence.*

"Love of the enemy" is the standard of active non-violence. It indicates the active working of soul-force whose quality is Love, transmitting the power of Truth to annul distinctions and to make the mundane and materially insignificant as precious as the materially dearest. It is the standard more so since this relation also is given a new quality based on the unison of being and accomplished by the power of Truth and Love. No material affinity (physical, emotional, mental, intellectual) can fulfill the moral and spiritual being since these affinities are essentially temporal and basically self-centered "taking-relations", as opposed to intrinsically permanent, soul-centered "giving-relations". The material affinities and relations are not self-sustained and yet self-preservation is their inborn tendency (*abhiniveśa*). To Gandhi there is no way to compare the two categories, as there is no way to compare the *satyāgrahī*'s death with non-retaliation and the soldier's death with hate while killing.

Motives, Quality of Acts and Change of Self: On the basis of the
karma theory, Gandhi believes that any good in an action shows up
in the resultant and accumulates from act to act while evil also
shows up but progressively dissipates itself as it disassembles and dis-
perses its own supporting structures. He qualifies his motive-oriented
ethics and axiology.

In particular, Gandhi believes that a right act accomplishes good
even if the motives are not good.

The chief moral efficacy of *satyāgraha* is precisely the change in
one who uses it sincerely even if with impure motives and ineptly. Its
whole purpose is the progressive conversion of such imperfect votaries. To the charge that his non-cooperators had motives of hate,
Gandhi replied that the end of hatred was retaliation while the end
of non-cooperation was not punishment that hate must wish, but justice that Truth required. He writes that, "The hatred of the non-
cooperator turning upon himself loses its points, purifies him, and
makes it possible for the object of his hatred to reform and retrace
his steps. Thus the non-cooperator starting as an enemy ends by becoming a friend. What does it matter with what motive a man does
the right thing? A right act is right whether done for policy or for its
own sake . . . policy being abandoned, if it does not produce the desired effect is not an argument against the morality of the act itself."[55]

Gandhi is defining "right act" as "right-making", an act which of
itself produces the moral good elaborated above. This is only a particular case of the basic ideal underlying *satyāgraha* that exact conduct is itself a *tapas* and has the capability to change the agent who
adopts it as his mode of action.

Gandhi writes elsewhere that his mass program was intended to
canalize hatred and transmute its self-destructive energies to constructive and life-giving ones. He believes that by teaching the masses
harmless but effective direct action, and inculcating the fact of the incapacity of the evildoer to do evil without sufferance or tacit alliance
and complicity of the good, the masses could come to feel that the
remedy lay in their own hands. They would cease to blame and wish
punishment to even the oppressor and seek only redress of the
wrong.

Gandhi claims that the permanence of the practical and moral effects produced by *satyāgraha* is the expression of its being accomplished by a spiritual and therefore eternal principle. It produces a material *conversion* in both the advocate and opponent, not a mere suppression of the original material elements or temporary and morally irrelevant change in their arrangement. Thus "relative permanence" is the basic criterion of non-violence of the strong.

Conversion, Not Suppression: In responding to charges that his fasts were coercive, Gandhi writes that they were not meant to achieve results external to the act except on very closely defined moral and spiritual conditions. He believes that these conditions must place the act in a different category from "coercion" or "compulsion" as ordinarily understood.

Gandhi believes that a true *satyāgraha* fast would achieve its effect by touching the soul, not the body and mind, of the opponent. His methods of *satyāgraha* were meant to have primarily the spiritual effect of awakening the permanent element in oneself and the opponent. This constitutes a spiritual rebirth and a moral conversion, and it produces the active quality of non-retaliation in the subjective makeup; these changes are then sustained by the permanent changeless soul which presides over the non-violent efforts. The one in whom the awakening and conversion occurs then partakes of the permanence.

A material method might produce a temporary suppression of violent tendencies, but with no material basis for maintaining the state gained. Third party alliances and ulterior motives that are a rallying point for material energies inevitably shift, or are voided, by the programmatic success they were intended to achieve; the empirical will itself is by nature changeable and shifty.

Finally, Gandhi claims an educative conversion in that as the opponent acts on non-violent ideals his actions will prove effective and this success will justify to him the beliefs and motives implied by those ideals, and produce an enduring firm and reasoned moral character.

ated his campaigns principally on the criterion of permanence.

Non-violence as a quality and force of the soul must exhibit the quality of permanence in accord with his ideological substitutions of the "eternal/ephemeral" and the "real/unreal" distinctions in the *"brahmasatyam. . ."* formula.

In 1946–48, when according to the non-enmity criterion the Hindu-Muslim conflict was proving his earlier campaigns to have been non-violence of the weak based on material force rather than soul-force, Gandhi said that non-violence of the weak, whatever its success in practical terms, was hardly an improvement on violence since it left the moral character untouched and produced a greater violence when the period of material satisfaction had ended.

Violence would reappear when forces keeping the violent pressures in check were withdrawn as when they were by the British Rāj leaving, the common objective of Independence having been achieved.

However, Gandhi maintained that the achievements of such a "limp and lame" non-violence were still comparatively miraculous because of the moral awakening in the demoralized and paralyzed masses, and because of the number of lives *not lost* that necessarily would have been lost had the movement been an intentionally violent one.

Gandhi drew on the Gītā's *karmic* view that no non-violent effort is lost, and on the scriptural assurance that "those who strive shall not perish." He concluded that even such non-violence of the weak must, with time and accumulated effects, achieve the spiritual and moral conversion characteristic of pure *satyāgraha*. This would progressively take the place of the imitation to the extent that it was motivated by a requisite minimal sincerity, because even a particle of true non-violence has effective potency while the mere form of it has *none*. A particle of the one must finally overpass any combination of the latter.

The dynamics of persistence, understood in terms of both the *karmic* law and the grace of God who completes all acts, makes repeatedly, renewed persistence in non-violent efforts (the mark of minimal sincerity) tantamount to a criterion of permanence. The contrast of such an adamantine spiritually inspired will with the vagaries of ordinary material purpose clearly indicates that this perseverance is a result of activity of the soul.

The radical nature of Gandhi's practical claims has been shown to be directly the result of the radical opposition of the material with the spiritual and its chief characterization as the oppositions of "ephemeral" to "eternal", and "unreal" to "real". The categorical nature of these oppositions justifies Gandhi's claims, though they appear *prima facie* unjustified when the empirical standpoint is tacitly assumed. Gandhi has added a dimension not covered by the *prima facie* case.

Underlying the conceptual divisions of the spiritual and the material or practical is the *advaita* (non-dualist) view that reality is impartibly whole. Therefore Gandhi finds all analytic distinctions to be only functional and pragmatic. They reflect only limitations of mental consciousness and human action as instruments of pure knowledge.

Gandhi's claims and methods are not meant to bypass categorical differences. They are meant to show how facts and conditions of applying soul-force to practical reality indicate the necessity to temper categorical understanding when deriving practice, while still acknowledging the necessity of retaining the dichotomous view for establishing functional ideals with which to assess practical potency and effects.

Basis of His Claims: The substantive basis of Gandhi's claims is the idealist's belief in soul as an eternal, all-powerful reality whose attributes cannot be cancelled by superimposition of the dual and relational empirical consciousness which yields only a functional reality and whose basis is the human mind and brain.

Gandhi does not conclude that this functional illusion can be ignored.

The illusion is functional for the human soul (see Chap. 1) in its efforts to realize its eternality outside of the superimpositional consciousness of mind and senses. Gandhi notes that the core of this consciousness, the problem of good and evil, is not illusory because reality and action are substantive factors which, relative to will, may be called "law".

According to Gandhi, man's struggle is to realize that this law relating his material being to Truth is not the insubstantial and associational appearance of lawfulness by which the ego-mind-body complex understands reality and guides its action. The two are not unconnected because the constitution of the material complex and of the material field is objectively lawful. The connection of these all, through the distinction between good and evil, is itself lawful. Gandhi believed that God, Good and Truth always are, and the illusion that they sometimes are not (ignorance) is what is evil, self-destructive falsehood.

But the illusion is spun out according to law and is made out of real materials. Dissolution of ego is the precondition of spiritual realization and without the illusion it could not have a self-dismantling mode of activity, that is, one based on essential falsity and unreality by which empirical and discursive consciousness could find the Truth by failure and contrast.

The ego-mind-desire complex will not recognize its fundamental ignorance of Self as soul, and of its own insubstantial nature. It does not see the distinct limitations and disabilities of its sensory and mental equipment for achieving more than a very narrow and immediate functional or pragmatic validity, and it does not see the enormity of its lack of objective and substantial data.

In arrogance (in the root sense of arrogation), trying to make up the difference between its views and the Real, the ego-mind complex *creates* a whole in terms of which it feels confident to act, and it follows the impressions of its own experiences and established tendencies of attraction and repulsion, like and dislike; it superimposes these on substantial reality, an imaginary order geared to securing its own growth and to the realization of its wants. The imagination itself is not unreal and its functioning is lawful, but its product is associational, a law unto itself, and not in accordance with objective moral law and spiritual or material fact—but in accordance only with past personal experience and the very narrow scope of understanding this that is allowed by the ego-desire structuring and project orientation that reduces most thought and reflection to mere processes of calculation.

Thus an evil thought is one based on illusion or falsity created by the "I" and "mine" sense. Action upon it and reaction analyzed in terms of it are not unreal and they lend to the illusion a sense of reality. The cause and effect ascription is not true; means and ends ascriptions likewise will fail ultimately.

Thus Gandhi's fundamental position is that evil is what lives only by sufferance of the Good and has no independent existence. The illusion is sustained because one acts in terms of it and to that extent gives it one's own reality, power and life. But, in fact, Truth alone exists and Love or *ahiṁsā* is its power which works according to law and binds all apparent diversity because it works without any regard to the illusory superimpositions of the innumerable ego-mind-body-desire complexes. Action upon Truth and non-violence will produce reactions that do not answer to illusory imagination based on empirically determined reason. These reactions so serve to rob this imagination of justification and to progressively defuse it through its own operation upon the new facts and relations thus produced.

According to Gandhi's ideology it can be said that Love is an infinite power because evil really has *no* power. *Ahiṁsā* must be infallible because nothing exists but Truth and law, of which Love is only the active and affective aspect. He feels justified in claiming that since all have the same soul and the same human constitution, non-violence as soul-force cannot fail to touch the soul of the opponent, to draw a response from it, and to reconstitute his material so as to re-establish reason and moral sense in him. This is the basis of his fundamental claim that pure suffering reaches the understanding where reason fails to, and that the unfailing efficacy of *satyāgraha* is based on the scientific necessities of interacting force released by the spiritual suffering of *tapas*.

Gandhi's fundamental argument is that the law of non-violence is the law of existence, and if this is so, never anywhere can it fail to respond. If it is "law", a *universal* tendency, then conscious non-violent action must immediately take effect and inevitably succeed.

Gandhi cites as his proof that amidst disorder order prevails, and amidst death and destruction life prevails; and in history he sees the persistent and cumulative evolution of conscious non-violence. He senses the persistent changelessness behind all that the senses perceive as changing and which the senses do not perceive. He sees its invariable spontaneous operation in the family.

Thus Gandhi believes that *ahiṁsā,* or God, will have its way non-violently regardless of whether or not an individual votary, or group of votaries succeeds in any specific programs for its realization.

Gandhi writes, "He who has completely destroyed the 'ego' be- /111
comes an embodiment of Truth. There is no harm in calling him
even God."[5]

Ex hypothesi the omniscient, omnipotent Reality will be infallible. And *ex hypothesi* omnipresent, the divine law and infallibility
must be universal.

Mundane, Corporate and Political: On the basis of his logical principle *"yathā piṇḍe . . . "*, the same law must apply to the large reality
as to the smaller, and if *ahiṁsā* is the law of individual and domestic
relation and of fundamental spiritual nature and its reflection in biological life, it will be the law of the less inclusive corporate, mundane
and political realities. The same invisible working of non-violent
forces will be found in institutional relations.

Gandhi's position bypasses philosophical problems as to whether
there are emergent laws for group or organizational psychology.
These are inherently false laws, holding only relatively to the particular epoch and culture that gives rise to the ego-desire centered regu-
larities they exhibit and are studied under. The permanent laws of
human nature are those upon the basis of which any emergent psychology—group, social or political—must itself be studied as a human science. The basic laws of humanity can only be laws of Truth
and non-violence and the common morality of self-restraint and self-
expression that Gandhi derives from the experience of *ātman*.

Gandhi believes man to be distinguished from brute creation by
his religious nature, the inherent urge to realize Truth and the capabilities of reason and self-restraint. He can know himself as *ātman*
and establish a spiritual life linking the practical and spiritual in himself. If this fundamental nature is respected all lesser aspects will follow harmoniously ("be added unto you").

Anāsakti is the only universal obligation. The mundane, corporate
or political contexts of action only present added application conditions. They cannot limit the power of Truth and non-violence. Truth
and non-violence work through energy transactions and qualitative
transformations occurring at a material level much more basic than
that of the energy-desire nexus. The laws of these various secondary
or emergent configurations of human relations and action, the application conditions of time, place and polis, derive from the relatively

more superficial transactions and transformations at the level of ego and desire, and these also ultimately rest on the foundation and laws of Truth and Love. *Anāsakti* reaches to this basis.

Dynamics of Suffering:　By Gandhi's logico-metaphysical principles, the fundamental principles of *satyāgrahic* victory are logically the reverse of what materially would mean defeat—the dynamics of self-suffering and contra-mundane additions of strength.

The first principle is that self-suffering of the *satyāgrahī* is transmuted into joy.

The active factor of *satyāgraha* is the purifying acceptance of suffering from the vantage point of spiritual realization or from living faith in Truth and non-violence. The only weapon of the believer in force and violence is the suffering he can inflict. The believer in violence believes that the greatest injury he can do, the greatest threat or leverage he has, is to deprive one of his body which is the only means of both sense enjoyment and spiritual realization—and the final means of retaliation as an "enemy".

But according to the moral criterion of *satyāgraha,* voluntary acceptance of death at the hands of the assailant is the *satyāgrahī*'s greatest weapon and its use constitutes victory for the Truth apart from which he has no wish or life. To Gandhi, the *satyāgrahī*'s aim is to suffer for his cause, since he believes that this is the only means of achieving it, and the cause is paramount, the only meaning of his life. The *satyāgrahī* therefore cherishes suffering and even death awarded him in the line of duty, that is, in battle. Violence aims at sustaining the ego-mind-body complex and fulfilling desire; non-violence aims at abolishing the ego-mind-body complex and extirpating desire. When necessary, voluntary cheerful loving submission in suffering death would most clearly demonstrate this opposition of values and have the best chance of converting the opponent and convincing him of the superiority of the *satyāgrahī*'s values.

In campaigning and mass movements also the law of suffering is that the purer and more intense the suffering the quicker the victory. Only quality is to be considered in the methods of suffering of *satyāgraha*. Numbers are a hindrance where there is not the moral training and discipline in which alone mass cooperative action can be spontaneous and not self-destructive.

Where highly innocent *satyāgrahī*s court the greatest suffering, the

campaign will need the least numbers to attain the practical success.
In material methods the loss of practicants or the intensification of suffering bring only defeat. The *satyāgrahī* welcomes new problems and complexities as sources of suffering and thus as a cause of the greater influx of soul-force, which itself is the source of unalloyed joy from within. This joy is necessary to meet the increased material resistance.

Gandhi believed also that time was on his side. The Truth that his sustained suffering is a *tapas,* worthy in itself, and truly the result of soul-force, is proved by patience that outlasts any empirically inspired infliction or resistance.

Empirical ego consciousness wastes energy in things that are not essential to its own aims. It is misguided by its false beliefs and perceptions. The *satyāgrahī*, on the contrary, does not "dignify trifles" and has a trained one-pointed interest in Truth. Though he accepts suffering and transmutes it to joy, he does not seek it for its own sake, and so his action is geared to efficiently minimize loss of energy that would be needed to sustain suffering that is not directly a part of his duty of non-violent resistance, or that would come as part of reacting to inessentials.

Gandhi believes that the *satyāgrahī*'s suffering is thus self-corrective, but limitless in its capacity to meet external causes that force him to use it as a weapon.

Finally, Gandhi believes that the final safeguard and guarantor of the *satyāgrahī* is God. The divine sanction and faith in it has been repeatedly shown to be the basis of Gandhi's radical practical claims. But in the present context it should be noted that whereas for the materialist the state of helplessness means necessary defeat, it is reaching the state of utter helplessness that insures the *satyāgrahī*'s victory. The sacrifice of the *satyāgrahī* is adequate and effective only when it takes him to the extremity of his material powers where his call for the help of the Divine itself completes the necessary negation of the claims of ego and desire. Only in this realized helplessness can the Divine have unobstructed use of him, and can his cause have benefit of the Divine infallibility and universality.

Contra-mundane Additions of Strength: The second reversal of material resistance is the *satyāgrahī*'s addition of strength through those circumstances which would weaken material methods.

Gandhi's criterion for non-violence of the strong is that the votary feels an accession of strength from the very act of disarming himself. If the physical act of abstention is in fact a symbol of the renunciation of the will to preserve one's separate existence by resort to violence, then alone is there an accession of strength from an influx of soul-force into the *satyāgrahī*'s material being.

Gandhi requires that the renunciation and action of the *satyāgrahī* include knowledge not only of the soul and his relation to it but also the perception, data and understanding which make action accurate and efficient. The *satyāgrahī*'s attention, perception and understanding are focussed on Truth and backed by Love so that his vision and action even in the mundane and common sense have an objective basis and source of power not possible to egocentric and desire-bound perception and calculations.

On the basis of the law of *puruṣakāra*, Gandhi finds a source of strength in the act of forgiveness. Only one who is stronger than his adversary has the capability to punish and kill as also the authority to forgive. He writes that one who practices forgiveness from the feeling and belief in his own strength builds this belief and strength into his character. Believing himself strong, the *satyāgrahī* acts on that belief and draws on his inner resources which by their own law must respond. These are inaccessible in mundane methods, where "forgiveness" is usually a cover for weakness to justify compromise and make defeat palatable.

The *satyāgrahī*'s new strength leads to success, and the *satyāgrahī* comes to believe more firmly in his methods. The cycle continues and he grows "from strength to strength."

According to Gandhi's axioms, the power of non-violence is proportional to one's power to kill, and the actual strength available by use of non-violent means is always more than that available to violent means. Gandhi compares the weak man's forgiveness and non-violence to those of a mouse who presumes to "allow" the cat to eat him and "forgives" him as if he might have "chosen" to vanquish and punish him.

According to the second moral criterion, Gandhi claims that in successful *satyāgraha*, the *satyāgrahī* gains for his cause the additional strength that is freely given by his newly won friend. The conversion postulated by *satyāgraha* is that of an enemy to an ally in the cause of Truth in which both are new co-victors—victors in the de-

mise of any cause of conflict and in the new cause of friendship and
mutual interest.

Lastly, the helplessness experienced as defeat by the materially centered opponent is greeted by the *satyāgrahī* as the condition of receiving God's power and guidance (previous section) which are promised to him. It is the *satyāgrahī*'s faith that the fulfillment of that promise is the Truth's fulfillment of itself in practical reality as universal and infallible efficacy. Gandhi's claim is that his experience of sixty years, and that of others closely associated with him, verifies that faith and justifies the assertion of his radical practical claims.

SUMMARY AND TRANSITION

This chapter concludes the exposition of Gandhi's philosophy and methods of non-violence. It has examined the basis of his radical practical claim for these methods.

In order to understand why Gandhi believed that his claim was justified, this section has examined the classical sources of his concept of *ahiṁsā* and principles of *satyāgraha*, their form as he adapted them from personal experience and experiments to practical application in modern conditions, and the criteria by which he guided and evaluated that application.

In Part II, Gandhi's concept of non-violence, his principles and methods of *satyāgraha* and his criteria for their evaluation will be critically examined in terms of the radical practical claim he believed they support.

The principle question in this examination will be whether Gandhi's claim that non-violence is always right and ought always to be applied is justified by his practical analysis of non-violence as a force to be applied by means of *satyāgraha*, and by his experience in its application.

If Gandhi's claim cannot be thus justified, can his concept and methods be criticized from the objective standpoint of the distinction between violence and non-violence and the problem of the justifiability of violence, force and war? Is Gandhi's ideological analysis adequate to the phenomena of violence and non-violence? Is it adequate to the problems of justification where two categories of reality seem to make their own separate but equally valid claims?

Part Two

INTRODUCTION

The purpose of this section is the examination of Gandhi's claim that violence is never justifiable.

Logically, this claim is merely the obverse of Gandhi's absolute normative claim and prescription that non-violence is *always right* and *ought always* to be applied; but it lays bare the counter-intuitive character of Gandhi's practical position. In fact, Gandhi's concept of non-violence and his *satyāgraha* were meant as part of his mission to propagate non-violence as a practical rejoinder to the commonsense argument for the justified use of force and violence.

This section first defines this orientation and aim of Gandhi's mission; second, it depicts Gandhi's argument in terms of the new debate that his work created on the problem of the justification of violence; third, it analyzes several basic confusions inherent in his concept and its application, evaluates his views on justifiability in terms of rightness and necessity, and establishes the commonsense counter-position, which defines a criterion of moral necessity for the use of violence and delineates the conditions of its practical application; fourth, the elements delineated in the foregoing critical analysis are applied to Gandhi's arguments against the justifiability of war, force and violence, and to his claim that *satyāgraha* expresses an objectively valid and universal moral law, which completes his argument in the practical sphere.

5. *Gandhi's Mission and the Context of His Argument: A New Debate and the Problem of Justification*

Introduction: This chapter examines how Gandhi's mission against the justifiability of violence restructures the way violence is ordinarily looked at, by questioning absolutely its justifiability that is ordinarily taken for granted. Gandhi may prove to be mistaken in the final assessment, and his mission may thus prove to have been fundamentally misconceived, but the issues raised in assessing his efforts to vindicate his *absolute* position are vital to examine when faced with the *absolute* violence of the now humanly achievable self-annihilation by nuclear warfare.

This chapter stresses that Gandhi's argument is based on arbitrary ideological elements, but also that his position gives a sound basis for elaborating and validating the general commitment to non-violence by starkly and insistently raising the question of its limits.

A. GANDHI'S PRACTICAL CLAIM AND THE ABSOLUTE RIGHTNESS
OF NON-VIOLENCE: ITS OBJECTIVE VALIDITY;
DISCOUNTING THE IDEOLOGICAL BASIS

Gandhi's radical practical claim is implicit in his concept, principles and criteria of practical non-violence. For him, rightness implies truth in its pragmatic and practical sense. These in turn imply the "ought" of rightness. Gandhi believes that his claim that non-violence is absolutely right and ought always to be applied is thus justified by his analysis of non-violence as a spiritual force and by his practical experience with *satyāgraha* in applying that force.

If Gandhi is correct that this cluster of implications is justified, aside from the ideological position that structures his argument, then it should be possible to evaluate his ideology and methods by critically examining his radical practical claim which embodies them.

This claim is not only the logical focus of Gandhi's entire effort, theoretical and practical, ideological and programmatic, but it provides the *differentia* between his and other conceptions and methods of non-violent action, and so provides also the focus of the new debate that it initiates.

An objective assessment of Gandhi's non-violence must simply and finally ask, "Is it true?" Is it practical, viable and reliable, aside from his compelling ideology? Are his analysis and claim consistent with the facts? Empirical? Practical? Moral? Spiritual?

Since Gandhi's concept of non-violence is derived from his moral ideology, his principles and methods of action from this ideologically constructed concept and his criteria from their practical application, the evaluation of these components of his philosophy of non-violence and the assessment of its practical, moral and theoretical validity are summed up in the question—Does Gandhi's radical practical claim stand if it is divorced from its ideological basis? Does his claim stand if we discount (1) the moral equation of violence with evil, (2) the programmatic aim of demonstrating universal applicability and (3) the prescriptions of moral authenticity and moral faith that outer conduct and inner states be made identical, and practical means be made convertible with moral ends?

Most fundamentally, and as a minimum, for Gandhi's non-violence to prove valid, it must be justified on grounds independent of the equation of violence with evil that is central to his moral ideology. The criteria of practical efficacy must be evaluated without interpretation through this axiomatic equation of his moral theory if they are supposed to justify the extension of that theory to the practical sphere.

B. GANDHI'S MISSION TO SHOW THE UNJUSTIFIABILITY
OF VIOLENCE, AND HIS ARGUMENT TO DEFEAT THE PROPOSAL OF
VIOLENCE AS A LAST RESORT

Gandhi took as his mission in life the exploration and propagation of non-violence.

Gandhi writes, "I have been practicing with scientific precision nonviolence and its possibilities for an unbroken period of over fifty years. I have applied it in every walk of life—domestic, institutional, economic and political . . . Its spread is my life mission. I have no interest in living except for the prosecution of that mission."[57]

Since Gandhi believes non-violence to be "right", and rightness to be not separable from practical potency, his mission is also to show that resort to violence is never justifiable even in the practical sphere. Again, he writes, "My mission is to teach by example and precept under severe restraint the use of the matchless weapon of *Satyāgraha* which is the direct corollary of non-violence and truth."[58]

Gandhi wished to totally undermine the prevailing belief that violence is justifiable and may even be morally required: "I must continue to argue till I convert opponents or I own defeat. For my mission is to convert every Indian, every Englishman and finally the world to nonviolence for regulating mutual relations . . . I must continue my experiments."[59]

The problem of justifying violence is ordinarily that of finding circumstances, needs and moral aims that are believed to override the general commitment to not seek gain by violent means, or to act violently for self-indulgent purposes. It is taken for granted that violence is at some point permissible if not required—at least in self-defense.

Prior to Gandhi's work and the advent of the atomic bomb, vindication of the justifiability of violence was not ordinarily questioned. It was Gandhi's problem to vindicate his claims that this justifiability itself was a moral problem. Because of his assimilation of the practical to the moral and the expedient to the religious, he raised, from a new point of view, the question of the practical justifiability of violence also.

The peace churches—Anabaptist, Mennonite, Brethren, Quaker, etc.—did not speak to the issues of universal practicability and perfect practical efficacy of non-violence. They did not give non-violence a scientific analysis. Their "witness" was theological and ethical. The peace movements have restricted non-violence to tactical use for programmatic aims. Quaker social and political non-violent activism, aside from its peace witness, has likewise addressed only a few institutions and relationships specifically related to overt and large scale reforms.

Gandhi's radical practical claim is not naive. It is a complex claim deriving from his sophisticated analysis of the relation of moral and practical realities and of the operation of moral consciousness.

The commonsense *prima facie* case against Gandhi is that surely /123
violence must be justifiable to combat insuperable evil or to thwart
the agent of greater violence, where one's abstention from violence
would amount to allowing that larger violence. To make sense of the
question of justifiability in opposition to the *prima facie* case against
him, Gandhi needed to supply the founding concepts and equations
of an ideology to make sense of his claim to rule out *a priori* all
question of the justifiability of violence.

But Gandhi's own position must be justified against the commonsense and *prima facie* case for justifiable violence. His analysis must
not only show that the force of the soul and the spiritual dimension
of reality are objective factors not considered by the *prima facie* case,
he *must show also* that these factors actually cancel the material
principles normally operative in such situations.

Since "justification" for one must be justification for all, Gandhi's
justification must bring about agreement in practice or action by al-
laying doubts raised by the *prima facie* presentation. It is to the
doubters he must defer and give a practical demonstration proving
the ideologically conceivable to be practically viable as well. He constantly repeated that example is the only effective argument in practical ethics. The viability of a whole class of actions which hitherto
had been matters only for moral imagination and conjecture must be
proven. Gandhi believed that by showing at least one example (or
better, a whole series) of practical success in the most difficult of
cases, the viability of the entire class would be demonstrated. Then
popular conversion from the general commitment to absolute faith in
non-violence would be only a matter of momentum and time.

Gandhi's argument is that violence is a completely negative concept. Destruction and harm are its *necessary* results. Evil is self-
destructive in essence, and violence is evil. Violence would therefore
require some positive and extrinsic justification; use of violence
therefore results in self-destruction and there are no positive results
attributable to violence qua "violence" that could possibly justify it.
Therefore, violence is always unjustifiable.

This is an ideological argument in that it assumes the equation of
the empirical appearance of violence with the concept of pure
evil. The argument is clearly circular.

The practical side of Gandhi's argument is his program for the
demonstration of his test cases. Since it is ordinarily believed (the

prima facie case) that violence may produce enough good to justify its properly limited use, or that it may be justified by the fact that there is no non-violent way to produce the same result which is considered to be a practical necessity in service of a moral good; then, if Gandhi can demonstrate that non-violence is a universal means, an always applicable and perfectly efficacious practical means, he can draw on the general moral commitment to non-violence and argue that it only need be extended similarly to *all* practical cases. Everyone knows non-violence is certainly right; they only need to be shown that it can also accomplish every good that violence was ever thought to achieve.

This leads to Gandhi's basic claim that therefore non-violence ought *always* to be applied and violence can have no justification.

In fact, Gandhi goes further and argues that violence could never produce the practical results it has claimed, and that his demonstration would help to dispel the false belief that the moral and practical are separable. On the basis of his moral ideology and metaphysics, his concepts of human nature and moral spiritual sciences, he argues that it is *always* possible, even in the worst imaginable case, to conceive a non-violent solution or discover correct application conditions.

Finally, the criteria of supra-material potency and necessary universal practical efficacy are built into the definition of his concept of non-violence of the strong, and since his practical claim derives from this criterion, its vindication requires both an ideological argument and the practical component of demonstration of viability.

The Last Resort Argument: The basic argument to justify violence is that it may be necessary as a last resort.

It is argued that in many circumstances there is no non-violent way to defeat an evil that one feels the moral obligation to engage and overcome. One feels obligated to resist evil and to preserve and protect the good. It is believed that *in itself* violence may be evil, but its *use* is not intrinsically evil. Maybe it *usually* is used as an instrument of evil, but it *may* also be used by the good as a last resort. Its use is redeemed to the extent that it proves to be morally effective in overcoming the evil intended, without moral loss from that use so great as to offset the moral gain.

In this argument expectation of success must be in a degree sufficient to override the natural moral desire not to be the agent of
harm, to cause damage or to destroy the peace. This is the *ultima ratio* criterion in justification of war.[60] Violence may be used as the
last resort against an incorrigible evil.

Gandhi's argument thus involves two components (1) the ideological component proving the universal rightness of non-violence, and
vindicating it as an absolute category, imperative and prescription,
superseding the ordinary general commitment, and (2) the practical
component to prove the *non-necessity* of violence even as a last resort, its strongest case.

A New Debate: Gandhi's ideology, methods of exact conduct and
especially his notable successes in their practical application bring
into question the commonsense justification of violence and the
commonsense *prima facie* case against Gandhi's practical claim.

A new debate is initiated by Gandhi's challenge to our commonsense intuitions, and the absolute dimension of his new concept, ideology and practice of non-violence seem to justify that challenge.

C. CONCEPT, CONTEXT AND MEANS; THE PROBLEM OF JUSTIFICATION

Having been long exposed to the ideal of practical non-violence
on a large scale and for political purposes, it is difficult today for us
to realize what a novelty it was when Gandhi produced the first *satyāgraha* campaigns in South Africa at the turn of the century and
later in India in the teens and twenties. They had neither the passiv-
ity of the Christian peace witness, nor the submerged anger of the
suffragette or non-conformist.

Gandhi's argument proceeded at a developed theoretic level as a
complete experimental moral philosophy which he wished to see become a full science. A counter argument would now have to meet a
developed metaphysics, spiritual and empirical analysis and extensive
practical results, besides meeting the traditional textual arguments
based on the exegesis of the non-resistance and love of the enemy
texts in the 'Sermon on the Mount' (Matt. 5:38; 5:43–44).

The context of the debate is also new, created by several factors of global significance for the question of the justifiability of the use of violence and the call to non-violence; the rise of totalitarianism and neo-fascism and the rise of international terrorism in reaction to them; the rise of neo-colonialism and the rise of guerilla insurgency in reaction to it; the immediacy of global response[61] to local events; and, the technological sophistication and desensitization of life.

Gandhi claimed that he was preparing his non-violent weapon and political program to meet just these historical necessities. But the principal new components of this context are the advent of the atom bomb, on the one hand, and of Gandhi's *satyāgraha*, on the other.[62] The atom bomb and the real possibility of nuclear war raise the question of an *ultimate* or *limiting case* of violence, i.e. self-annihilation as the intrinsic result of absolute evil.

If the law of violence means that there is an ever greater retaliation to every violence perpetrated, then nuclear conflict is the limiting case of that escalation. The atom bomb is potentially the demonstration of the equation of violence with evil. Gandhi believed that the atom bomb did present that limiting case, proving "the futility of all violence."[63]

But Gandhi asks the further, most pertinent question: where has that spirit of evil and violence gone if violence not only cannot reach the root of evil but must increase that evil by the escalation of counter-violences? Gandhi says that it must inevitably lodge in the hearts of the victors.[64]

The advocate of violence looks at *satyāgraha* as Gandhi's contribution to the traditional debate about the justification of violence, but from Gandhi's standpoint, *satyāgraha* ends the debate over justification and establishes a new debate—or rather it ends all debate as to the possibility of any such justification.

Gandhi's claim includes the capability of non-violence to meet and defeat even atomic violence. He calls this the "age of the atom bomb" and he opposes non-violence to it as the "only force that confound all the tricks of violence put together."[65] Gandhi writes that, "Before it [non-violence] the atom bomb is of no effect. The two opposing forces are wholly different in kind. The one moral and spiritual, the other physical and material. The one infinitely superior to the other which, by its very nature has an end. The force of the spirit is ever progressive and endless. Its full expression in the world makes it unconquerable."[66] And further, "Violence can only be effectively met by non-violence. This is an old established truth. The questioner does not really understand the working of non-violence. If he did, he would have known that the weapon of violence, even if it was the atom bomb, became useless when matched against true non-violence."[67] Violence refers to the same human breast as ever, only the destructiveness of its instrumentalities has come to more nearly picture its absolute character.

If the advent of the atom bomb as representing absolute violence is admitted to have changed the whole structure of the debate on the justifiability of violence, then Gandhi's *satyāgraha* must once again radically metamorphose the debate in presenting his absolute counter-claim.

The atom bomb cannot solve the problem of peace; its advent only makes peace more urgent.

Not the Prima Facie Case: Gandhi's work raises a categorical problem of justification which is against the general moral commitment to non-violence and the practical and moral *prima facie* case, both of which come from moral common sense. If he is correct about the logic of escalation to nuclear self-destruction as the inevitable culmination of *any* lesser political violence, the commonsense argument cannot be admitted. The *ultima ratio* argument must in that case mean only resort to suicide.

The commonsense *prima facie* case and general commitment subscribe to the moral criteria that violence would be justified if (1) a lesser violence will defeat the agent of greater violence without producing a greater evil in the process, or (2) abstention from violence would aid the evil that one feels obligated to engage and resist. This balance of moral results can be considered the distillation of the traditional argument in justification of violence. Gandhi's ideological equation of violence with evil rules out this criterion since it insures escalation to self-destruction in atomic war, leaving no results to be balanced.

Since use of violence for Gandhi automatically involves inadmissible propagation of evil, it could only deepen the involvement of evil in the world, and in the present world situation in its state of technological sophistication and moral immaturity, this must translate eventually to nuclear confrontation. Both Gandhi's practical and ideological arguments yield the same result.

Not a Naive Claim: Though Gandhi's practical claim is in dispute of "common wisdom", it is not a naive and vague moralism. It is intended to enunciate a general categorical situation and confirmed scientific law.

Gandhi tries to (1) model moral law on physical law and necessity, and yet retain (2) the notion of freedom that is definitive of moral action,[68] and (3) the prescriptive form and force of the moral imperative. He represents his claim not as a naive ideological assertion but as the scientific statement that, given certain conditions, the appropriate form of action and release of energy must result necessarily in the consequences projected according to general laws.

Failure of results must indicate insufficient regard for application conditions. Gandhi writes that, "Peace is not attained by part performance of conditions, even as a chemical reaction is impossible without complete fulfillment of the conditions of the attainment thereof."[69] The application conditions refer to *both* spiritual and material states, the analysis of which rests on complex and sophisticated moral theory of the categorical relation between the qualities inhering in those conditions and their respective forces, and in the moral will. The laws, application conditions, and correct modification and modulations of the moral will and subjective states are givens, facts.

Efficacy and precise results are dependent on one's accuracy and comprehensiveness of knowledge and judgment, as in any scientific application. But the introduction of spiritual *facts* and laws as a necessary component of the analysis, experiments and prescriptions, and of the admittedly new order of destructive violence of atomic warfare, all combine to give new meaning to the problems of explanation and justifiability; these new factors go beyond the scope of common sense and the casuistry of the general commitment that seemed previously sufficient.

If Gandhi's claim represents simply the naive ideological dogma it first seems to, it could be readily discounted as only a subjective preference. But since his ideology itself rests on a sophisticated metaphysical analysis of spiritual, moral and phenomenal realities as these meet in human nature and action, his claim bears initial inspection as representing a wider objective investigation.

Justification: If violence as such is *prima facie* unjustifiable, arguments for its justification must refer to extraneous elements such as necessity in the cause of violence, character of results, practical success or motivation. When these refer to subjective conditions they may be called moral justifications; when they refer to objective conditions they may be called practical justifications.

If Gandhi's assimilation of the spiritual, the moral and the practical is valid, then justification by results will be a single criterion, whether the results are subjective or objective, moral or practical. The immediacy of moral results consequent on moral effort will assure the more remote and diffuse practical consequences.

But the question is whether this synonymy and assimilation are valid. Does it answer to the facts of human spiritual evolution, moral consciousness and practical will and action? Or, is this assimilation merely imposed by Gandhi's ideology?

Justifiability: If Gandhi's synonymy is not assumed then the problem of justifiability is raised alongside the question of the morality of will and intent. The problem is again raised of *proving* that both subjective and objective factors of motive and results are equally moral considerations. The debate between Gandhi and the advocates of violence is outside the current extensive technical considerations of deterrence, balance and theatre strategies to stem atomic escalation, et al.

For Gandhi the self-destructive nature of violence as evil is axiomatic, leaving no result to possibly justify it, but for the advocate of violence this necessarily self-defeating character of violence is precisely what is in question. From the empirical and commonsense standpoint, Gandhi's argument only *assumes* the equation of violence with evil; he must still prove or justify it. Without Gandhi's ideological superstructure this "inevitability" of self-destruction is an empirical and so an *open question* rather than a self-evident axiom.

By his equation of microcosm and macrocosm, Gandhi equates violence, force and war as all terms for the same evil.[70] The second part of his argument against the justifiability of violence is *satyā-graha*, which he offers as a complete substitute for violence, even for the violence of war.

Gandhi writes,

Up to the year 1906, I simply relied on appeal to reason. I was a very industrious reformer. I was a good draftsman, as I always had a close grasp of facts which in its turn was the necessary result of my meticulous regard for truth. But I found that reason failed to produce an impression when the critical moment arrived in South Africa. My people were excited . . . there was talk of wreaking vengeance. I had then to choose between allying myself to violence or finding some other method of meeting the crisis and stopping the rot, and it came to me that we should refuse to obey legislation that was degrading and let them put us in jail if they liked. *Thus came into being the moral equivalent of war.*[71]

If, on the basis of our general moral commitment to non-violence, it is admitted that violence should have an intrinsic moral justification aside from any extrinsic result, then Gandhi, by his equations of violence with evil and violence with force and war, provides two moral arguments against any possible justifiability of violence.

D. TWO ARGUMENTS AND A "DEPENDENT" ABSOLUTE CLAIM

Gandhi argues for this unjustifiability by means of his metaphysical and scientific analysis of the facts of violence and non-violence, and by his practical demonstration against the *ultima ratio* or last resort argument. His absolute claim is strangely for both conditional and "perfect" practical efficacy.

The elements of Gandhi's ideology and the components of his arguments are simple and not numerous; but their elaboration in argument, theory and practice is complex. To unravel this complexity we will focus on Gandhi's practical claim as it functions theoretically in the problem of justification, and practically in the context of the new debate. We will examine its two roles and the mixed validity of his two inquiries, scientific and ideological.

Theoretical Inquiry (Examination of spiritual facts to vindicate a universal claim and prove the absolute rightness of non-violence): Gandhi's ideology and praxis were developed specifically to vindicate the application of the spiritual analysis of reality to the problems of evil and violence.

Gandhi's aim was to give a material basis for his moral presentiment that non-violence constituted a universal and absolute moral principle. Whatever the disorder and violence apparent in the world, it coheres and evolves and taps in mankind that consciousness of self as one spirit, one and the same in all, in which all force and law necessarily succeed in subverting all violent forces.

From this *advaitic* viewpoint, violent material forces are only distortions of this "one and only real force"—but observed at a less fundamental, and therefore only partial and less self-knowing level of its activity. Thus non-violence is actually always operative, and evil or violence is only an appearance to unseeing human consciousness.

Thus non-violence is *potentially* of universal application, given the factual existence of all as having the same soul and the same spiritual reality subtending, encompassing and overpassing all merely empirical or outer appearance.

Practical Inquiry (Examination of the justifiability of violence by practical factors that prove its non-necessity): Because the problem of justifiability logically involves a practical component, Gandhi proposed to fulfill his mission to defuse belief in the necessity of violence as a last resort by devising and demonstrating a non-violent sanction.[72] Since the passive resistance of classical non-violence must be materially weaker than the forces it opposes (having abdicated the opponent's means without replacing them with another force its equal or greater), Gandhi's search was for just this substitutable force and sanction. This was his discovery of soul-force, whose instrument is the non-violent action of *satyāgraha*.

Absolute "Dependent" Claim (Absolute claim for perfect practical efficacy, non-naive in granting its conditional and dependent nature): Gandhi's radical claim rests first on the conception of soul-force as a force factually superior to all material forces, and second, on the actual possibility of bringing that force to bear on material reality to yield practical results. His ideology is intended to describe the spiritual facts of this potency and its practical possibilities. His praxis is meant to demonstrate this practical viability. His claim has a necessary component descriptive of the nature and laws of real forces and a conditional component dependent on moral perception, will and activity that self-consciously expresses that nature and law in practical terms.

Though according to his conception it is assumed that the force of non-violence is potentially indefeatable, Gandhi can offer a conditional analysis of how to bring that potentiality to actual tangible and determinate results. Ultimately, the *satyāgrahī* can fulfill only the negative empirical conditions of adequacy of training and preparation (the 18-point constructive program; remembrance, repetition and congregational chanting or singing of Rāma, the Name of God), intensity and accuracy of application (knowledge and wisdom), and sufficient restraint to dismantle the ego-desire complex and to discern the truth or legitimacy of the means and the cause. The positive conditions of adequate faith and accession to power are the province of divine grace and purpose. The truth of the cause and adequacy of the self-sacrifice are themselves conditions of that grace.

Gandhi's absolute claim thus insures both compliance with moral law and with projected actions as these might express the law. The operation of the moral law of non-violence is an existential postulate, true *ex hypothesi*, manifesting as soul-force the use of which is a matter of judgment, experiment and discovery. But since this force is "moral", it is lawful in its operation, objectively valid, and optional in its self-conscious activation and use, a law of freedom.

Core of Non-retaliation: Gandhi's problem of justification thus has two aspects: (1) the commonsense general commitment and general explanation and "science of *satyāgraha*", and (2) the possibility of a limiting case, addressed by his practical experiments in test cases of extreme violence (particularly his plans for defense against Japanese invasion,[73] his Noakhali "pilgrimage" and his Calcutta and Delhi fasts).

Non-retaliation, connecting the practical and the ideal, provides
the core of both inquiries.

If human existence is under constant assault by evil or violence of inner passions and desires, non-retaliation must be the constant moral guide in spiritual introspection and self-inquiry. Its systematic use constitutes the essential practice of moral self-purification, since it provides an operational definition of love, capable of molding the moral will—the ideal of *sthitaprajña* or a naturally reactionless state of consciousness, its *sine qua non*.

If all energy is fundamentally on an impartible continuum of reality, this principle must be capable of meeting even the limiting case of all-out war and threat of nuclear conflict with exact conduct determined by it. In meeting this limiting case, it would prove the supremacy of *ahiṁsā*, the power of love. This successful demonstration would exemplify Gandhi's defining criterion.

Science: A brief introspective practice of non-retaliation in thought, word and deed readily demonstrates the validity of Gandhi's principle of non-retaliation for reconstituting moral consciousness. It progressively stems harmful and blinding reaction that is inherent in sensory and mental life. Daily life experience demonstrates the validity of his analysis of the vicious circle and escalation of violence, and the necessity for unilateral abstention as a self-evident moral and practical first requisite.

These analyses of escalation and the circle of violence provide the moral and theoretical rationale for non-retaliation as the mechanism for realizing and extending the general commitment to non-violence as also a generally valid practical position.

Ideology: But can Gandhi's ideological commitment to his exceptionless non-violent exact conduct defeat the claims of the traditional limiting case arguments of last resort and moral necessity?

Gandhi's arguments for the general commitment based on the ordinary functioning of non-violence as non-retaliation are derived from common experience and reflect his scientific and experimental attitude; they are sufficient to justify a general claim. But his argument for non-retaliating exact conduct as an exceptionless practical instrument is deeply rooted in his ideological thought.

Though his procedure of inquiry into the practical force of non-violence in these limiting cases may be acceptable as "scientific" to the extent such a complex inquiry can be expected to be,[74] his interpretation of his findings and subsequent claim do not stand independently of their ideological foundations and superstructure.

In the following chapter, the conditions of objectively evaluating this ideological component are established. On this basis, we examine Gandhi's claim as it challenges the necessity criterion and last resort arguments that would limit non-violence to only a generally valid, and not absolutely valid, moral practical principle.

6. *Standpoint of an Objective Evaluation: Scope and Limits of Gandhi's Non-violence*

This chapter will establish, from a commonsense position, an objective standpoint independent of Gandhi's ideological position. From that standpoint, it will define contrasting views of the necessity criterion as it enters the debate on justifiability through the last resort argument.

This prepares the way for the examination, in Chapter 7, of Gandhi's discarding of this criterion in the application of his ethical theory against the justifiability of war, and, in Chapter 8, the application of his practical theory to supersede that criterion by demonstrating the viability of the practical substitution of methods of *satyāgraha* for those of war.

A. PROBLEM OF EVALUATION

1. *Objective Standpoint*:   An objective evaluation must take as its vantage point some criterion or comprehensive view that stands independently of the ideology to be evaluated.

Internal Invulnerability of Ideology: From within his ideology, Gandhi's claims are invulnerable. His experiments also cannot "prove" the validity of his ideology since these are interpreted through his ideological terms. His fundamental ideals are also invulnerable since they are isolated in a separate category as regulative ideas and conceived *ex hypothesi* to be not fully realizable in the empirical medium.

The critical examination of Gandhi's philosophy of non-violence requires *ab initio* discounting his ideology. At the same time his moral and practical claims and results, and the ideology itself, must be subjected to critical inquiry in the light of a wider more general philosophical investigation. Is his ideological analysis adequate to the facts of violence and non-violence, and do these facts preclude the question of the justifiability of violence, force and war, as he claimed?

Necessity of Practical Criteria: The question of this justifiability is a necessary one given that the practical justification of non-violence is a logical component of a moral ideology. If Gandhi cannot assure *a priori* that non-violence will work in every possible practical context, if he cannot independently justify his radical claim, then the question of justifiability of violence is again opened, and inquiry is returned to the fundamental moral problem of *drawing the line* between violence and non-violence in practical yet morally supportable terms.

The moral analysis of this distinction logically involves the justifiability of either an absolute claim on the side of non-violence, or a conditional one on the side of violence. In either case, the justification must be a moral one since the starting point of the inquiry *is* the moral point of view; that is to say, the general commitment to non-violence on the basis of an original moral preference.

2. *Criteria:* Beyond this fundamental agreement on a moral framework and starting point, there is need of further criteria in terms of which to evaluate Gandhi's work without assuming a counter ideology.

Experience, Common Sense and the Test Case: Experience must provide the criterion in the form of commonsense justification and its *prima facie* case.

Experience is a common basis for judgment and action when it yields results that none would argue against on the basis of experience alone (without reference to ideological or theoretical rationale). In the present context, experience gives the commonsense criteria for justifying violence against the moral presentiment of our general commitment, i.e. the last resort, necessity and balance of moral qualities in the practical outcomes. Another criterion is choice of means that preserve the good.

Without going outside common sense and experience, the traditional criteria for just war give a comprehensive summary of this position that is difficult to disagree with without raising theological issues. Ellul summarizes these criteria in his reflections on *Violence*, seven conditions must coincide to make a war just; the cause fought for must itself be just; the purpose of the warring power must remain just while hostilities go on; war must be truly the last resort, all peaceful means having been exhausted; the methods employed during the war to vanquish the foe must themselves be just; the benefits the war can reasonably be expected to bring for humanity must be greater than the evil provided by the war itself; victory must be assured; the peace concluded at the end of the war must be just and of such a nature as to prevent a new war.[75]

Ellul writes that the basis of this "dogmatic" position is "the conviction that man can retain control of violence, that violence can be kept in service of order and justice and even of peace, that violence is good or bad depending on the use or purpose it is put to."[76]

These seven criteria can be characterized as an analysis of conditions believed sufficient to guide the well-intentioned party in realizing his "conviction" when violence *does seem to him necessary*.

These criteria might all be reduced to the single criterion of insuring that the outcome of the violence be greater good than the evil of the means necessitated. In commonsense terms, these are the two criteria referred to earlier: (1) a lesser evil, the good use of violence, should succeed in defeating the agent (intending) of greater violence, and (2) abstention should not aid the evil agent in perpetrating the violence he espouses to realize his own ends.

Unless survival itself is a sin, an original evil, some such analysis justifying necessary violence as moral must be allowed.

It has been shown that in some sense Gandhi takes just this position and makes a sin of embodied existence and possessive attachment to the body and corporeal life. According to that position, birth in physical form necessarily brings more violence into the universe; violence is *ex hypothesi* evil, and life therefore is inherently evil or sin. Then enjoyment of life must be greater sin as enjoyment implies greater activity and greater mutual competition for use of limited resources, including, at the extreme, for sheer occupation of space and domain. Greater activity is more violence and more violence is more evil and greater sin.

But this argument is at variance with the Upaniṣadic analysis that sees the universe as a place of play, abundance and mirth, in which the realized being, identifying himself even with creation as "food of food", finds in it pre-eminently the joy of taste, not the pain of violence.

The Taittirīyaka Upaniṣad ends in such a chant of wonder and delight, revealing the transfixing aspect of even the most mundane:

> ... He who is this (Brahman) in man, and he who is that (Brahman) in the sun, both are one (III:10:4). He who knows this, when he has departed this world, after reaching and comprehending the Self which consists of food, the Self which consists of breath, the Self which consists of mind, the Self which consists of understanding, the Self which consists of bliss, enters and takes possession of these worlds, and having as much food as he likes, and assuming as many forms as he likes, he sits down singing this Sāman (of Brahman): "Hāvu, hāvu, hāvu!" (III:10:5) "I am food (object), I am food, I am food, I am food! I am the eater of food (subject), I am the eater of food, I am the eater of food! I am the poet (who joins the two together), I am the poet, I am the poet! I am the first-born of the Right (ṛta). Before the Devas I was in the centre of all that is immortal. He who gives me away, he alone preserves me: him who eats food, I eat as food. 'I overcome the whole world, I, endowed with golden light. He who knows this, (attains all this).' This is the Upaniṣad."[77]

Universalizability, Heteronomy and Confusion: Aside from variance with one of his own basic sources, Gandhi's extreme position does not bear initial inspection on the universalizability criterion of general moral theory. By this criterion one looks at the practical consequences should everyone act on the principle in question to its fullest logical conclusion.

Were *all* the good to suspend physical resistance and choose self-immolation, the *sine qua non* of *satyāgraha*, would there be any one left to be or to do good? Evil, being violence in its very nature, is self-destructive; life's purpose under such a moral regime could only be self-destruction, making life itself intrinsically evil. Why need it ever have been created?

But Gandhi insists on absolute exemption from taking life[78] as the basis of morality as non-violence.

Thus life appears to be the highest value from the standpoint of Gandhi's methods. Yet from the standpoint of his theory and cause, the aim and value of life is its exhaustion.

Gandhi's moral position is fundamentally flawed by a heteronomy that is built into its structure by his attempt at the same time to make ends and means convertible and yet emphasize and exploit their practical distinctness. He maintains two standards.

Granting the absolute nature of moral law and commitment, the criterion of universalizability helps one to realize the consequences of his actions in logical terms that reveal the full dimensions of that commitment, action or exemption. On the one hand, Gandhi uses this criterion to meet practical objections to his methods, but on the other hand, he ignores the consequences for his own arguments in support of those methods.

By ignoring, or only selectively emphasizing the criterion of universalizability, Gandhi creates a cluster of confusions in his philosophy of non-violence, both at the theoretical and practical levels. His arguments against the commonsense criteria depend on arbitrary postulates, axioms and assumptions that reflect these confusions.

Gandhi's equation of micro- and macrocosms allows the criteria of the just war to be seen as criteria justifying the use of violence in general, so these are inadmissible to his theory. They leave open the question of where the line between violence and non-violence is to be drawn, which he does not. To common sense this is always a matter of particular individual, circumstances, situations and outcomes.

But Gandhi's ideological notions blur distinctions, confuse categories and misdirect valuations, making categorical differences look equivocal. He tries to *annul the need* to draw such a line by justifying his exceptionless rule of non-violence. But justifications follow only from ideological constructions that are formulated to support those assimilations and confusions of otherwise distinct terms and categorical realities.

The evaluation of Gandhi's philosophy of non-violence thus involves (1) demarcating the valid core of his concept and methods which coincides with the general commitment of commonsense morality, but which he also uses to annul the commonsense limitations to that common basis, and, (2) examining the way in which Gandhi's methods of *satyāgraha* embody those confusions in his attempt to use them to justify overriding those criteria.

3. Valid Core of Two Inquiries: Non-retaliation

Correct Analysis of Violence as Retaliation: Gandhi's singular contribution to non-violence theory is his radical practical claim and his comprehensive principle of non-retaliation, as both the moral and the practical core of non-violence.

Gandhi calls this a self-evident principle accessible to anyone with the capacity to reason. He writes that, "Non-violence does not require any outside training. It simply requires the will not to kill even in retaliation and the courage to face death without revenge. This is no sermon on *ahiṁsā* but cold reason and the statement of a universal law."[79]

Though Gandhi does not claim more than to have applied, on as "vast" a scale as he could, an "ancient" principle found in all religious texts, it must be remembered that before his efforts in non-violence, and the efforts of those who followed him, there was no general acceptance of non-retaliation as a general moral principle and no entertainment of it as a moral law.

Gandhi is correct in stating that the operative principle in human affairs is "an eye for an eye" and that vital belief in this principle and the mistrust it incurs, regardless of nominal moral professions to the contrary, is still the ruling fact in human relations, both personal and political. Nevertheless, Gandhi's clear analysis and incessant application make evident the true status of non-retaliation as the working and definitive principle transforming the general commitment to non-violence into a practicable ethic of love.

Exploratory Instrument: The Last Resort Argument. The use of this principle as an exploratory instrument greatly extends the last resort argument, if it does not, as Gandhi hoped, prove the last resort argument fallacious. Its failure as an absolute principle need not vitiate Gandhi's philosophy and method of non-violence in general, as is clear from the above. Granted the proven practical power and value of non-retaliation so far as Gandhi demonstrated it in his *satyāgraha* campaigns, it must be seen how greatly he widened the scope of the non-violence espoused in our general commitment, and how much more force he put behind the last resort argument for those who might now assert it after pushing the new non-violent methods to the limit.

B. RIGHTNESS AND NECESSITY

The problem of justifying violence using arguments of last resort, balance of good results and use of *prima facie* morally legitimated means seems to involve a special kind of necessity or conferring a special moral quality on necessity. In assessing the problem of justifiability it is essential to become clear about the distinction between rightness and necessity, both as Gandhi understood it, in terms of absolute non-violence, and as understood by proponents of the justifiability of violence, in terms of violence and non-violence as relative categories.

Characterizing this necessity is central to both the problem of justifying violence and Gandhi's claim that the problem of justifiability itself arises only because of false views of the nature of violence and non-violence.

The next two sections examine why Gandhi thinks that necessity is ruled out as a moral argument justifying violence, why his position is inadequate to the problem and under what circumstances necessity *is* a moral argument for the use of violence. The second section examines how the necessity criterion *must* be applied to preserve its moral and justifying character.

1. *Gandhi's Position: Defining Necessity by Dichotomy Confuses the Analysis of Violence.* It is an important contribution to the new debate on justifiability that in his ideology Gandhi draws a radical distinction between "rightness" and "necessity" with respect to violence. By identifying violence with evil he makes it a moral term and isolates it from the difficult arguments involving the complex logical and apparently neutral notions of necessity.

Necessity and Self-Deception: In answer to the question did he believe there was moral progress in the world, considering the large scale violence that seemed to be itself growing without hindrance, he said that there was definite moral progress because at least now man did not justify his violence and laments his inability to abstain from what he knows to be wrong.

Gandhi insists that one remain clear about what he is doing. Where there is Truth there is hope of finally defeating evil. He asserts that true moral self-consciousness robs evil of the strength that it gains through false justifying arguments. Honest recognition is sufficient to disarm these tendencies whether in one's own moral consciousness or in a prevalent ideology. But self-deception insures that the growing dominance by evil is ignored and allowed its full sway.

Gandhi argues that violence is unjustifiable not only because it is *prima facie* evil, as all admit, but also because acknowledging claims that necessity can be substituted for moral legitimacy leads to self-deception; and this self-deception (essential untruth) strengthens the evil that was intended to be destroyed by the violence one had justified in the name of necessity.

Arguing in the name of necessity is itself, therefore, an instrument of self-deception and so an evil. This is Gandhi's ideological argument against accepting necessity as a justificatory argument legitimating violence—the brutalizing of oneself by use of violence and the general material damage are not undone by sophisticated arguments.

The advocate of the justifiability of violence claims that violence is sometimes necessary to, and does in fact produce, tangible redress of wrong and defeat of aggressive evil. Gandhi's development of the praxis of non-violence and the method and history of *satyāgraha* constitute his argument against this claim.

According to Gandhi, such practical necessity is itself the product of insufficient faith in non-violence. The advocate of necessary violence suffers a self-fulfilling misplaced faith which inevitably succumbs to arguments of practical necessity instead of sustaining non-violence past apparent necessity to that point of moral effort and modulation of spiritual and material states where the force of non-violence first becomes effective on the practical level. According to Gandhi, such arguments from "necessity" are themselves *evil* since they interfere with true non-violence, which alone is morally valid and which alone gives a true or permanent practical solution.

Simplifying Moral Reality: These arguments are based on Gandhi's initial ideological position which establishes a strict dichotomy and clear opposition of categories and terms. But it is such clarity that is most in doubt in practical applications.

At the basis of Gandhi's entire thought and methods is the ideological equation of violence with evil and the resultant characterization of "violence" as an "evil in itself". This is also acceptable as a starting point to the commonsense position of a general commitment to non-violence. But the further assumption that *use* of violence by moral agents can never be good or produce good claims no such general agreement.

The original equation can stand in a provisional way, but this does not as an absolute support Gandhi's second claim as he believes it implicitly does. He argues that "two wrongs don't make a right". Again, in practical contexts rather this is what appears to be an *open question* that needs to be investigated. It evokes an argument not simply answerable by dichotomous thinking. The moral starkness of characterizing all violent activity as "evil" may mislead if one needs an analysis of action (including subjective agency) that is distinct from a physical description of activity alone. In the analysis of moral action, "use" involves agency separable from activity as an essential factor to be independently characterized if moral ascription is not reduced to empirical terms.

The agent would seem to be "external" to the "activity" in a morally relevant sense. At the very least, there would seem to be a complexity in *types* of ascription involved, even it if were granted that moral dichotomy is in some formulation sufficient to describe the moral mix of the situation. It is enough for the present argument to note that the problem is fundamental, and its solution cannot be assumed without examination as Gandhi's analysis does. That the situation is "moral" and not reducible to merely empirical terms is still a common ground for argument.

The starting point for both positions is the general moral commitment to non-violence which cannot be overridden by any non-moral necessity, i.e. any necessity where violence might be conceived as an end in itself. Gandhi's analysis closes the question of a limit to that commitment as he claims that a line cannot be legitimately drawn in terms of rightness and necessity. But, again, this is a question to be investigated and not *ab initio* foreclosed by ideological commitments.

Gandhi's ideology constructs a dichotomous view of a static existence of properties and qualities by its radical opposition of good and evil. This excludes the third element, basic to Gandhi's position also, i.e., the intervention of spirit (call it will) whose activity *ex hypothesi* is not conditioned by or explicable in terms of good and evil. *Gandhi cannot rule out the question of justifiability and necessity when his dichotomous view does not address all categories involved.*

The spiritual reality is not represented in Gandhi's opposition. But it is fundamental to the analysis of practical violence and non-vio-

144/ lence since this is a problem of action and agency. An opposition of
categories drawn in terms of only properties and qualities, moral or
otherwise, would be inadequate to the analysis of dynamic reality,
where action and use are implied over and above mere existence of
qualities and properties, whether natural or moral.

The Critical Standpoint: Defining Real Necessity.   The question
for critical examination of Gandhi's philosophical position is
whether, given the complexity of the dynamic moral situation (whose
admission is common to both Gandhi's ideology and the commonsense general commitment), stark dichotomous arguments against
the justifiability of violence can be sustained. Objective examination
must ask *what a justifying necessity must look like* once the ideological bases and constraints are discounted.

The commonsense *prima facie* criteria for the balance of good and
evil are the correct starting point. It makes no presumption but looks
at moral reality as it is presented in common experience. It has the
backing of general non-ideological argument, viz. agreement in
common uninterpreted experience. The general commitment is very
strong and relies on the same basic moral preference as does Gandhi's position.

Gandhi has no extra-ideological grounding above this agreed
moral preference for generally ruling out violence and for completely
ruling it out on any other than moral grounds. He offers no objective
ground for insisting on conditionless rightness, especially if "rightness" conceptually includes "working" or "efficacy". He cannot offer better than ideological, assurance of an actual infallibility. Gandhi's grounds for ruling out extension of the necessity criterion are
categorical but his categorical analysis is based on real confusions.
But the *same* moral preference supports *going beyond* the general
commitment when it is believed a moral purpose can be served. It is
incumbent to ask what this limit might look like.

A radical compelling necessity alone could override such a fundamental moral commitment and *prima facie* unjust or harmful and destructive means. The basis of such a necessity can be found in the
original commonsense criteria—the question of "means" brings in
the factors of agency and results which are not covered by the static
dichotomy of good and evil.

The commonsense position requires that this necessity be radically moral. The use of violence must itself be *necessary*. It must be not only allowable but *morally required*, since the basis of having the general commitment at all is the moral presentiment that is foundational to the consciousness it represents. Yet this use of violence must respect the evil nature of violence which is inexpungible and does not subside under influence of any external factor. It must be just this specifically evil nature of violence that makes it morally required, or the necessity involved will not be stringent enough on moral grounds. The violence resorted to must be *just the thing needed*, not admitting any surrogate or substitute, if it is to insure that the necessity be radical and overriding in moral terms. Only a necessity which is the absolute negation of the general but fundamental commitment can satisfy the moral stringency assumed in that commitment.

The evil means, violence, must be chosen just because only that evil means, being in its nature self-destructive, is believed capable of serving a wider moral interest than that involved in the immediate ends/means transaction—local injury and damage may be healed and repaired, while the evil itself will be hastened to self-destruction by turning violence against violence, evil against itself.

Thus Gandhi rightly insists that any justifying necessity would have to be required by the nature of violence as radically evil, and that less than this radically moral requirement would fail to respect the truth that all violence is evil in itself. Gandhi, however, believes further that no good can be produced as an emergent quality superseding the evil in the original means, and if this is so, then all such arguments for the moral necessity of resorting specifically to violence, as occasionally the *only way* to satisfy the moral requirement to protect and propagate the good, are specious and self-deceiving.

Necessity of Fighting Evil: The question is, how does the question of justifiability and radical necessity arise from the common-sense and experience-grounded point of view if it is agreed that violence is radically evil in itself and, as an end in itself, must be morally condemned? It is not claims of inadvertance, inevitability or incapacity that require such justification. These are only pleas to be "excused" and cannot provide a basis for positive action. Justification to be "moral" must be from conscious deliberate choice, as Gandhi repeatedly stated. The question arises from the challenge to justify the morally active assertion that violence is necessary for fighting evil itself—for which no excuse is needed, and which is to be morally demanded and commended.

"Fighting evil", and particularly its overt and extreme form as war, is the limiting case that Gandhi seeks to override, but which the commonsense view believes must be upheld. That Gandhi has significantly widened the scope of practical non-violence and established its conditions and means well beyond any previous conception, proving how extensive and active a power non-violence is, does not affect the commonsense recognition of a necessarily limiting case. Evil is to be beaten by any means. Self-defense is no sin. This is the instinctive, healthy commonsense outlook.

The fight with evil is the focus of both of Gandhi's inquiries: his valid core of inner moral exploration and moral self-culture in the battle with evil within, and his attempt to explore and eradicate the supposed limits of practical and outer non-violence. This active fight with evil is thus also the principal notion for examining Gandhi's ends-means distinction that is central to his philosophy of non-violent action. It focusses the problems of the relation of macro- and microcosm, of moral will and moral action and of evil and violence.

The next section examines Gandhi's arguments against the justifiability of war, representing in macrocosm the non-justifiability of any and all violence, and representing his approach to the limiting case of moral necessity in the practical sphere generally.

2. *Commonsense Position: Defining Moral Necessity, A Real Need for Violence*:   Common sense derived from tradition is more likely true to experience and valid for practical affairs than any one man's theory, even when it is presented in such an appealing moral, ideological dress and is backed by sixty years of such an intense and wide moral inquiry and experimentation. If "non-violence" involves, finally, comparison of intuitions of a legitimating balance of good over evil evolved through historical experience of whole races, versus one man's experience and limited justifying ideology, clearly common sense must be preferred without the need to counter the "perfect proof and clarity" or moral "self-evidence" of the ideologue.

It must be noted that Gandhi felt that his non-violence would be no contribution until he could produce a substantial example of non-violence of the strong. He died believing he had not: "Admirers have given me credit I do not deserve. I am not able to testify that India furnished the world with a good example of non-violence of the strong and therefore as a substitute for armed resistance against an aggressor. India undoubtedly has shown the efficacy of passive non-violence as a weapon of the weak. But useful as it is as a substitute of terrorism, I claim no newness or merit for it. It is no contribution to the peace movement."[80]

We need not be as perfectionist as Gandhi to appreciate his extension of the non-violent principle and means as a theory of action, regardless of its limitations in answering to his final criteria and concept. We must see how far this admission weakens his challenge of crucial commonsense intuitions.

Violence Morally Required by Its Own Evil Nature: "A House Divided. . .". We must clearly characterize the radical necessity that would require the use of violence.

It has been shown that only the contest of fighting evil, which would call for active moral choice of violence (for its evil nature), could initially justify the use of an intrinsically evil means.

The *prima facie* case is that use of violence with no further purpose than to act violently and do violence, to be or feel violent, is a fundamental evil. As a negative concept without further qualification its only resultant is harm, both to the agent and the environs.

Admitting pleasure as a good, it could be acknowledged that in fact there is no possible resort to evil except in terms of the expression and feeling of power involved in the perpetration of the violence. Evil indulges in this power to gain that pleasure at the price of self-destruction. This would separate "use of violence" from "evil of violence" initially, and breaking the equation of violence with evil, would suggest as now equally viable the use of violent power for good, viz. the good of destroying the evil agency that would use violent power only for evil purposes.

Criteria are needed for when violence is necessitated and justified by that necessity.

We begin with the commonsense criteria of balance of good over evil results either when evil is defeated by use of violence or when abstention would increase the violence that evil would do.

But this only says that evil should be defeated, not *why* violence is *required*.

To satisfy the radical moral requirement for use of violent means, the means must be dictated by the nature of the evil itself. The form of evil is destruction with no purpose beyond destruction. Its pure form and inevitable result is self-destruction. Violence is its mechanism and the medium of its expression and operation. The "defeat of violence" would mean hastening evil's self-destruction, and restriction of the violence and resulting damage to evil's own vehicles.

"A House Divided. . .":   The only assurance of defeat in battle is "when a house can be divided against itself."

External means are intrinsically fallible. They leave success subject to chance. Defeat or stultification and minimization of evil cannot morally be left to chance methods where there is a principle available assuring defeat if its methods can be discovered and accurately employed. Evil must, in principle, be defeated if once turned against itself.

By parity of reasoning, this position represents the opposite of Gandhi's argument that "two wrongs don't make a right." In a practical equation such "wrongs" and "rights" are not so clearly and exclusively identifiable. Nor results so clearly delineable. Production of a positive right is not the only possibly desirable outcome of two violent actions which, considered in themselves, are two evils. To avoid otherwise certain evil is also a legitimate moral or "right" outcome. In moral terms, such a result might be considered emergent, or combinatory and not simply additive as, by analogy, a chemical reaction rather than mechanical mixture.

To introduce the ideas of "wrong" and "right" as simple pairs coordinate with "evil" and "good" as Gandhi does, as if they were similarly simple qualities or properties, is to narrowly dichotomize while ignoring the complexity of the action situation. The action situation involves the dynamics of motive, agency, action, aim and purpose, and results in their vital totality not simply as static factors analytically separable or as fixed ideological points.

Required to Control Evil by Its Own Methods: How Evil Functions, a Rationale.   According to this argument, entirely counter to Gandhi's, violence, evil's tangible form and chief means, *must* be used against evil and against intentional and aggressive violence in order to most nearly assure its defeat.

As a philosophical principle rather than a moral or practical maxim, "A house divided against itself cannot stand", does not depend on activation by, or accuracy of moral intuitions, themselves not clearly separable from moral sentiments. Nor is it modified by variations in material conditions. This maxim fills the dual role of a "dependent absolute" that Gandhi asserted of his practical claim; we need only the mechanism of its activation and operation in the material situation and against the particular material form of evil's action in order to guarantee its efficacy. Its logical status as a universal at least is not in doubt.

The status of Gandhi's moral principle of "two wrongs. . ." is doubtful as a universal and so is arguable as the present analysis illustrates. Its lawfulness is a postulate, not an analytic character.

By this argument deceit as well as overt violence can be justified as valid moral means in the fight with evil, as ways of turning it against itself by enlisting its own methods. This is the theoretical argument. As a philosophical principle, it applies universally to soul-force as well as to brute-force, even if *de facto* it has no relevant application to soul-force.

On the practical side, this principle makes a calculable form that clearly delineates the necessity involved.

Gandhi considers deceit a violence because of the tangible damage that results. Damage is assessible and there seems no reason, outside of the assumption of Gandhi's ideological position, why the balances involved in that assessment should not figure in the overall valuation of the action as morally justifiable. However, the principle behind the calculations must reflect the radical moral necessity criterion if their outcomes are to justify a particular action of violence or deceit. This is illustrated in the following:

An episode often brought to challenge Gandhi's mission against the justifiability of violence and untruth for good ends is that of Bāli and Śrī Rāma in the Rāmāyaṇa, depicting the life of Śrī Rāma, the incarnation of God in his attribute of Truthfulness. This epic, along with the Gītā, was Gandhi's chief "companion" and guide in *satyāgraha*.

In this epic, Rāma kills Bāli, a vānara chieftain, by shooting from behind a tree while Bāli is engaged in another battle. This is not truthful open combat. Gandhi answers only that he could not vouch for the truth of everything in the epic but would deny that Rāma was the incarnation of Truth if he did, as an historical person, fight by such violent and untruthful means.

The story makes a fundamental point in the present context. Bāli had chosen a boon that in any fight he would gain half of the opponent's strength and retain all of his own. Thus mathematically not even the incarnation of God could defeat him through ordinary material forces. To engage Bāli in direct conflict would mean for Rāma to surrender half of his own strength and so necessarily to succumb to the quotient of Bāli's strength added to that half of his own. But the special purpose of incarnation is the defeat of rampant and otherwise insuperable evil which is irreversibly winning against all the forces of good in the outer moral battle.

Hence, here is depicted the necessity of Truth itself—the essence of goodness—to use deceit and violence as an indisputable mathematical necessity if once it is admitted that the good must be protected and that the truth of categorical limitations on operant forces must be respected. That also is truth, which cannot be expunged if the play of dualities is to be maintained. Existence as we know it depends upon maintenance of real distinction and limitation.

Universalizing Gandhi's position and valuation would be tantamount to canceling all relative Truth and hence all created evolving existence. But as Gandhi acknowledges, maintenance of this play is the purpose of incarnation (Gītā IV:7–8).[81]

As a single event, the story simply tells about a diabolical choice of boon, but its universal implication is patent. In relations of conflict and resistance, forces are divided equally through the transaction (force meets equal and opposite reaction). But where qualities and tendencies of good and evil are involved, the factors of will and intent materially supersede and redistribute the energies and modify the spread of forces.

Ex hypothesi it is the nature of evil to take without limit. Evil desire and the will to aggressive expression and aggrandizement of ego are insatiable. The fundamental maxim of its action is "all for me, none for all else." The essence of evil is aspiration to realize a radical division and possession of the "goods" and "benefits" of existence and relations, exclusively for itself or to parcel out as its private dominion.

The logical outcome of interaction between two such agents is mutual destruction. The nature of the good is to give to the limit. Thus while the good freely gives more than half of its force and resources, the evil takes the half naturally extended and retains its own, making realization of its own intent materially inevitable if

goodness persists in its goodness without qualification. *Ex hypothesi* /151
this intent is pure evil, pure will to destruction and self-aggrandizement with the non-resisting and unprotected good naturally as its
prey.

The principle of Gandhi's non-cooperation is the "moral truth"
that evil has no existence apart from that lent it by the good. This
need for protection of the good, whether helpless by lack of material
strength or non-resisting by choice and moral conviction, would be a
criterion for use of violence if that violence alone would defeat the
evil that intends destruction of the good. The dynamics of material
force and resources require that the good, in confronting and engaging evil, abstain from its goodness as the disposition to give freely.

Gandhi admits that human nature is a mixture of good and evil.
One can never know if evil is active and has such a diabolical power
as Bāli's. One does know that evil by definition takes all and gives
nothing, that in the *limiting case* it excludes all freedom if not existence of all others; that by nature it aspires to that limiting case; and
that it would, if it could, choose to win the diabolical boon for its
own purposes.

Gandhi also admits that humanity is still evolving. There is no
principle to assure that all human bodies possess an evolved human
brain and matured mind or moral sense. Violence and brutality, or a
demonic disposition, may be literally its delight. There may be an active ego structure and desire principle but not yet any material or
mental basis for evolving reason or moral character or for the restraint in favor of others that moral culture and social life require.
There may be no point of leverage for the self-suffering technique
and soul-force of *satyāgraha* to take hold of and operate on. In such
a case, would not *only* brute-force be capable of restraining brute-
force? By hypothesis, Gandhi's *satyāgraha* requires an active mental
medium as intermediary between spiritual and brute elements.

If victory is assured in principle only by dividing the nature
against itself, i.e. use of evil means to destroy evil, and if violence is
the chief form of all evil's means as Gandhi rightly asserts, then, the
good are *obligated by moral necessity to use violence* against evil.
Even the mathematical necessities of the empirical situation support
the moral analysis. From where can any stigma arise?

Gandhi's Rejoinder: Hate Not the Doer but the Deed: Gandhi's
argument is more complex however. He does not speak of using non-

violence against evil itself. He advocates violence and even hate against the original evils of hate and passion.[82]

But according to Gandhi, the doer should not be identified with the evil deed or with the evil that ensnares him. Hence non-violent methods of non-cooperation with evil should be devised that break the sustaining connection between the evil impetus and its present material vehicles and agencies. Gandhi argues that it is precisely the force of violence, used by the good to resist evil by counter-violence against its vehicles, that actually sustains the evil.

This does not cancel the argument from the principle of dividing the evil against itself. It correctly indicates that the unlimited aspiration to dominate by force and the wish for a guaranteed supremacy and superseding strength are always operative in the principle of evil.

But since evil is never purely manifest, the *relative* support given to evil by an opposing, overt violence is precisely what is to be weighed against the damage that violent opposition inflicts on evil. It severs evil's connection with these vehicles by which evil exercises its tendencies. This exercise is what gives them strength and gathers force.

As empirical categories, good and evil are on an equal footing. They both rely on material vehicles and the medium of physical actions for their growth and maintenance. Therefore, calculations of the balance of good and evil must be made in terms of effects upon their vehicles and activity. These are tactical and strategic considerations of means. They can be morally evaluated *only* in terms of the ends they serve, i.e. whether they produce an ultimate balance of good or evil as the prevailing force in the locale or the world.

Gandhi argues that the force of non-violence acts directly on the evil principle.

This argument is based only on his ideological interpretation of the categories of spiritual and phenomenal reality and their relations. Unless he can support this argument with practical results, its assertion is not justified sufficiently to meet counter-ideological claims of the commonsense position.

Gandhi is arguing on the basis of a confusion of categories of force. He may say that *ex hypothesi* the force of spirit is finally the only reality and is necessarily more powerful than any combination of its partial phenomenal derivatives. But in the sphere of practical activity the categorical requirements of the diverse forces, which alone maintain dual nature in existence, must be respected. There, vi-

olence and non-violence will only have *relative* values and potencies,
varying with material circumstances and with the specific situation
and agents. Remember that Gandhi places good and evil in the "empirical" realm when reality descends to the level of duality.

*Gandhi states that if non-violence is not the law of our being and
species, then "my argument falls to pieces" and "recrudescence" of
violence is inevitable.* But there is no logical or textual guarantee that
in fact this recrudescence is *not* inevitable and is not a necessary feature of our world.

Rather, examination without ideological bias suggests that evil
and good are equally necessary factors which sharpen, shape and
sustain each other, progressively refining the thought, feeling and
sensibility of their agents, giving the soul a progressively clearer
self-expression.

As mentioned earlier, spiritual texts do not bear out Gandhi's position either. He was at odds with the orthodoxy throughout his career. Science argues for entropy and possibly recurrent "big bang"
and disintegration cycles. Experience shows that the best of the good
only comes out in response to opposition. There is validity to the
quip, "what would you do if all your problems were solved; what
boredom would life be in a perfect universe!"

Human sensibility and moral sense seem to progress by engagement with evil. If so, it would not be an unforunate circumstance
that evil were as much a necessary constituent and law of being of
phenomenal evolution as is goodness. *The necessity to engage evil
with violence would naturally be a limiting condition to the principle
of non-violence, necessary to completely define it and to express its
full potency.* According to this analysis, non-violence need not be absolute in order to be morally stringent and spiritually efficient.

Though the difficulty of applying Gandhi's principle is great, that
there was a rule to apply without question of its applicability and
that it ought to be applied, would remove a very significantly
stimulating, and sharpening question from the problem of moral
growth—and perhaps its basic question and primary mechanism.

This balance and opposition seems an essential feature of the self-
realization that Gandhi aims at through non-violence. Gandhi cannot
so easily claim that only his view and methods are valid or that only
his rule or something of the same absolute order must and ought to
be applied.

Gandhi's Partial Validity, But Non-Necessity: Gandhi supports his arguments that "two wrongs can't make a right" and that non-violent force alone can penetrate to the root of evil (without creating the counter-productive and self-defeating evil of violent reactions in its own vehicles) by referring to the intrinsic nature of the opposition of soul- to brute-forces. They cannot be righted off and neutralized. A good act does not cancel the damage already done by the bad action. This confuses force with the properties that manifest with its use and with its application conditions.

Since Gandhi subscribes to the *advaitic*, non-dual, view of reality and so considers force to be fundamentally single and a continuum, therefore, the same force can manifest contradictory properties.

That Gandhi has discovered a spiritual force which has the properties he claims and operates in the way he explains, need not be discounted. He set out to discover a force fitting specific moral criteria on the basis of a particular metaphysical view of Truth, ideological interpretation of spiritual reality and creation and certain hypotheses about the relation between spiritual, moral and practical realities. That he discovered such a force and a mechanism of action does not justify his claim that this set of properties, principles and methods of action is the *only* one capable of realizing ultimate moral and spiritual aims.

By Gandhi's own admission, those aims have a reality and knowability that is outside of any categories through which they may be characterized and manipulated. The "only" that he attaches to those constraints and conditions merely reflects that the principles and criteria he appeals to are those derived from his categorically confused and materially unjustified presuppositions. On the basis of common sense and common uninterpreted experience and judgment, it may be concluded that there is a moral practical limitation to use of non-violent means beyond which such abstention from violent means constitutes an evil; and the realization of this limit must be calculated in terms of practical (dual) categories, properties and results. These are characteristics of practical reality that *must* be dealt with if defeat of evil is to be assured, i.e. destroyed by its own means; turned against itself.

Still, Gandhi may be justified in asserting the assured efficacy of his *personal* practice of non-violence.

If it is admitted that *karmic* adjustment of external results and of moral and spiritual fruits is made by a divine agency, according to

faith (Gītā IX:25) and trueness to one-self, Gandhi's personal moral
authenticity may serve as the decisive moral consideration above the
mere mechanical and numerical adjustment of empirical factors. But
if someone abstains from violence on merely formal or mechanically
reasoned grounds without the authenticity of unabridgeable faith
that Gandhi is possessed of, then non-violent action cannot succeed
beyond some definite point. It will very likely serve the cause of evil
if used blindly without both the living faith Gandhi required and the
wide awake attention to tactical considerations, required in its strategic use. This is common sense. To the extent Gandhi's methods depend on material conditions, to that extent his practical claims are
dependent and must respect practical reality in operating with its
forces.

Failure of Gandhi's Position to Respect Categorical Truths: The
primary principle of action and the fundamental laws of force must
be derived from the realities through which they operate. Assimilation of categories amounts to abridgement of truth, regardless of the
ultimate singularity of reality outside of the categories of ordinary
active sense and mental consciousness.

Thus in practical affairs the principle of self-division is a constitutive principle and supersedes moral maxims. Moral maxims can apply only by analogy and according to mediating conditions that must
be satisfied to validate their application. Our analysis finds the
house-divided principle, in this case the necessity of using evil means
against evil, more fundamental than Gandhi's principles of non-
violence. Then Gandhi's attempt to annul the *prima facie* claim for
the necessity of violence to defeat evil as a last resort must be considered invalid both morally and practically.

Gandhi's Failure of Common Sense: What leads Gandhi to support his position by choosing a moral axiom rather than a neutral
examination of categorical realities? How does he support his position against the *prima facie* case in favor of the strongly counter-
intuitive claim that non-violence would necessarily defeat a Hitler?

If the "house-divided" argument is correct, a Hitler, an insuperable evil, can only be defeated by turning its own means against itself
using the laws of those forces that act through the practical medium.
Violence and deceit would be justified by the larger violence intended
and prepared for by the agent of evil thus destroyed. This is so much
non-violence as could be wished. There is no reason other than ideo-

logical preference to suppress the periodic recrudescence of evil as malicious violence, or to assume that such violence is not the law of empirical reality. Common sense sees evil through history repeatedly reassert itself, reconstituting its vehicles after each destruction. The battle goes on with no millennial termination.

Since so far as human effort and moral evolution are concerned, goodness is the sustaining principle against evil; the question is, what conditions define the necessity criterion in practical application in human affairs, so that this essential goodness is preserved? If a Hitler must be opposed by force at what point exactly must such force be applied?

These are the questions that the criteria of the just war are meant to specify.

3. *Last Resort: Conditions of Applying the Necessity Criterion*:
Defining the Good Use of Violence: Preservation of Goodness.
The conditions of applying the necessity criterion must be such as to insure not merely the greatest numerical human survival rate but to insure that the use of violence leaves the moral principle intact by which even the minimum survival rate of two could regenerate and evolve the race and sustain the pursuit of spiritual realization.

The moral principles are those which not only insure survival but insure also progress in quality of life, which is to say growth, refinement and self-expression of the spiritual element.

Gandhi writes, "Spirit is that moral being which informs the human body and which is imperishable. Spiritual progress is that which promotes the realization of that imperishable essence. What retards the progress of my neighbor must retard mine."[83] For Gandhi, character is the moral element of personality that supervenes and steadily evolves beneath the continuous wash of phenomena. Character, by this "relative permanence," represents the spirit.

The conditions for necessarily meeting evil with violence must insure the continued existence of the moral prerequisites for this culture of character and sustained spiritual growth.

If morality has its tangible form in rules and articulated principles, the engagement and aftermath must be prosecuted in ways that preserve those rules intact as a whole regardless of partial abridgement necessitated by the principle of meeting evil by its own means. This

abridgement of moral rules is in fact a purely tactical requirement
when the opponent is incorrigibly evil and indefeatable by other
means.

This condition defines the last resort criterion for assuring the
moral character of the justification by necessity. Though the violence
used is in itself evil, if enough strength is put behind it, empowering
its unique capability of overcoming evil, then the conditions of its
moral use must reflect the wider good that is to be preserved by the
partial or momentary and pointed suspension of "goodness" in its
form as restraint and non-use of violence.

Sincerity and Clarity: Evil is characterized by its specific intent
and readiness to use violence as a means to achieve any purpose it
happens to entertain and believes violent use of force will accomplish. It has no regard for collateral damage perpetrated by those
means. Delight in the release of violent energy for its own sake, the
exhilaration coming from any release of energy, is the limiting case
defining evil's use of violence.

The good use of violent energies, intended to destroy evil, must be
opposite this. The violence must be a last resort, sincerely, hesitat-
ingly and regretfully engaged with full cognizance of its nature, its
likely and unwished-for collateral effects and the severity of the necessity involved. Whatever violence is used must be fully believed to
be necessary and must be operated fully and only to the purpose of
insuring that its use will result in less harm than would have oc-
curred by not engaging the evil violently. Even in this engagement the
violence must be most narrowly constrained to the purpose of overcoming the particular evil opposed. This purpose and its clarity, sincerity and singularity legitimize the intent.

Factual judgments of wisdom and sincerity, etc., are not at issue.
They will always be questionable from without and subject to decep-
tion from within.

In violent engagement with evil, preparation of the moral will and
clarification of the moral intent are matters of "peacetime" and constant moral self-culture—exactly as is preparation for active *satyāgraha*.

The fact of having constantly worked to achieve such moral
strength and clarity stands as surety that one's wisdom and sincerity
in crisis will be authentic and optimal, though the training beforehand cannot function as a criterion.

Gandhi argued similarly that the force of *satyāgraha* was only a last resort necessitated by the incorrigibility of opposition and conflict. He stated that perhaps the final argument against challenges of uninformed or insincere application could only be a deferring to one's past constant efforts. The accuracy of judgments and purity of will and intent, the moral integrity and depth that can be assumed to have evolved only through constancy of effort over time and variousness in scope of practice, can alone give depth and credibility to the last resort justification, whether for use of violence or of *satyāgraha*.

Patience, and Restraint in Use of Violence: Thus the restraint involved before resorting to violence is, to the degree possible, both test and proof of purity of that intent; one is to use non-violence "as much as one can, for as long as one can."

First, this serves to awaken what dormant or obstructed good may be present, possibly obviating the need to overtly fight evil with evil. Gandhi's practical claim was, without independent justification, based on the belief that it had an absolute power of non-violent force to awaken the good in the vehicle and to enlist it in non-cooperating with evil, thus subverting the agent of evil from within.

Second, this patience and sustained restraint assures the purity of the resort and the moral character of the necessity and engagement to the agent, the opponent and to neutrals or potential allies as well. Evil would not "take the pains" implied in the restraint of "long, hard" non-violence. Evil's aim is pleasure and self-aggrandizement, and minimization of its own suffering necessitated in gaining these.

Third, this restraint defuses evil's defensive challenges and stands out against counter-justifications, first, by the material sacrifices it involves, and second, by the maintenance of the moral beneficence required to sustain the restraint.

These are similar conditions to those Gandhi puts on the last resort argument for *satyāgraha* which he takes also to be a drastic measure and limiting case. But for common sense and the *prima facie* case, these conditions do not postulate necessary abdication and forfeiture of moral principles simply because of entrance into violent engagement, as Gandhi believed must occur automatically. These conditions merely insist on the equal necessity of maintaining that moral status through the conflict—whatever the violence required.

Intelligence and Objectivity: Fourth, the use of violent force must be intelligent. It must be clear-sighted and to the moral purpose

to insure that the means are kept to that stringency of balance and
minimum assertion required by the specific necessity to be met.

As Gandhi insists, hate and anger are the essence of violence—its
subtle and first form. Intelligent use of force is possible only when
these are absent and when, therefore, perception, understanding and
keenness are optimally objective and active. This insures that the violence is maximally restricted to the evil resisted.

Peace, an End and Aim, Not a Means: The final condition is res-
titution to the harmed of all that can possibly be returned or repaid;
the establishment of a just peace on a new cooperative and giving
basis.

This is made possible by the morality maintained and retained intact throughout the conflict by the judicious abridgement of some of
its rules as dictated by the moral necessity addressed.

*This just peace and new friendship are in fact the substance of jus-
tification by the last resort argument.* Such use of violence is a clearly
moral last resort to save that moral basis necessary for returning to
and maintaining the moral and spiritual evolution whose life, action
and existence the upsurge of evil has challenged.

Sum: The moral appropriateness and practical effectiveness of
these conditions for accurately applying the necessity criterion can be
understood in full contrast with Gandhi's claims only in light of the
categorical realities they and Gandhi anticipate or ignore—the law
of practical reality which itself dictates this necessity to defeat evil by
its own means in the limiting case, and a law of being that assimilates the practical into the moral, allowing of no such limiting case.

Though the demand of the *prima facie* case and the counter-
intuitive practical conclusions of Gandhi's non-violence make it easy
to doubt the validity of his radical claims, the severity of the argument for necessary violence and the strength of the general commitment to non-violence make it difficult to accept the logical conclusion against Gandhi's appealing thesis.

It is necessary therefore to examine why Gandhi's position is confused and does not support the moral preference that he wants to
give it.

Gandhi's *satyāgraha* is meant only to demonstrate practical viability in order to defuse false belief and change action. He does not
claim that this demonstration would *prove* the validity of his position. Only the logic and truth of his concept and arguments could do

so. But the study of his methods has been shown to be necessary for gaining full insight into his concepts since these include his practical claims and aim as essential components. Examination of Gandhi's application of his concepts in the context of war and the final resort to *satyāgraha* will therefore provide the necessary critique of Gandhi's confusions in his denial of a limit to the general commitment to non-violence.

The two next chapters examine Gandhi's practical application of his ideological components. This application is meant to supersede the necessity criterion and thus provide the basis for his arguments against the justifiability of war, and for *satyāgraha* as its viable, non-violent, complete moral and practical substitute. It is shown how this application is fundamentally misconceived and produces both categorical and valuational confusions.

7. Critical Examination of Gandhi's Views on War: The Limiting Case in Conflict, Violence and the Last Resort Argument (Real Necessity: Application of the Objective Analysis of the Limiting Case, I)

The necessity criterion represents just those real limiting conditions to the application of non-violence which Gandhi wishes to annul and supersede in his ideological exploration.

In the last chapter, Gandhi's ideological components and the confusions inherent in his position have been adumbrated while establishing an objective standpoint. As theoretical elements these may be acknowledged to suffice for giving a rationale to the general commitment. It is shown in this chapter how the practical application of those elements produces confusions when the application is meant to supersede the limits inherent in that general commitment as understood by common sense.

This chapter and the next examine in detail how Gandhi's views on the justifiability of war and his proposed substitute for war fail to dispose of the necessity criterion which is a real necessity since it represents the inherent limits of the practical component of non-violence.

A. NON-RETALIATION AND THE IDEOLOGICAL INTERPRETATION OF THE MAXIM "TWO WRONGS DON'T MAKE A RIGHT"

Gandhi repeatedly draws upon the maxim "two wrongs don't make a right" as an expression of moral truth when he argues against the justifiability of any violence and insists on the use of *satyāgraha* to dissolve all conflicts. He uses the maxim to express, generalize and justify non-retaliation as the chief operative principle and core of his practical non-violence concept and methods, *ahiṃsā* and *satyāgraha*.

First it is necessary to ask why Gandhi's position is so appealing and yet repelling. It apparently has the certitude of self-evidence, yet it raises doubts when it opposes fundamental moral intuitions. The maxim "two wrongs . . ." has the rhetorical force of mathematical certainty and the immediate appeal of a common sense truism. Gandhi draws upon this force in expounding both his ideology and practice.

The rationale of his arguments in justification of his practical claim as it is expressed in this maxim is, however, fundamentally flawed when he applies it unconditionally. He must apply it unconditionally in order to explicate that claim and to defeat the last resort and necessity arguments. His ideological interpretation of this maxim hides a circularity. The feeling of certitude thus stems from Gandhi's ideological constructions and definitions, in which this circularity appears as a "self-evidence".

The circularity gives the feeling of logical certitude; this feeling is reenforced by the fundamental sentiments stirred up by the strong moral general commitment. This feeling leads to confusion when it is frustrated by equally basic intuitions that arise when the formula is used to justify superseding the *prima facie* limit of that general commitment.

If the two "wrongs" are mutually retaliatory actions based on a will and intent to reprisal and injury, then they clearly cannot produce a "right". They cannot produce the "end of retaliation" which defines "good" in Gandhi's non-violence. The two wrongs, being defined as retaliations, will necessarily lead to an escalatory chain of reprisals that necessarily end in mutual exhaustion or mutual destruction. Or, if there is a victor there will be bitterness and sense of injustice. The resolution is by force, not reason. It is inherently tainted with personal and arbitrary judgment and vindictiveness. These are the seeds of the necessary counter-action that must come when there is no principle of restraint operative.

Gandhi generalizes the principle to thought and speech activity. He argues that since these retaliations proceed from fear, anger and hatred accumulated from continuing reprisal and injury, there is no escape from the cycle of violence. He believes he can deduce unilateral non-retaliation from this *factual* situation and, therefore, as the *only* practically valid principle of *moral* action.

The original violence of aggression is clearly not morally justifiable, and if the only result of retaliatory violence (also aggressive in quality if not by original intent), besides immediate injury, is the escalating cycle of counter violence, there is no result left to possibly justify that secondary or defensive violence either.

Gandhi finds it incumbent upon the one who "knows better" to break the chain.

Gandhi writes that "it was no answer to say that similar or worse things had happened (there) . . . it would be improper to institute comparison of evil doing. Even if the whole world did wrong, should we do likewise?"[84] We should note that this is one of Arjuna's arguments in the Gītā, for not entering the battle for justice (I:38–39). In the Gītā, "knowing better" becomes the argument for pacifism and Arjuna's knowledge of a moral rule is translated to grounds for desisting from action.

Gandhi challenges retaliation as an absurdity: "They could not secure justice by copying the evil ways of one another. If two men go out riding and one falls down, was the other to follow suit? That would merely result in breaking the bones of both."[85] Professions of rightness or of redeeming purposes are either hypocrisy and self-deception, or ignorance of the nature of retaliation as unredeemable violence.

Gandhi argues that by definition the retaliatory motive excludes all other aims, regardless of appearance to the contrary. It is "logically" all-consuming and, therefore, only a knowing renunciation of it (unilaterally if necessary) in all its manifestations can lead to a "right". By Gandhi's metaphysics of action this means a knowing renunciation of all personal motives. Two blind retaliations "logically" cannot produce a good, a non-retaliatory, non-reactive response, according to this conception.

By his logico-metaphysical principle of "yathā piṇḍe . . ." Gandhi concludes, with "mathematical" certainty, that war is merely the fullest manifestation of the "fact" that mutually escalating retaliation is the form of violence at every level, and that this definition logically encompasses the physical as well as the mental and verbal spheres of activity. The same "two wrongs . . ." maxim applies absolutely in the context of war as it does in all lesser relations of violence.

But again, though Gandhi's analysis is simple and straightforward, it is neither naive nor simplistic.

Writing about the incalculable Hindu-Muslim violence of 1946–47, Gandhi states that "India knows, the world should, that every ounce of my energy has been and is being devoted to the definite avoidance of fratricide culminating in war."[86] He is engaged in a delicate analysis of the situation in terms of war and non-violence. Again, Gandhi stresses the "logical" connection between practical options and outcomes. Note the similarity of the situation below with that depicted in the Gītā:

> Gandhiji said in his post-prayer speech that he had been an opponent of all warfare. But if there was no other way of securing justice from Pakistan, if Pakistan persistently refused to see its proved error and continued to minimize it, the Indian Government had to go to war against it. War was not a joke. No one wanted war. That way lay destruction. *But he could never advise anyone to put up with injustice. If all the Hindus were annihilated in a just cause he would not mind it.*[87]

> He was wedded to non-violence for all time and could never advocate war . . . he was merely pointing out the various possibilities. India and Pakistan should settle their differences by mutual consultation and failing that fall back upon arbitration. But if one party persisted in wrong doing and would accept neither of the two ways mentioned above, the only way left open was that of war. They should know the circumstances that prompted his remark.[88]

But Gandhi seeks to avoid misinterpretation and writes:

> Not a single mention of war in my speeches can be interpreted to mean that there was any incitement to or approval of war between Pakistan and the Union . . . I claim that I rendered a service to both the sister States by examining the present situation and definitely stating when the case of war could arise between the two states. This was done not to promote war but to avoid it as far as possible . . . was it wrong to draw public attention to the logical steps that inevitably followed one after another? . . . India knows, the world should, that every ounce of my energy has been devoted to the definite avoidance of fratricide culminating in war.[89]

It should be noted how carefully Gandhi maintains the balance of his statements to keep the distinction between "understanding" the conditions of war, its causes and circumstances, and advocating, justifying or even allowing war. Yet he does allow and even advocate it with his very posture. It is also arguable that it was in his power to call for a general mutiny, or to intervene directly with the authorities and he *chose* not to.

For purposes of the present argument it is enough to note that /165
(1) Gandhi considers the chain of events "logical" and "inevitable",
and that (2) he does not himself feel the non-violent power to break
that "logic of events", and that (3) he does not "mind" the war for
justice. All of this is tacit abdication of his practical claim, an abdication not nullified by qualifying disclaimers. His inconsistency is patent here.

Gandhi did feel justified, however, given his disclaimers, in asserting universal scope for his principle, and in taking war to be the
prototype of violence.

To accomplish this universalizing, Gandhi has to make the contents of the maxim the circumstances of its practical application
homogeneous at a more fundamental level than the facts and experience drawn upon by the counter-intuitions of common sense and the
prima facie case when they define an overriding necessity that seems
to cancel the moral maxim.

This is the locus of the cluster of confusions which leads Gandhi
to a *prima facie* untenable position and which does not on clarification support retaining that position against the *prima facie* intuitions.
Here is rooted his confused and falsifying (not its technical sense)
analysis positing the moral and practical homogeneity of the spiritual
and practical spheres.

Since in Gandhi's view, war is the basic form and fullest culmination of violence, the appropriate focus of this critical investigation
is (1) his analysis of the genesis of war as he derives it from the
Gītā, and his judgments in actual instances of war that he dealt with
during his sixty years as an active war-resister; and, (2) his *satyāgraha* intended as a complete substitute for war (representing all violent methods in any conflict).

It is necessary to see, in concrete contexts and in detail, how
Gandhi's ideological and homogenizing interpretation of the key
maxim is bound by confusion and contradiction and how it fails to
do justice to the real situation.

B. GANDHI'S ANALYSIS OF WAR IN THE GĪTĀ AND JUDGMENTS
OF ITS JUSTIFIABILITY

1. *Misuse of Logical Principles of the Identity of Micro- and Macro-cosmic Reality: Confusion of Basic Distinctions.*

According to Gandhi's principle of micro-macro-cosmic identity, *"yathā piṇḍe . . ."*, examining his views on war is equivalent to examining his views on violence in general.

War is only the outermost and externalized form of violence (whose roots are always internal—affections and dispositions of the subjective material makeup). The shape and quality of all violence are the same. The same laws are found operative and the same moral rules and methods apply. War involves the same entanglement in outer form—binding retaliations and escalation of violent reprisals that the Gītā elaborates in the escalation of the violence of desire and anger (II:62–63).

But the Gītā and the Mahābhārata are not only the source of Gandhi's analysis of war and violence and the justifiability problem, they are the *locus classicus* of these issues.

Gandhi finds in the Gītā the depiction of the moral battle within, but he elaborates on this in his judgments about physical war and in his analysis of the pacifist position and methods of war resistance.

Though it may not be incorrect for Gandhi to point out an analogy and parallel here from the standpoint of principle, he is not justified in reversing the direction of his application of this logical principle to assert *from the standpoint of perception* that the "ideal" and the "real" are identical. That the "Truth is the truth" and "what is true within is reflected without" are valid propositions, notwithstanding.

Real and Ideal: Appearance and Reality. The problems Gandhi wants to solve by this principle are the identification of violence with intention and motive and the proper characterization of violence and non-violence for moral application to practical purposes.

It is a confusion to base a theory of practical moral truth on the application of a logical principle without modifying it for application from the practical standpoint; Gandhi does this in his *satyāgraha* and his radical practical claims. He uses these not as instruments of inquiry to guide investigation and to focus and clarify perception, but as *a priori* rules to determine moral definitions and principles of action.

From an *a priori* moral standpoint, on the basis of his assimilation
of the real to the ideal, Gandhi justifies his assimilation of the spiritual, practical and moral. He seems to be incognizant of the categorical differences that enter when the assimilation is reversed and the significant difference becomes precisely that of appearance and reality. He is aware of this as a fundamental problem in explanation and judgment when he tries to convey the difficult truth that the *same* act can be prompted and guided by entirely different motives which determine opposing qualities and sets of results. This is a decisive recognition in terms of the present argument.

Gandhi writes that, "the question raised . . . is of very great importance and has always caused me the greatest difficulty, not so much in deciding upon the action to be taken at a given moment but in justifying my conduct in terms of *ahiṁsā*. For the same action may outwardly be taken by the believer and the unbeliever. At these times the motive alone decides its quality."[90]

But Gandhi writes also that, "Non-violence of two persons occupying different positions will not outwardly take the same shape. Thus the non-violence of a child towards his father would take the shape of conscious voluntary submission to this violence when he loses his temper . . . The father would take the child to his bosom and instantaneously sterilize the child's violence. In each case it is of course assumed that the outward act is an expression of the inward intention."[91]

Supporting the inference from appearance to reality is a large problem in any theory but Gandhi does not address it on the theoretical level. He merely assumes the unmodified reversal of the micro-macro-cosmic identity principle, and ignores the categorical truths by insisting on the primacy of absolute, ideal truth as if regard for the latter cancelled validity of the former. This disregard of difference and distinction ignores the non-commutivity conferred on the principle by the practical context of its application.

For the core and most extensive part of Gandhi's analysis, this assimilation functions as if valid since it is all within the category of phenomenal reality. The principle functions, as Gandhi wishes, to raise one's sights towards guiding ideals. But this causes confusion and leads to contradictions in the limiting cases where he shifts categorical perspective without regard for categorical realities, and for the requirement of a cross categorical perspective.

Confused Valuation of Life: Peace at Any Price. Because of this assimilation and confusion of categories, the real and the ideal, the apparent and the real, Gandhi places too high a value on life, giving it an absolute value when it is only a relative category.

In spite of recognizing the spiritual principle as fundamental existence, Gandhi values transient life as if it were permanent existence. He makes its protection and quiescent state, i.e. non-violence and pacifism, his absolute values and aims.

In answer to the argument that he strained the Gītā into an allegory just to support this idealizing, Gandhi writes that though ". . . the Gītā . . . is not a treatise on non-violence nor was it written to condone war . . . What I have done is . . . to give an extended but in no way strained meaning . . . I hold that the logical outcome of the teaching of the Gītā is decidedly for peace at the price of life itself. It is the highest aspiration of the human species."[92]

From this valuation, Gandhi derives the imperatives for total non-violence and for proving the unjustifiability of war by any moral value, supposed necessity or putative practical result.

2. Views on the Justifiability of War and Violence: Analysis Vitiated by Ideological Homogeneity from Wrong Use of Identity.

Justifiability: War Is in No Way Justifiable. Gandhi repeatedly states that he finds war to be an "unmitigated evil",[93] unjustifiable under any circumstances or for any cause, even for the defeat of insuperable evil—directly contrary to the *prima facie* criteria introduced above. To illustrate:

The tyrants of old never went so mad as Hitler seems to have gone . . . with religious zeal . . . he is propounding a new religion of exclusive and militant nationalism in the name of which any inhumanity becomes an act of humanity to be rewarded here and hereafter . . . If there ever could be a justifiable war in the name of and for humanity, a war against Germany, to prevent the wanton persecution of a whole race, would be completely justified. But I do not believe in any war. A discussion of the pros and cons of such a war is, therefore, outside my horizon or province.[94]

Gandhi writes more specifically, "I do not believe in short—violent—cuts to success . . . However much I may sympathize with

and admire worthy motives, I am an uncompromising opponent of
violent methods even to serve the noblest of causes."[95] But were not
"motives to decide?" It must be asked: "Why then, only 'not here'?"

Again Gandhi opposes to the putative moral worth of war (as
having only a temporary value derivative specifically from and for
the particular and localized situation) his absolute moral value of
non-violence, which he holds is universally valid and not temporally
conditioned by any circumstantial provisos.

Gandhi understands this value to be *true* practical expedience and
efficiency, since thus any supposed moral value or apparently justifying "good result" of a particular war will necessarily be cancelled
in the long run, whereas non-violence, as an *ultimate* and *comprehensive* value, has the *practical consequence* that it alone can permanently break the circle of violence. Every violent attempt to do so,
though "justified" on every other ground, must *in fact* fail to realize
permanently that practical translation of ultimate value which is
really the basis of any serious justifying arguments. According to
Gandhi's assimilation of categories and valuations, "permanent
breaking of the circle of violence" is merely the practical and physical counterpart of ultimate moral value.

Thus Gandhi concludes that peace and non-violence are the same
thing.

Gandhi asserts that ignoring the ultimacy of non-violence results
in mere change in the form of violence and extension and deepening
of the original violent motivation, "for ultimately, force, however
justifiably used, will lead us into the same morass as the force of
Hitler and Mussolini. There will be just a difference of degrees."[96]

The root fact of violence is that no matter what justification and
arguments are made from the standpoint of abstract valuation, divorced from the equation of the moral, practical and spiritual, what
we call violence *can only* in fact instigate opposition and produce a
mirror reaction in the opponent. It merely deepens the violence and
brutal proclivities in agent and victim both.

Note that for Gandhi, appeal to principle is identical with appeal
to expedience—intrinsic evil *cannot help but* lead ultimately to bad
results, and he writes "To Every Briton" of the World War,

I appeal for cessation of hostilities, not because you are too exhausted
to fight, but because war is bad in essence. You want to kill Nazism.
You will never kill it by its indifferent adoption. Your soldiers are do-

ing the same work of destruction as the Germans. The only difference is that perhaps yours is not as thorough as the Germans. If that be so, yours will soon acquire the same thoroughness as theirs, if not much greater. On no other condition can you win the war. In other words, you will have to be more ruthless than the Nazis. *No cause, however just, can warrant the indiscriminate slaughter that is going on minute by minute.* I suggest that a cause that demands the inhumanities that are being perpetuated today cannot be just.[97]

In terms of the new debate on justifiability and the advent of the atom bomb, Gandhi reaches the same conclusions. He points to the logic of the debate as another and final proof and unavoidable vindication of his arguments in the practical sphere. He wrote in 1946,

So far as I can see, the atomic bomb has deadened the finest feeling that has sustained mankind for ages. There used to be the so called laws of war which made it tolerable. Now we know the naked truth. War knows no law except that of might. The atom bomb brought an empty victory to the allied arms but it resulted for the time being in destroying the Soul of Japan. . .

The moral to be legitimately drawn from the supreme tragedy of the bomb is that it will not be destroyed by counter-violence. Mankind has to get out of violence only through non-violence. Hatred can be overcome only by love. Counter-hatred only increases the surface as well as the depth of hatred.[98]

To the question: "Had it (the atomic bomb) antiquated non-violence?" . . . Gandhi's reply (was)

"On the contrary, non-violence was the only thing that was left in the field. It is the only thing that the atom bomb cannot destroy. I did not move a muscle when I first heard that the atom bomb had wiped out Hiroshima. On the contrary, I said to myself, 'Unless now the world adopts non-violence, it will spell certain suicide for mankind!!' "[99]

For Gandhi, the ultimacy of incipient atomic violence throws into relief the ideal status, character and superior practical potency of non-violent force (a spiritual force) and the ultimacy of non-violence values (a spiritually based ethics, axiology and pragmatics).

Thus, in Gandhi's view, the atom bomb had not only not "exploded" his "faith" in non-violence, but had "clearly demonstrated . . . that the twins (Truth and Non-violence) constitute the mightiest force in the world. Before it the atom bomb is of no effect. The two

opposing forces are wholly different in kind, the one moral and spiritual, the other physical and material. The one is infinitely superior to
the other which by its very nature has an end. The power of the
spirit is ever progressive and endless. Its full expression makes it unconquerable in the world."[100]

According to Gandhi, not even the pretense of justifiability of violence and war is thus possible, given the contemporary world situation of nuclear armament, immediate global impact and amplification of minor and local violence or conflict, with its probable rapid
magnification and escalation to global and nuclear proportions.

Further, according to Gandhi, the possibility of justifying violence
and war by success, when used against large nations or super powers
by oppressed and weak nations, is logically ruled out; "You cannot
successfully fight them with their own weapons. After all you cannot
go beyond the atom bomb. Unless we can have a new way of fighting imperialism of all brands in the place of the outward one of
a violent rising, there is no hope for the oppressed races of the
earth."[101]

Thus for Gandhi there is *no possible justification* for "war on
war", judged on any possible criteria of results, spiritual, moral or
practical. The thing itself is evil and there is absolutely no ancillary
consideration of results possible; no justification is possible given the
contemporary situation. Therefore, non-violence alone has the potency to solve the problems usually addressed by violence; and so
non-violence *ought always* to be used!

This is the conclusion Gandhi has consistently sought in the practical demonstration of his radical claims.

The suicide implicit in violence is unavoidably visible in its nuclear
expression. Gandhi takes the analysis he has given of violence in general to be vindicated and demonstrated by the logic of the atomic debate. *In one sweeping practical display is revealed the final poverty
and impotence of violence and the corresponding potency, viability
and necessity of non-violence.*

But Gandhi caused difficulty for other absolute pacifists by his not
only allowing war but actually supporting the call to training in arms
and war, and himself participating in the Boer War, the Zulu Rebellion and recruiting for the British in World War I.[102]

As shown in Chapter 1, the fundamental value in Gandhi's idealism is Truth and its first form is authenticity. Gandhi writes that

though he participated as stretcher-bearer and recruiter in three acts of war,

> My repugnance to war was as strong then as it is today; and I could not then have, and would not have, shouldered a rifle. But one's life is not a single straight line; it is a bundle of duties very often conflicting. And one is called upon continually to make one's choice between one duty and another. As a citizen not then, and not even now, but a re-former leading an agitation against the institution of war, I had to ad-vise and lead men who believed in war but who from cowardice or from base motives or from anger against the British Government, re-fraining from enlisting. I did not hesitate to advise them that, so long as they believed in war, and professed loyalty to the British constitu-tion, they were in duty bound to support it by enlistment. Though I did not believe in the use of arms, and though it is contrary to the reli-gion of *Ahiṁsā* which I profess, I should not hesitate to join an agita-tion for a repeal of the debasing Arms Act which I have considered amongst the blackest crimes of the British Government against India . . . And I have not hesitated only recently to tell Hindus that if they do not believe in out and out *Ahiṁsā* and cannot practice it, they will be guilty of a crime against their religion and humanity, if they fail to defend by force of arms the honor of their women. And all this advice and my previous practice I hold to be not only consistent with my pro-fession of the religion of *Ahiṁsā* out and out, but a direct result of it.[103]

Gandhi explains further that, "Life is governed by a multitude of forces . . . Non-violence works in a most mysterious manner. Often a man's actions defy analysis in terms of non-violence; equally often his actions may wear the appearance of violence when he is abso-lutely non-violent in the highest sense of the term and is subsequently found so to be. All I can claim for my conduct is that it was, in the instances cited, actuated in the interests of non-violence."[104]

Gandhi admits that his arguments in explanation of "choice of duties", or "necessary compromise" in the interests of the principle of non-violence that he wanted thereby ultimately to someday govern all conduct, may be a self-deception "I claim to have done every act described by me for the purpose of advancing the cause of peace. That does not mean that these acts really advanced the cause of peace. I am merely stating the fact that my motive was peace . . . What is possible, however, is that I was weak . . . I observe daily how capable we are of utmost self-deception. For the time being, however, I am not aware of my self-deception."[105]

Or, his reasonings may be badly expressed. He reiterates and insists that no result in action or argument can compromise the essential unjustifiability of war and violence. He writes that "there is no defense of my conduct weighed only in the scales of *Ahiṁsā*."[106]

Gandhi adds that ". . . for me the matter does not admit of reasoning beyond a point. It is one of deep conviction that war is an unmixed evil . . . But conviction is one thing, correct practice is another." (Note, "Gandhi's ultimate appeal is to "conviction.") Because of the very nature of the analytical problem, reason often confutes itself in applying principle to practice; "The very thing that one war resister may do in the interest of his mission may repel another war resister who may do the exact opposite, and yet both may hold the same view about war. This contradiction arises because of the bewildering complexity of human nature. I can only, therefore, plead for mutual toleration even among professors of the same creed."[107]

And, Gandhi concludes, "I would therefore urge . . . fellow war resisters not to mind my faulty or incomplete argument and still less to mind my participation in war which they may be unable to reconcile with my professions about war. Let them understand me to be uncompromisingly against all war. If they cannot appreciate my arguments, let them impute my participation to unconscious weakness. For I would feel extremely sorry to discover that my action was used by anyone to justify war under any circumstance."[108]

Gandhi's chief argument for his participation in war was, ". . . though as an individual I was opposed to war, I had no status for offering effective non-violent resistance. Non-violent resistance can only follow some real disinterested service, some heartfelt expression of love . . . I felt that . . . by sufficient service I could attain the power and the confidence to resist the Empire's wars and its warlike preparations."[109]

Unless he was totally non-cooperative with the government and "renounced to the utmost of . . . capacity the privileges it offered . . . ,"[110] Gandhi could not avoid direct participation and service that might shorten the war and give him status for propagating non-violence.

Gandhi believed that living in an evil, warring society was as deeply supporting that evil as direct participation in war, and since he could not without suicide non-cooperate with a society and government that he believed to be basically good for the world, he must therefore openly and directly support it in its life and death struggle.[111]

Gandhi places war-participation *in the same category* as his helpless killing of any life by possession of and action in the human body. He explicitly equates war with all fundamental violence: "My opposition to and disbelief in war was as strong then as it is today. But we have to recognize that there are many things in the world which we do although we may be against them. I am as much opposed to taking of life of the lowest creature alive as I am to war. But I continually take such life, hoping some day to attain the ability to do without this fratricide."[112]

Gandhi's aid to those sincerely believing in violent means was only so that they would be receptive to his true *ahiṁsā* when they had become "bold and strong" through their own methods, but had disavowed them when they found that their methods finally failed them.[113]

Thus, from every possible angle Gandhi denies the equation of justifiability with any form of necessity, factual circumstances or principle, for whatever reason.

Denying justifiability of war, Gandhi denies any practical, moral and spiritual efficacy to war and all violence whatsoever. Even that complicity in war which is intended to further the ideal and force of non-violence and which involves a certain necessity of unavoidability in the given circumstances, cannot *justify* the violence. It cannot undo the evil or avert its necessary consequences; injury once done is unmitigable and the evil cannot be annulled.

The two components of Gandhi's view, argument and activity, have their logic and consequences in parallel and not in combination; therefore, "two wrongs cannot make a right".

Gandhi's Interpretation of the Gītā as a Pacifist Document: Outer Form of the Moral Attack on Inner Causes. Thus against all orthodoxy, Gandhi argues that "the author of the Gītā never advocated violence. It is a sermon on non-violence."[114]

Most importantly, in spite of Śrī Kṛṣṇa's direct command to Arjuna to fight (Gītā II:3, II:37, XVIII:59) to protect justice and fulfill his *kṣatriya* (protector's) duty, in service of society, Gandhi writes that "I do not believe that the Gītā teaches violence for doing good,"[115] and, that "I have the courage of saying that Krishna never taught violence in the Gītā."[116]

Gandhi argues that the Gītā would be meaningless as a sectarian treatise describing a minor historical event, and not worthy of being spoken by Lord Kṛṣṇa.[117]

He argues that Kṛṣṇa's advice to Arjuna has to do specially with Arjuna's particular situation and dilemma of facing a war of fratricide, though clearly in protection of justice.

Gandhi praises Kṛṣṇa as a teacher for giving Arjuna exactly what he needed in the historical situation, inciting him to duty in an age where the question of participation in war was raised only in terms of caste duty or cowardice. He writes that, "Arjuna was not averse to killing in general, but only to killing his own relatives. Therefore, Krishna suggested that doing one's duty, one may not treat one's relations differently from other people. In the age of the Gītā, the question, whether one should or should not wage war, was not raised by any important person."[118]

Gandhi writes that war then was no more looked upon as an abridgement of *ahiṁsā* than cereal eating is today. War posed the problem of conflicts of duty in a forceful and poignant way but there is nothing in this that is intrinsic to the problem of action in the context of war.

But the duty of a warrior is a particularly vivid case and lends itself to poetic narration. It also represents the universal struggle of common everyday experience that Gandhi takes as the archetype of conscious moral experience. Gandhi reveres Kṛṣṇa for presenting the universal and eternal doctrine of *ahiṁsā* under the severe constraints of such arguments justifying participation in a small local war, one historical event.

To Gandhi the eternal battle is the inner one against passions and the ego-sense. It is the moral battle inviting universal study, and according to Gandhi the Gītā teaches the battle's science and practice as the Yoga of Equability—peace which comes by renunciation of fruits of action and non-attached duty. These are the means of controlling the senses and the mind (as discussed in Section II), and ultimately thereby destroying the passions and rooting out the very sources of violence and war;[119] clearly a universal teaching. But in the narrative this teaching is locally applied to the historical situation and may appear more restricted than it is.

Gandhi asserts that the purpose of the Mahābhārata is to depict the struggle of man in his eternal ascent and to declare the way of right action.

According to this interpretation of the Gītā, the outer narrative form merely depicts Arjuna's dilemma of duty in order to instruct those caught in the consequences of past actions and commitments. This raises no question of non-violence.

Gandhi considers Arjuna's arguments for pacifism to be valid if they are understood to support the *universal* moral doctrine of absolute non-violence and pacifism.

But Gandhi believes that Arjuna has no status to raise these deeper questions because, as Śrī Kṛṣṇa rightly explains, Arjuna's aversion is not sincere and creedal, arising from urgent commitment to an eternal ideal. It is only an expression of attachment and the resultant fear of killing close relatives, friends, teachers and elders.

Generally, it is really social reality that constitutes one's "moral" reality. Kinship cannot determine activity in terms of objective social norms; social duty must carry an overriding obligation if the larger social unit is to survive. Arjuna is no believer in non-violence and pacifism as a universal ideal and law; he must at least be impartial in wielding violence and his battle skills—not for exclusive benefit of personal relations.

Gandhi concludes that the advice of Śri Kṛṣṇa "to fight" speaks only to this moral minimum demanded of Arjuna in his particular circumstances and cannot be generalized.

Gandhi writes,

It was not in a spirit of *Ahiṁsā* that Arjuna refused to go to battle. He had fought many a battle before . . . He fought shy of killing his own kith and kin. Arjuna never discussed the problem of killing as such . . . Sri Krishna . . . told him "Thou hast already done the killing. Thou canst not all at once argue thyself into non-violence. Finish what thou has already begun." . . . to say that the Gītā teaches violence or justifies war, because advice to kill was given on a particular occasion, is as wrong as to say that *Hiṁsā* is the Law of Life, because a certain amount of it is inevitable in daily life.[120]

Gandhi writes further,

Not that the actual physical battle is out of the question. To those who are innocent of non-violence, the Gītā does not teach a lesson of despair. He who fears, who saves his skin, who yields to his passions, must fight the physical battle whether he will or not; but that is not his Dharma [law, path of conduct in the widest sense]. *Dharma* is one and one only. *Ahiṁsā* means *Mokṣa* and *Mokṣa* is the realization of Truth. There is no room for cowardice, and despair is not the way. *Better far than cowardice is killing and being killed.*[121]

According to this reading, Arjuna's arguments are only counsels of fear and they bear no relation to moral argument. They could not possibly support a universal teaching.

Confusion of Basic Categories: The Logic of Gandhi's Over-Valuation of Life.

(1)   Arjuna's Pacifist Arguments Universalized—Gandhi accepts Arjuna's arguments on their own merit and uses them repeatedly to elaborate his own position, but he universalizes them through his ideology.

(a) Arjuna sees no good in killing kin (I:31), and would not slay them even for heaven (I:35), much less for an earthly kingdom.[122]

(b) How could he be happy killing kin (I:37); they *are* kin, and with memory of killing kin to get victory, how could the fruits of that victory be enjoyed (II:5)?

(c) The very fruits of victory were wanted only for those who have renounced those fruits to fight for me, or whom I will kill to gain those fruits (I:32–35).[123]

(d) Sin and pain here and demerit in afterlife are the only results of killing kin (equating evil with violence, as Gandhi does).

(e) Even the patent guilt of the opponent cannot justify those who know better what the results are of doing likewise in return (Gandhi's "two wrongs . . ."); for that can give no good results (since (d) is assumed true) (I:39). It necessarily leads to destruction of the family—its virtues and traditions, the caste order, the ancestors passed away but supported by family ritual—and hell is the result for all—an end to the entire social and moral order as these are so deeply and fully developed in Indic corporate consciousness, tradition, sentiment and ideals (I:38–45).

(f)   And from these arguments, Arjuna draws the conclusion, based on fear and attachment (that Gandhi finds to be a universal moral injunction), better to die unresisting and unarmed with the happiness at least of not having added to evil and sin (I:46–47); better to forsake victory, fame and every reward (II:5).

(2) Confusion of the Moral with the Spiritual: Arjuna's final state is disabling grief and paralysis, unable to decide or act decisively (II:6–8). The essential result will be mass fratricide or social suicide; from the natural point of view, kin-killing strikes at the very root of order and justice of which "family" (blood and body relations) is the foundation.

All of these arguments are based on calculations of desire and fear of result. With no higher standard there can be no decisive outcome. The dilemmas arise because worldly values cancel each other out in "moral calculations" based on them; as "worldly" values they set each other at nought, each looks equally valid and none can decide the moral question which is not simply a matter of facts, desires and fears.

Śrī Kṛṣṇa will go on in the rest of the Gītā to establish a framework of values, and of spiritual facts demonstrating the validity of those valuations, so that action can have an *objective* basis outside of material or social relations and motives. Material relations, motives and institutions have no permanent basis. In the final analysis they reduce to the mere advocacy of changing perceptions, decisions, aims, affectations, affiliations and sentiments. Duty without attachment, *anāsakti* of Gandhi, is the practical form of that teaching.

Gandhi, however, by the confused use of the *"yathā piṇḍe . . ."* principle, reads from Śrī Kṛṣṇa's argument the doctrine of non-killing:

> World is "brother" and killing brother is essential sin
> Killing any is killing "kin"
> _____
> Any killing is necessarily "sin"!

Delusion as to the Truth of Reality, nature and self-identity, as soul and spirit, *ātman* and *brahman*, and as to their empirical reflection in the oneness of all life, leads to the false view that "kin/non-kin" determines "right/wrong".

The practical doctrine and ethics of both social- and self-realization, that both the Gītā and Gandhi derive from these fundamental spiritual facts, is that Truth of conduct by right effort is effort to fulfill the duties of one's station in larger social life in accordance with one's present material and spiritual status and state, and one's stage in moral and spiritual evolution, *svadharma* (Gītā III:8 & 19, XVIII:47).

Right effort at duty is possible only with objective perception,
which implies unconcern about results, since they are not within
one's control (II:47, XVIII:13–15). Objective perception and pure
impersonal reason are possible only with equability resulting from
this inner renunciation of one's fixations on doubtable consequences
and personal fruits (II:48).

Such right effort at self-duty, regarding and serving wider Truth
(*anāsakti* and *yajña*), by itself leads to realizing the freedom (*mokṣa*)
inherent in soul or Self. But Gandhi adds that "Truth of conduct"
can be non-violence and absolute pacifism, only because Truth of existence and life *entails* the brotherhood of all life without exception
(Īśā Upaṇisad, 1).

(3) Confusion of the Ideal with the Phenomenal: Gandhi interprets the first verse of the Īśā to enunciate this foundational fact.

Citing this verse and using the principle of "*yathā piṇḍe . . .*",
Gandhi extends "ideal reality", as known in realization, to phenomenal reality, as met in action and conduct.

It is essential to note that Gandhi cites the domestic model as both
his ideal and his principle of inquiry in *satyāgraha*. Interpreting it as
an expression of his logical principle of micro-macro identity, he assumes that it is self-evident and self-validating as a moral principle
and standard of conduct.

This is the basic confusion of Gandhi's position.

Assuming the ideal standpoint, Gandhi denies the truth of categorical (empirical, phenomenal and practical) reality. The micro-
macro-cosmic identity principle properly functions to *clarify* identities and distinctions—to become correctly aware of the truly
distinguishable realities which are being realized as identical at a
more fundamental level of their existence, and which will *appear*
identical only as they are assimilated to a progressively deepening
perception.

The identity principle cannot be used as Gandhi attempts—to create an *a priori* rule of action, presupposing the content of a perception that is not possible from the standpoint of ignorance and bondage. The basis of such a rule is imagination, not perception. The
problem of practical application of the ideal, which was the topic of
the second section above, depends on the accuracy of analogies
brought to substantiate and justify all equations, assimilations and

definitions upon which the final applicational formulae and practical methods and techniques are based.

Thus in his stipulation that *svadharma* be also *ahiṁsic*, Gandhi is arguing from analogy as if in possession of the knowledge-viewpoint of the realized man, while in fact, and as he acknowledges, his knowledge in these areas is merely informational, gathered from study and reflection.

Argument from analogy, and the guidance of experienced judgment, presuppose the knowledge-standpoint and direct perception of the guide. Gandhi disclaims this for himself and while acknowledging belief in the traditional doctrine of *guruvāda* (learning from a teacher with direct knowledge, mastery and command of the subject; experienced and realized), he disclaims any guidance, correction and validation from such a realized and knowing person.[124]

While the Īśa may accurately express a foundational spiritual fact, the logical principle does not support Gandhi's use of this fact to make the practical world "kin" in his ideal sense of the term, as if the categorical difference in realities did not exist. It is by this invalid commutative use of *"yathā piṇḍe . . ."*, confusing the standpoint of appearance and intent with that of substance and action, that Gandhi assimilates the real and ideal and justifies assumption of *either* standpoint, as his argument and aims require for support of his ideal, ideology and methods of non-violence.

On the one hand, Gandhi erases the distinction between spirit and body (or institution) in order to justify his claim, ideology and *satyāgraha*, and on the other hand, he reinstates the distinction in order to deny the validity of mundane violent methods.

Thus Gandhi's ideology makes reality—ideal and phenomena, substance and appearance—*homogeneous.*

From a categorical standpoint and from a reality that does not support a factual presentation of the unity of reality, Gandhi assumes that his dichotomies are comprehensive and mutually complementary. Not proceeding from the factual judgments of perception or guidance this dichotomous presentation does not correctly *inform* action. It *superimposes* an arbitrary praxis supposed to be justified by the comprehensiveness and rational clarity of the imposing ideology. Gandhi *assumes* an ideal of family behavior, a model of identical behavior towards non-identical reality.

There is simply no justification for granting Gandhi's assumption
that his model constitutes *the* ideal.

Gandhi's very extensive experience would be more to the point, but experience, however extensive, cannot justify assertion of an *eternal* principle and exceptionless practical rule. Neither is there anything in the spiritual facts of impartible existence and creation by a single Lord and Father to justify his assertion of the moral ideal as he interprets it for practice by his domestic model.

On the basis of our general commitment to non-violence (whatever the basis of that commitment itself), it may be agreed that in all cases Gandhi's loving ways are *preferable* to forceful ways.

However, it cannot be presumed that by analogy with Gandhi's model of brotherly treatment the ideal treatment of a stranger must be non-violent—unless one has first agreed that the non-violent treatment of Gandhi's model *is* the domestic ideal and one's blood brother and kin must necessarily be so treated.

This is the question not the solution. The "ought" has been read into the ideal on the basis of which the facts have then been interpreted and so the question as to what material form the facts (action and envisaged results) *should* take is again foreclosed instead of openly investigated.

This problem is not specific to Gandhi but is merely the nature of praxis as the instrument of ideological investigation of the ideal and its revisionary reduction to practice. Gandhi is perhaps unique in so thoroughly constraining himself to prescription of means and attitude and only very reluctantly and with self-conscious unreality of poetic expression, venturing descriptions of ideal outcomes,[125] fully admitting their tentative, remote and wholly suggestive character.

Nevertheless, Gandhi's advocacy of principle and means is tantamount to utopianism. He translates these to action in programs of specific reform propagated as immediate steps to definite, if not ruling, ideals and end-states.

Here again responding from the ideological posture, Gandhi has taken as a self-evident axiom what is principally in question. The simplicity of his doctrine, its fidelity to our own general commitment and the ideological and practical force he invests it with, give that general commitment a new and irresistible appeal. Nevertheless, its basis is arbitrary and its conclusions unsupported.

It seems that Gandhi has simply taken our general commitment to non-violence and turned that into a pure ideal. If so, his ideal merely depicts the logical and practical limits of what is morally given and already accepted *a fortiori*. Nothing in the Īśā says what it is to be a "brother", nor admonishes not to kill one's brother.

A rival ideal, from common sense, may be to fearlessly and lovingly take one's brother to task when that is needed. At the limit of the general commitment the use of violent force may be argued to be the fulfillment of the ideal, which tests even filial love by its strength to use even violent force without succumbing to its passional side effects.

Either ideal is arbitrary with respect to the spiritual facts as adumbrated.

However, Gandhi's ideal is the assertion of an only single, if utterly devoted, belief and investigation, while the commonsense ideal is the product of generations of moral inquiry at all levels. Again, it derives from a very much wider range of circumstances and experiences, whatever the special characteristics of Gandhi's individual extraordinary, larger scale and more magnified moral experiments.

(4) Confusion of the Moral with the Practical: Gandhi does believe that moral justification is also a matter of practical justification and says that a moral principle that did not produce tangible practical results is meaningless.

But in order to satisfy this requirement the results must be "moral", and so again the argument is circular.

If Gandhi's definition of the moral as the non-violent, *ahiṁsic*, is not assumed, then failure to defeat what would otherwise be called evil (or an agent of greater violence) must defeat his claim. Gandhi often admits defeat but retreats to his circular argument to avoid these implications—his own effort not being *purely* non-violent, or morally perfect practice, perfect efficacy should not be expected.

Gandhi cannot rely on characterizing the force of *satyāgraha* as "spiritual" or on adumbrating the "spiritual" nature of foundational fact. These do not imply a necessary rule of behavior unless again, an ideal of action has been presupposed in the analysis of the factual situation; but then that "ideal" cannot be proven by the facts alleged to support it.

Nor does the fact of a force's inherent superior power guarantee its predominance or even sufficiency in every application. The route from "theory" to "practice" cannot be so casually predetermined.

There is constantly the unavoidable paradox of the moral ideal: if a moral ideal is meaningless unless it can also produce results when acted on, then that ideal is valid only to the extent it proves itself in practice, and then where is the original self-valid ideal, and where is the special practicality that was supposed if now the self-valid ideal is gone? No *a priori* efficiency can be asserted on its behalf so long as its action depends at all on the material medium and mechanism in and through which it manifests as practical effects.

3. "Non-violence/Violence", Not an Absolute Distinction: Right-making Factors.

Need for Accurate Analysis of the Action Situation: Motive, Intention, Results. It is because Gandhi's assertions are grounded in the general commitment rendered limitless by the micro-macro identity principle, and by his intense experiments of action designed and carried out *as if* this commitment was an absolute that the maxim "two wrongs don't make a right" seems self-evident and the natural unchallengeable expression of the ideal. It thus seems to confirm the moral validity of his non-retaliation.

But the second "wrong" is not necessarily wrong unless there is justification for asserting the identity of static fact and moral, dynamic reality independently of Gandhi's commutative use of *"yathā piṇḍe . . ."*. He merely *asserts* that moral reality *must* be identical with moral appearance and the second "wrong" becomes an unequivocal logical term. The assertion ought to be without prior interpretation of (1) appearance as "violence identical with evil", or (2) "outer reality *nothing more than* expression of interpreted substance." Interpretation of the relation of appearance and reality substitutes for its investigation. Again, with ideological assertion and experiment it is the validity of the prior interpretation, the very interpretive apparatus, that is in question.

However, the situation is more complex than can be understood through Gandhi's homogenizing dichotomies. In the analysis of this situation there are factors of motive and of total results, besides the immediate quality of the action. Scientific inquiry would seek to analyze and not to legislate the role and relevance of motive and total results in determining the full moral dimensions and consequences of situations of action.

Since Gandhi admits morality must manifest practically in production of good results over evil, it is necessary to understand this requirement ("balance of utilities") in the uninterpreted context of the complexity of action which involves agency and use as independent factors.

Violence may be intrinsically evil as a quality of action, as the general commitment accepts. But the wider uninterpreted view does not assure that this quality is the *only and final* determinant of the good/evil quotient and that other emergent factors may not be discovered that are equally or more determinate of this final quotient. There may be a real resultant quality of the transaction as a whole, qua moral. This analysis of the moral resultant as an outcome of multiple factors and possible emergent qualities allows the possibility of showing how *use* of violent action can produce less evil —how the second "wrong" may be found not to be wrong in the context of the whole transaction. This would be to suggest that ends as a whole may justify otherwise morally invalid means. Again, at least still an allowable question.

Gandhi's analysis of violence as a quality equated with evil, and thus the absolute determinant of moral validity and sole basis of moral justifiability, is the result of assuming an *a priori* dichotomization; it is not the result of *looking at* the situation for its component parts, contributory causes, moments and possible emergent and discoverable qualities.

But Gandhi also goes behind the immediately evident quality of action and results when he asserts that non-violence should not be equated with mere non-killing and that, though often violent and non-violent action may look alike, motives are decisive of the moral quality and final outcome at every level. Hence, only divine judgment can truly know that quality of intent and real aim. For man this is a practical judgment about the immediate quality of the outer action and likely immediate consequences. But the accumulating results progressively reveal the full moral dimensions and subtler moral qualities of the transaction.

Nevertheless, in elaborating on the violence or non-violence of his own participation in war or on the character of any act in terms of violence and non-violence, and in analyzing its justifiability, Gandhi finds motive, not outer form, decisive.

Gandhi would rather forfeit argument and stand by conviction, if argument seems to betray his purposes in justifying that conviction. *He retains or cancels at will the distinction between quality of act and quality of motive.* But Gandhi's equation of the moral and the practical makes it necessary that motive or qualities, as criteria, have tangible counterparts in the form of practical results.

If life in the body is constant battle, and if practical life merely mirrors this, every act and state must be a compromise between non-violence and violence (according to Gandhi's strict interpretation of material reality as "violent" in nature). The votary must act so as always to extend the scope of non-violence, and to push back the dividing line in justification of that particular act.

Gandhi writes that, "Indeed life is made of such compromise. *Ahiṁsā*, simply because it is purest, unselfish love, often demands such compromise. The conditions are imperative. There should be no self in one's actions, no fear, no untruth, and it must be in furtherance of the cause of *Ahiṁsā*. The compromise must be natural to oneself, not imposed from without."[126]

Gandhi argues for a "violence/non-violence" distinction relative to circumstance and act. He will not let the motive of compassion redeem the existential involvement in violence or evil. Rather, he insists that the outer shape of the act necessarily compromises and qualifies the motive. This is an important point to detail:

"*Ahiṁsā* is a comprehensive principle . . . The saying that life lives on life has a deep meaning in it. Man cannot for a moment live without consciously or unconsciously committing outward *hiṁsā*. The very fact of his living—eating, drinking and moving about—necessarily involves some *hiṁsā*, destruction of life, be it ever so minute. A votary of *ahiṁsā* therefore remains true to his faith if the spring of all his actions is compassion, if he shuns to the best of his ability the destruction of the tiniest creature, tries to save it, and thus incessantly strives to be free from the deadly coil of *hiṁsā*. He will be constantly growing in self-restraint and compassion, but he can never become entirely free from outward *hiṁsā*."[127] And, "In life, it is impossible to eschew violence completely. Now the question arises, where is one to draw the line? The line cannot be the same for every one. For, although, essentially the principle is the same, yet everyone applies it in his or her own way. What is one man's food can be another's poison . . . Evil and good are relative terms. What is good under certain conditions can become an evil or a sin, under a different set of conditions . . . At every step he has to use his discrimination as to what is *ahiṁsā* and what is *hiṁsā*."[128]

Gandhi works out a practical solution, but his theory remains in contradiction: "Life is an aspiration. Its mission is to strive after perfection, which is self-realization. The ideal must not be lowered because of our weaknesses and imperfections . . . One who hooks his fortunes to *ahiṁsā*, the law of love, daily lessens the circle of destruction, and to that extent promotes life and love; he who swears by *hiṁsā*, the law of hate, daily widens the circle of destruction, and to that extent promotes death and hate."[129]

Yet, again, Gandhi insists that there *can* be only one criterion and allows that there *is* one principle for drawing the line of justifiability of apparently violent uses of physical force, viz. that it be an act of love, and so of *ahiṁsā*, in its most basic sense, that the only active motive be the good of the recipient of the act. That line is absolute; "Once you admit the lawfulness of the use of physical force for purposes other than the benefit of the person against whom it is used as in the case of a surgeon against his patient, you cannot draw an arbitrary line of distinction."[130]

Is the motive determinant or only the instrument of necessary compromise and participation in evil?

Non-violence and Violence: Justification by Balance of Results. A modified reading would allow a type of justifiability by results, a balance of good over evil, even in terms of non-violence and violence.

This would of course violate Gandhi's strict ideology, unless he allows the motive of non-violence to have a *sui generis* quality and special material expression that is not liable to the previous categorical characterization. He makes no such provision, but this is the effect when he speaks of non-violence as a force and assigns to its ideal a *creative* power of initiating spontaneous action. This, in practical effect, eliminates subjective, material, intermediary formations and impulsions.

In this case, "motive" would denote only a set of statements that are the inspired *result* of reflection on the action of that force in moral consciousness, and this would answer to Gandhi's description of the irresistible inner voice that, according to him, is the inseparable cognitive aspect of the activity of non-violence (of soul-force) within oneself.

This again has the consequence that since the "motive" comes into play in practical application, it must still have an overt material counterpart to satisfy the strict ideological equations. This can only be expressed as a balance of such non-violently produced material components with ordinary mediately magnetized or agitated ones, whose movement cannot but be tainted by empiricality, i.e. inherent violence and evil. The motive must in some way *materially* decide the outcome if it is to figure in the moral cum practical justification.

Gandhi gives the following very telling moral "physics":

Passive resistance . . . is a misnomer for non-violent resistance. It is much more active than violent resistance. It is direct, ceaseless, but three-fourths invisible and only one-fourth visible. In its visibility it seems to be ineffective, e.g. the spinning wheel which I have called the symbol of non-violence. In its visibility it appears ineffective, but it is really intensely active and most effective in ultimate result . . . A violent man's activity is most visible, while it lasts. But it is always transitory . . . But the effects of . . . non-violent action persist and are likely to grow with age. And the more it is practised, the more effective and inexhaustible it becomes, and ultimately the whole world stands agape and exclaims, 'a miracle has happened'. All miracles are due to the silent and effective working of invisible force. Non-violence is the most invisible and the most effective . . . I may say all kinds of sweet words to you without meaning them. On the other hand, I may have real love in me and yet my outward expression may be forbidding. Then outwardly my action in both cases may be the same and yet the effect may be different. For the effect of our action is often more potent when it is not patently known. Thus the unconscious effect you are making on me I may never know. It is, nevertheless, infinitely greater than the conscious effect. In violence there is nothing invisible. Non-violence, on the other hand, is three-fourths invisible, and so the effect is in the inverse ratio to its invisibility. Non-violence, when it becomes active, travels with extraordinary velocity, and then it becomes a miracle. So the mass mind is affected first unconsciously, then consciously. When it becomes consciously affected there is demonstrable victory . . . When the spirit of non-violence pervades the people and actually begins to work, its effect is visible to all.[131]

Thus Gandhi notes (see Chapter 6) that many acts of non-violence are necessary to yield one visible non-violent resultant.

On our modified reading, the motive *materially* decides the quality and justifiability of the act because through it the resultants of many more acts than the present one alone are brought into combination. The final resultant may never be considered purely non-violent (which Gandhi's strict dichotomy of motive and act forbids), nevertheless, it will necessarily have an identifiable distinctive action corresponding to the contributory motivations of preceding acts. The assessment of that balance may be independent of any characterizations of single forces. It may be that only results, the necessary practical expression or materially accountable counterpart of the moral motives, are calculable. But this is enough, since they merely signify the initiating (motive) ratios.

Thus even according to Gandhi's strict reading of the equation of moral and practical, non-violence can be legitimately defined as the balance of total non-harm over immediately present harm, regardless of the appearance of the forces used.

But Gandhi further mistakenly identifies "violence" with immediate results of force as if that were the whole phenomenon; so he continued to contradict himself even as he ceaselessly tried to answer "conundrums" about the apparent failure of non-violence in terms of the necessity of combining several resultants spread over time as they empirically mature to give one tangible non-violent result. The 100 or so volume corpus of his writings documents his more than sixty years' attempt to answer these "conundrums" of his critics—he himself constantly posed them in ceaseless self-examination. The contradictions could not but remain since they are built into the terms of that reflection and examination.

The contradictions remain, partly because though Gandhi requires that motive decide character of similar looking actions, he gives no scientific (or otherwise) analysis for this in consonance with the rest of his ideological analysis, and its pragmatic and experimental investigation of how this differentiation is discovered. This merely avoids the above implications for the problem of justification.

Though Gandhi's definition of non-violence and his analysis of non-retaliation are reasoned out as if on scientific lines, connecting real effects of moral qualities with forces governed by laws and predictably manipulable, he invariably falls back on abstract and moralistic reasoning in problems of justification and the application conditions of his practical doctrine. He cannot independently identify the ideal homogeneity between categorical realities that his theory of justification requires.

No "Ideal" War: Gandhi stressed that war is an "unmitigable" evil unjustifiable on any grounds. Yet he acknowledges that it evokes admirable bravery and many other noble and intrinsically good qualities and actions; "War is an unmitigated evil. But it certainly does one good thing, it drives away fear and brings bravery to the surface."[132] And, "if war had no redeeming feature, no courage and heroism behind it, it would be a despicable thing, and would not need speeches to destroy it."[133]

Thus, Gandhi acknowledges that war is a complex fact and that there is no unmixed evil in the world or in human nature. He can conclude that war is an unmitigated evil, absolutely unjustifiable only if he assumes that war can produce evil effects that are of ideal purity (i.e. produce no good at all) regardless of its non-ideal material mechanism.

If war is a material fact and does not have only ideal reality (if the inner battle is not the only "real" war), it can only be considered absolutely disallowable by the imposition of an absolute dichotomy of real and ideal which superimposes an ideal quality on phenomenal activity, as Gandhi attempts by equating violence with evil.

If in the world there is no unmixed evil and real war must have some good, then on what grounds can the justifiability of war be analyzed as if it were an ideal existence? Without justification Gandhi identifies the ideal "concept" of war with the "fact" of war. Therefore, war in the real world might be justified by a real overbalance of *facts* of bravery, nobility, charity, etc., as its real outcomes.

Against this conclusion, Gandhi has argued that no cause *could* justify war's "indiscriminate slaughter" (which he demonstrates to be the *logical* conclusion of *all* war) which was so fully exhibited in the prelude and beginnings of World War II. But the logical extreme has in fact never been realized, as Gandhi himself asserts in his arguments to establish that non-violence is the law of being.[134]

By common sense we can know that *logically* at some point the good must overbalance the evil. By definition each war would be necessarily an exercise in self-annihilation and the first and only one possible would long since have demonstrated its ideal purity in leaving behind no empirical history to look back on now and no now to look back from.

Gandhi cannot dogmatize from his concept of ideological purity that all war *must* degenerate to an absolute barbarity. Neither is there more validity to his analysis of non-violence than to that of war, nor less to war than to his *satyāgraha*, so far as they must be treated on a par as equally ideal concepts or equally factual states.

Gandhi has said of the Gītā, as a text on "eternal verities", that its logical outcome is "peace at the price of life itself." *He writes also that "the first condition of non-violence is justice all round in every department of life,"*[135] and that peace is impossible without non-violence and truth.

Then the outcome of justice must be more fundamental than that of peace, and a balance of justice, a materially just war, should be justifiable in terms of non-violence. It can be argued that in fact the world has gone on after war because whatever the appalling aspect presented in terms of violent means and physical suffering and devastation, nothing short of that could have destroyed incorrigible evil and saved the modicum of justice on which the succeeding order could be based and continue to evolve.

Given the whole complex fact of war, its many actions, motives, operative intentional states, not to mention sheer physical magnitudes, why does Gandhi withhold the logico-moral certification of "justified" from the complex reality of war?

War *never does* reach its logical conclusion and admittedly has many noble aspects. If the aim is truly corporate and mass application and widening the scope of non-violence in the world rather than individual propriety and salvation, then analogies are available by which to ascribe the same love, motives and surgical activities to the large scale reality of war as to states and activities of the individual.

Such analogies can be derived from the criteria of the just war.

The application of the categories of good and evil through the dichotomy non-violence/violence magnifies the outer destructive aspects of war, as well as its moral destructiveness, and gives a distorted but compelling depiction of the fruits of war and violence. Gandhi disallows justification analogous to the just war model in order to retain the ideological purity embodied in his equation of violence with evil. But this equation itself only reflects his more basic assimilation of appearance to the ideal—and that again is based on an unsupported imputation of commutativity to the micro-macro identity principle in its practical application.

Again, it is evident that Gandhi's arguments pro and con justifiability thus are woven throughout with categorical confusions.

Gandhi argues, finally, by idealizing the relation of means and

ends as if here also a complex fact (the entire action) could have a
morally meaningful outcome only in purely moral terms.

Gandhi gives the law of *karma* a simplistic punitive interpretation
and by interpreting war as a simple, single wholly evil action, a
single totally bad end is assured and logically no new material order
can emerge. But this ideally bad end also can have no material counterpart and Gandhi is again arguing ideal goods against ideal bads in
terms of ideal realities and relations. He is again bypassing the categorical reality in terms of which the practical efficacy of non-violence
must ultimately be calculated if he also wishes to sustain the equation of the moral and the practical. His moral physics and metaphysics are inadequate to sustain both his ideological presuppositions and
the practical outcomes.

When Gandhi writes that not even a "noble end" could justify violence and war, he adds the practical rider that "experience con-
vinces me that permanent good can never be the outcome of untruth
and violence."[136] But "experience" cannot teach that "permanent"
evil is the definite outcome of violence. Defference to experience as if
it had such a logical function indicates the *"a priori"* is merely ideological. Again, Gandhi confuses categorical realities at a fundamental
level of his analysis.

Finally, Gandhi does allow, even require, moral support for the
exploited victim against the exploiter and aggressor.

His moral support extends naturally to non-violent assistance. He
writes, "If war is itself a wrong act, how can it be worthy of moral
support or blessings? I believe all war to be wholly wrong. But if we
scrutinize the motives of two warring parties, we may find one to be
in the right and the other in the wrong. For instance, if A wishes to
seize B's country, B is obviously the wronged one. Both fight with
arms. I do not believe in violent warfare, but all the same, B, whose
cause is just, deserves moral help and blessings."[137] And, "Whilst all
violence is bad and must be condemned in the abstract, it is permissible for, it is ever the duty of a believer in *Ahimsā* to distinguish between the aggressor and the defender. Having done so, he will side
with the defender in a non-violent manner, i.e., give his life in saving
him."[138]

The limitation to non-violent means is of course the ideological requirement but, given the claim's acknowledgment that a right is at
stake, the ideological commitment to only specially designated means

stands out thereby as arbitrary in even greater contrast to the commonsense position of the general commitment to non-violence. If the end is admittedly good how can any means that actually achieve it be considered wrong? Gandhi's contradiction of this follows naturally from such a narrowed view of what constitutes the action and its effects, as his ideological and arbitrary conception betrays in such cases.

All of Arjuna's and Gandhi's arguments against war, based on identification of highest values with narrowly defined material results, fail to win confidence for absolute pacifism as a valid or viable answer to the present necessities of impending war to protect justice.

4. Svadharma and Anāsakti: The Spiritual Content of Gandhi's Ideal.

Gandhi misinterprets not only the practical categorical reality but the spiritual as well by his interposition of the homogenizing moral dichotomy and principles.

Gandhi's biased use of the micro-macro identity principle and the resultant confusion of appearance and reality, and of reality and ideality in terms of violence and non-violence, lead him to a contradictory analysis of the moral standard as heteronomous and of *anāsakti* as a contradictory, morally qualified state.

Fundamental Heteronomy: Formal and Universal Standard of Self-realization (Svadharma)/Ideological Standard of Practical Non-violence. In the one direction, Gandhi imposes his moral ideal on practical reality and in the other direction, he imposes it on spiritual reality.

Gandhi's synonymy of the spiritual, moral and practical does not represent the non-dual *advaitic* reality and the micro-macro-cosmic logical principle, but the superimposition of an *external* form and standard. Thus the ideological assumption of the moralistic viewpoint results in that radical heteronomy introduced above in the explication of Gandhi's overvaluation of life. This is the origin of the heteronomy of ethical standards which was shown to extend to the roots of Gandhi's philosophy of non-violence.

According to *advaitic* principles, *"yathā piṇḍe . . . "* would be interpreted to reveal the same one reality both transcendent of and im-

manent in material existence and life. It would not extirpate the difference between the categories of being and becoming, ideal and real
or existence and life, which do have their functions in practical and
moral consciousness.

The reflection of this logico-moral identity principle and *advaitic*
basis is properly the Gītā's principle of *svadharma* (that duty unique
to oneself) which Gandhi accepts as the unique, simultaneous means
and expression of the individual's progressive self-realization. Freedom is the result of this self-less action.

Interpreting the Gītā, Gandhi writes, "If each does his duty selflessly according to his nature, he will reach perfection . . . A man remains free of sin when he performs the task naturally allotted to him,
as he is then free from selfish desires; the very wish to do something
else arises from selfishness. For the rest, all actions are clouded by
defects as fire by smoke. But the natural duty is done without desire
for its fruits, and thus loses its binding force."[139]

Gandhi gives the Gītā a moral interpretation of material existence,
characterized there as "movement", and movement characterized as
necessarily "violent" and therefore evil. Therefore, unless he admits
that there can be activity, friction, etc. without an evil quality being
produced, then uniquely dutiful action of *svadharma*, even aside
from his heteronomous ethics of non-violence, cannot result in free
action and freedom from reaction or consequences.

To hold the duty ethics of the Gītā, as a means of acting without
binding results, the possibility is required that all immediate "tearing", "friction", "violence", etc. that seem inherent in activity, be
completely cancelled either by an emergent counter-quality or by a
neutralizing and balancing of forces observable when a larger resultant or wider perspective is assumed. Therefore Gandhi's ideological
equation of violence with evil and these with activity, vitiates the attempt to establish a viable duty ethics that would produce free action
as a means to spiritual realization.

According to the principle of *svadharma*, the rightness of each action is totally and uniquely determined by the entire history of the
jīvātmā (evolving self). The utility of the action is determined by the
degree to which it either bypasses or dismantles the ego-desire complex or strategically satisfies and strengthens it, geared in either case
to the single aim of immediate self-expression as means, and to ultimate self-realization as end.

This interpretation makes spiritual utility and moral rightness identical on a purely formal basis—the concept of an evolving manifestation of the individuated yet non-dual permanent spiritual principle. Only a principle of action that determines conduct to realize in its totality each unique line of self-evolution, can have universal application.

Only such a principle gives a standard of action and valuation that is wholly formal from the standpoint of every material formation, yet wholly determined from the standpoint of spiritual self as self looks out from that formation upon the field of material reality as unity and totality.

But Gandhi's ideology interposes the moral form and standard of non-violent exact conduct which creates a second standard (heteronomy) that is not entirely formal. It has material conditions. This *must* at points oppose a standard (*svadharma*) which *requires* that there be no such external determination of the shape conduct.

Anāsakti: Also Heteronomously Interpreted: Gandhi's spiritual position is also self-contradictory.

Gandhi writes, "*Anāsakti* transcends *Ahiṁsā*. He who would be *Anāsakta* (selfless) has necessarily to practice non-violence in order to attain the state of selflessness. *Ahiṁsā* is, therefore, a necessary preliminary, it is included in *Anāsakti*, it does not go beyond it . . . whilst we are in the flesh and tread the solid earth, we have to practice *Ahiṁsā*. In the life beyond, there is no *Hiṁsā* or *Ahiṁsā*."[140]

This state is preeminently the state of dispassion, non-attachment and equilibrium. It is of the nature of spirit and *ex hypothesi* not affected by modifications and movements in phenomenal reality. Hence *Anāsakti* is simultaneously for Gandhi the *sine qua non* of non-violence as means, and the transcendent aim of non-violence as end.

Since *anāsakti* is Gandhi's name for the state beyond the *guṇas*, it is therefore beyond *hiṁsā* and *ahiṁsā* which describe qualities (*guṇas*), actions and forces. He defines *hiṁsā* morally from the standpoint of motive and intent, so that "*Hiṁsā* is impossible without anger, without attachment, without hatred, and the Gītā strives to carry us to the state beyond *Sattva, Rajas,* and *Tamas* to a state that excludes anger, hatred, etc."[141] More fundamentally, behind all *hiṁsā* is found "the desire to attain the cherished end."[142]

Gandhi writes that in the "balanced state of mind, of mental equi-
poise"[143] (Gītā II:55–72), *himsā*, violence and killing, are impossible because that state "can be achieved . . . (only) after killing all
your passions. It is *not possible* to kill your brother after having
killed all your passions."[144] And, "A man who is free from the action of the pair of opposites is *incapable,* like the perfect man of the
Bible, of injuring any living thing on earth."[145]

Thus, Gandhi reads into the state of *gunātīta* (state beyond *gunas*
or qualification) (Gītā XIV:19–27; II:45) the moral opposition of
violence/non-violence through his ambivalent, ideologically constructed concept of "violence", defined equally by the description of
outer action as by motive and intentional state.

Gandhi thus also reads into the factual state of *gunātīta* the moral
heteronomy that characterizes and distinguishes his non-violence.
But a correct interpretation and practical use of *anāsakti* must recognize its definitive character as beyond any quality or opposition at
all—moral as well as natural. Its interpretation, for moral ideological purposes, may explore its practical relation to moral action in
terms of favored moral distinctions or properties as Gandhi does. But
the definitive character of the state must not be assimilated to the
interpretation.

The very differentia of *anāsakti* from the material and moral
states, given in the Gītā and Upanisads (Gītā II:45, XIV:19–27,
XVIII:40; Katha Upanisad III:1:3; Śvetāśvatara Upanisad IV:5;
Chāndogya Upanisad VI:4:1) is its status beyond good and evil and
its realization independently of these qualities.

Gandhi is at variance with his sources. His *"anāsakti"* superimposes on the non-moral end-state the moral means and criteria that
he ideologically favors for its realization.

Moral Imagination: Cannot Solve Moral Dilemmas, But Only Re-
enforce Falsifying Dichotomous Views. The essence of Gandhi's argument is that the Gītā teaches non-violence as an ideal *and* a means,
and the man of equability, *sthitaprajña, anāsakta, gunātīta,* cannot
be imagined to be violent. Gandhi's moral imagination cannot disso-
ciate outer violent action and subjective states of anger, hate, etc.
that experience seems to show him are invariably at its root.[146]

Gandhi describes the state of *anāsakti* as beyond the *gunas* and
then contradicting himself, says that that "state excludes anger, (and)

hatred" (of *rajoguṇa*). Gandhi writes, "I can even now picture to my mind Arjuna's eyes red with anger every time he draws the bow to the end of his ear."[147]

The question of moral truth is not a question of the scope of one's individual moral imagination. Artistic or moral inspiration and imagination may lead to great discoveries in these fields but they cannot substitute for scientific or logical inquiry. Whatever the vividness of Gandhi's moral imagination, the intensity and breadth of his moral experience or the dramatic appeal of his rhetorical argument based on these, they cannot of themselves validate his ideological analysis and radical practical claim.

Confuses Outer and Inner Battles: Identifying violent appearance of activity with essential *hiṁsic* violence (the inevitable expression of anger, hate, fear, etc.), and drawing the sharp contrast between inner and outer reality with the spiritual and moral on one side and the material and evil on the other, Gandhi insists on the allegorical interpretation of the Gītā in order to justify his conclusion that "the author of the Gītā never advocated war or violence. It is a sermon on non-violence. Fight, without anger and passion, *can only* be spiritual."[148]

But again, Gandhi is saying that the "spiritual" *is not* a status outside of *prakṛti*, beyond determination by the *guṇas*. He is describing categorical facts but again reading in the ideological dichotomy that makes a logical necessity of equating violence with evil motives.

Gandhi goes so far as to assert that realization of this state has (1) the subjective consequence that "where detachment governs our action, even the weapon raised in order to strike an enemy falls down out of our hand,"[149] and (2) the objective consequence that though of "a humble man, who has reduced himself to zero it may be said that he does not kill though he kills, this does not mean that the man inspite of his humility may kill and yet be unaffected by the killing. For, no occasion *can* arise for such a man to indulge in violence."[150]

This analysis clearly does not leave the *anāsakta* indifferent to the presence or absence of the *guṇas* as the state of *guṇātīta* requires.

Gandhi, for whom struggle[151] and the inner moral battle are the *sine qua non* of spiritual and moral growth and evolution, writes that "The Bhagavad Gītā is a purely religious, not historical treatise . . . it deals with the war that is eternally waging between the forces

of evil and good, Ormuzd and Ahriman, Hyde and Jekyll, in the human breast. We cannot do enough violence to all the evil passions
that well up on that little *Kurukṣetra* (the field of battle)."[152]

Gandhi believed that "the Gītā represented the eternal duel between forces of evil and good, and inculcated the duty of eradicating
evil within us without hesitation, without tenderness."[153] The real
battle is only the one within, against the mind's submission to the
prevailing distinctions and motives of "I" and "mine" and the attitude it gives rise to of attachment and repulsion. These are the roots
of sin and the radical origin of all conflict, inner and outer.[154]

The real battle is against compulsion by sense life and desire
which, when one has not the vision and the assistance of the Lord,
are more powerful than any individual can withstand.[155] The real
battle is the individual effort to attain and maintain that "confidence
in soul-force" by which "everything else becomes easy as a matter of
course. And desire and anger and their countless hosts hold no terror
for him who has mastered the senses, the mind and the intelligence,"
by the soul which is "the greatest of all."[156]

According to Gandhi's reading of the Gītā, the inner battle is the
only real battle and recourse to and reliance on soul-force is the only
real means of waging it. Thus the condition of realizing the potency
of and enlisting soul-force is the exact conduct of Truth and non-
violence and the non-cooperation strategy of *satyāgraha*.

It may be admitted, on the basis of the general commitment and
the commonsense *prima facie* reading, that the inner battle is primary and must continue without letup. Unless the conversion and
disarmament (realization and renunciation) take place within, negotiation and external disarmament will accomplish nothing. The logic
of the recrudescence and escalation of violence is patent as long as
the motives of competition that initiate and sustain conflict are not
decisively and materially dealt with.

But it is an arbitrary conclusion of Gandhi's analysis that this is
the *only* battle and that *only* this inner battle is spiritual, moral and
effective.

If, as Gandhi has acknowledged, the spiritual state of *anāsakti* is
transcendent of all material states and is a natural master in complete control of all phenomenal activity, then there is nothing with
which he can counter the commonsense analysis of a moral limit to
the abstention from external violence outside of his self-contradic-

tory restriction of spiritual utility and moral rightness to subjective purity (*sattva guṇa* and *satyāgraha ahiṁsā*).

A spiritual "strategy" (as opposed to a moral ideology and praxis) of expanding the scope of non-violence and of diminishing that of violence would respect the categorical realities of the battle with evil. It would recognize the necessity at times of physically destroying the vehicles of evil by which that evil has throughout history sustained its dominance over the good and perpetrated further violence in absence of any obstacle to exercising its self-interested motives.

There are many instances in Indic classical literature where the paragon and exhibitor of the eternal ideals[157] (*avatāra*) himself, from the inner standpoint of *guṇātīta*, self-mastery beyond the passions, called upon and commanded the passion of anger in order to sustain battle against evil, using violence against evil in the way Gandhi ideologically rules out.

8. Critical Examination of Gandhi's Satyāgraha: Again, a Limiting Case in Conflict, Violence and the Last Resort Argument (Real Necessity: Application of the Objective Analysis of the Limiting Case, II)

A. SATYĀGRAHA: FAILURE OF GANDHI'S FINAL RESORT AND COMPLETE SUBSTITUTION

Gandhi's Moral Metaphysics Defeat His Practical Ethics: Reopens the Question of Balancing Good and Evil.   As shown in the previous chapters, Gandhi's analysis of the external conduct of war and the internal battle with the passions, and of the spiritual state and moral ideal in terms of which he argues for the unjustifiability of violence, are circular. They have for their only support his personal experience and the self-certifying logic of his otherwise arbitrary and ideological moral standpoint.

The *key* to criticism of this position is the fact that by his analysis of the ideal state, in terms of the *guṇas* and the moral qualities of *hiṁsā* and *ahiṁsā*, Gandhi actually negates the ideal overriding potency by which he justifies his radical practical claim.

Without the assimilations of the ideal with the real, and substantial moral content with outer appearance, the questions are again opened as to whether (1) "two wrongs" cannot make a "right" and produce a resultant balance of good over the initial wrong or evil of violent means (2) when and where this may be the case, and (3) where the line of justifiability defining the violence/non-violence distinction in material practical terms is to be drawn—if protection of life is not the ultimate value and automatic guiding moral principle?

Protection of Life: Value Equals Potency, the Key Equation in Gandhi's Argument.   Gandhi's practical argument that *satyāgraha* gives sufficient "warrant" against the necessity of last resort to violence depends on sustaining practical non-violence in the face of the *greatest conceivable* violence. Protection of life (peace) then becomes the *highest* moral value, the *most potent* expression of the superiority of spiritual reality and force.

But Gandhi confuses spiritual reality (or the Divine element in soul-force) on the one hand, with ultimate moral value and peaceful protection of life on the other, as equally valid expressions for the same *potency* and *practical* mechanism. This is the key to understanding the role of *satyāgraha* in Gandhi's wider argument and mission.

In this chapter the origin of this confusion, and its role in Gandhi's argument of *satyāgraha,* is examined on the basis of the previous critical analysis and the role of *satyāgraha* in Gandhi's mission to close the question of justifiability.

It is shown that Gandhi merely *constructs* his moral-metaphysical "laws" to objectify his a priori valuations and validate his methods, practical philosophy and claim. This "objectification" compounds the confusions. Trading on the general commitment, and the fundamental moral sentiments it expresses, further obscures the objective content and actual scope of his principles.

Lastly, in a positive critique, it is shown that Gandhi's *satyāgraha* is a coercive force which does not operate in the way he presumes, and therefore does not satisfy his own criteria of non-violence. It therefore constitutionally cannot fulfill the role Gandhi claimed for it in his argument and mission.

Life, the Chief Value: Wrong Aim and Methods, and False Views

1. *False Views and Values*

Assumes Equivalence of "Highest Value" and "Supreme Potency": If phenomenal reality is not analyzed simply as right or wrong, good or evil, violent or non-violent, and the complex fact of war is not analyzable by these distinctions alone, *who can say a priori* what the moral balance will be and where the line of justifiability is to be drawn?

Gandhi avoids the issue by *assuming* the equivalence of highest value and supreme practical potency. Then a method expressing this value may be said a priori to be eminently practical and guaranteed success. But this assumption rests on false views.

Factual Reality, a Moral Mix; Not Determinable a priori: An inappropriate use of "*yathā piṇḍe* . . ." produces a false view of reality based on the resultant confusion of categories.

The confusion is a factual one. Reality of action and of human nature are mixed so there *is no a priori* way to determine whether good or evil, reason or unreason, non-violence or violence divine or demonic, is going to be active at the moment, or if it will be susceptible to non-violent counter action.

The problem of justifying or morally supporting war depends on a complex analysis of justice and injustice, usually with no one side clearly just or in the right, and with no obvious symmetrical distribution of justice and rightness.

Gandhi accepted that Hitler's claims against the allies had a good deal of justice on their side and that the allies had caused much of the injustice which gave rise to his power in Germany. The allies also were no ideal exhibitors of democratic principles and non-exploitation. On the contrary, they thrived on colonial exploitation and oppression, aside from the gross injustice of the Versailles Treaty.

But Gandhi draws the line at Hitler's refusal to use non-violent means of adjustment of claims and to seek mutual negotiations or independent arbitration.[158] According to Gandhi's assessment, Hitler's claims may be justified, but he is definitely *wrong* and a propagator of evil in his choice of violence to adjudicate his claims.

Confusion of Material Destruction and Death of Body with Killing and Loss of Life: In line with Arjuna's arguments, Gandhi consistently points to the violent and destructive results, loss of life and destruction of property, as the primary proof of the futility of war.[159]

Gandhi cites the entire epic of the Mahābhārata as the demonstration of the futility of war: he points to the equal loss suffered by victor and vanquished alike, and the almost total physical annihilation involved, as well as the loss of an entire civilization—a totally "empty" victory.[160]

This interpretation is the result of his inappropriate use of the micro-macro-cosmic identity principle and the confused view of reality produced by the invalid assimilation of the ideal and the real.

Śrī Kṛṣṇa's argument in the Gītā makes clear the distinction between *ātman* and not-*ātman* by means of the grammatical proposition that what is the "soul" neither "slays" nor "is slain" (Gītā II:19-21, XVIII:17). But by his moral interpretation of the *ātmic* state as *anāsakti*, Gandhi confuses the native reality of the soul with its expression in life. This transfers values across categorical boundaries and produces both theoretical and practical contradictions between aim and method.

2. *False Aims and Methods.*

It has been shown that though Gandhi argues metaphysically for the highest reality of soul and the oneness of creation as the necessary basis of morality, he in fact assigns the highest value to life, and in support of absolute pacifism, calls for "peace at the price of life itself."

"Law of the Sword"; Not a "Law":   Gandhi calls brute-force and use of violence and its circle of retaliation the "law of the sword". To call it a "law" is to introduce confusion through rhetoric.

The "law" states that those who live by the sword die by the sword.

Gandhi writes, "I have no hesitation in redeclaring my faith in reason, which is another word for non-violence, rather than the arbitrament of war for the settlement of disputes or redress of wrongs. I cannot emphasize my belief more forcibly than by saying that I personally would not purchase my own country's freedom by violence even if such a thing were a possibility. My faith in the wise saying that what is gained by the sword will also be lost by the sword is imperishable."[161]

This "law" thus provides for Gandhi an argument for non-violence and pacifism that has the popular appeal and reassuring self-certitude of the maxim that "two wrongs don't make a right."

But this is not a "law" since it does not exclude dying by the sword if one does not live by it.

There is no law-like connection between antecedent and consequent. Further, if it is accepted as a loose expression of the law of *karma* or of a "homely" maxim whose meaning is "clear enough" and valid as a "general guide", then it admittedly is not a "law". The question remains why worry about dying by the sword if one believes a higher value might be served by the risk (or even the certitude) of death in its use. To quote it as an ultimate guide to conduct is to make saving one's life the highest value since it makes the saving one's own life look like the only reason for refraining from the use of force in defense of anything.

Gandhi, of course, does not advocate this passive moral posture from self-interest. But he does retain the argument that life is the highest value and says that non-killing, refusing to yield the sword even for self-defense, is the highest expression of this value.

Also, it is critical to note that there are certainly things one would *die for*; Gandhi used the moral weapon of "fast unto death." It is not simply "life" then that has the highest value, but particular life in particular circumstances—one's own as a last resort.

If ultimacy of value involves also universality of scope, as Gandhi's scheme of valuation requires, this removes life from the "highest value" category.

This may appear mere common sense. It is this common sense that Gandhi displaces when he argues ideologically, yet invokes when he prescribes for practice. One feels frustrated in trying to deny him, yet somehow unconvinced.

Non-retaliation: Self-defeating Principle at the Logical, Practical and Moral Limits.   According to the axiology of *satyāgraha,* for realization of any other value, only self-suffering unto self-immolation and self-killing are to be used. This is meant to express respect for life as a value higher than any other end sought.

The non-violent means thus express "ultimate value". Their use is an end in itself, since they are defined as the only morally valid means to realize *any other* values and ends; they may not be violated to achieve an ulterior end or to realize another value. As the *only allowable* means, they paradoxically represent the highest value. Translated to practice this would mean life itself gained by its giving.

Gandhi thus contradicts himself by making life the highest value and severest *satyāgraha,* the *only* moral means, its exact and most potent practical expression. One must not kill yet one must kill oneself to fulfill the highest value for realization of which self-killing is the preeminently moral and practical means.

Gandhi thus places "self-killing" in a separate category by making it logically the means of fulfilling an ultimate value.

Universalizability Criterion: Paradox of Highest Means Equated with Ultimate Ends (Fallacy of Assuming Their Ideal Identity).   The contradiction can be made evident in the *reductio ad absurdum* produced by universalizing.

One can imagine that if *all* good people simultaneously used the method of self-immolation in defense against evil-up-in-arms there would be no one left in the world to be or do good.

The good, dedicated to such an ideal and value of non-violence, would in fact be destroying the very good that their methods were meant to defend and realize. This blocks the argument that even if self-destruction were the only material result, still moral ennoblement of the world would justify the extreme method of non-violent defense.

Against the commonsense and *prima facie* case arguments of a limit to the general commitment, Gandhi argues that to die not trying to kill-in-return is of a *sui generis* moral order, while to die in the act of killing, even in self-defense, at best expresses moral weakness. But to common sense this is to make a *virtue* of dying at the hands of evil.[162]

Thus, unless the equation of violence with evil is assumed, choice of death at the hands of evil has the absurd consequence, by the universalization criterion, of pointlessly destroying the thing avowedly most valued—the moral order—and of gratifying the agent who is violently opposing realization of that value.

Ideological Axioms Cannot Replace Commonsense Assessment: If there are values higher than embodied life, e.g. justice, which Gandhi acknowledges as the condition of peace, then destruction of other embodied life must be equally as justifiable as destruction of one's own life in defense of that moral principle.

Justice should be a higher legitimating value. The argument that such violence would necessarily produce a counteracting quality of evil and self-defeating retaliations (whatever the momentary appearance of justice so gained) depends again on the assumption of Gandhi's equations. It has no justification in general human experience. The commonsense position is testimony to precisely this denial.

If Gandhi says that defense or protection by violence are impossible for the really perfect man who *ex hypothesi* alone could wield them without producing evil, the reply is that a higher ideal is enunciated in the Gītā—which Gandhi has both acknowledged and denied, as previously shown.

According to the classical interpretation of the Gītā, the *guṇātīta*, having no passionate motives in him, may nevertheless be inspired by motives of protection of the just and good life for the world in general.

Serving this end may in fact be the realized being's only purpose in maintaining the system of his material bodies (physical, vital, mental). It may move him to violence without any intermediary motive of desire or self-interest. This would not be *hiṁsā* as Gandhi defines it, though he does not admit it as a possibility.

However, that the world does in fact sustain itself by both types of force is acceptable both to common experience and to Gandhi. That a realized man might be the vehicle for violent forces used against evil looks contradictory *only* against the background of Gandhi's ideological interpretation of the Gītā.

Textual authority, inadequate "warrant": Assumes the Ideal It Is Intended to Validate as Universal. Gandhi claims the support of all scriptures and saints for his interpretation.[163]

But in fact, Gandhi stood against overwhelming opposition from
both hagiographical and textual arguments to the contrary. Agreement with his interpretation of the general commitment is not at issue. But Gandhi's attempts to annul its limits are either confuted by textual history and hagiography, or, at best, they are only tangentially addressed, since Gandhi's experiments open new fields in the application of non-violence that are peculiar to his interpretation of its principles.

That there simply is not the universal avowal of life as the highest value and of non-violence as its definite highest and purest expression is demonstrated by the nearly universal denial that his views met. It should be remembered that Gandhi's radical practical claim is "radical" and itself may be taken as the differentia of his from all other philosophies of non-violence, whether spiritually based or mundane.

It may be said that "the views of one *knowing* one may stand against the false views of 1 million who are ignorant", but singularity also is no definite criterion of Truth.

Gandhi tried to put forth a new ideal and to live up to it entirely. He may be "all wrong" or terribly right. In any case, his choice of exemplars of *satyāgraha*—Socrates, Prahlāda, Mīrābai, Daniel—still only exemplify a chosen ideal. Citing these examples cannot *prove* the ideal's validity. It perhaps clarifies it and shows its beauty.

Against these may be placed the examples of Rāma, Kṛṣṇa and Jesus (in the temple), which cannot be explained away if the explanation draws only on ideological *a priorisms*.

B. LAW OF BEING: GANDHI'S BASIC ARGUMENT AGAINST VIOLENCE AS A
LAST RESORT

Faulty Claim to Scientific Validity: Satyāgraha, a Tool of Ideological Inquiry; Non-violence, No "Law" of Being. It is necessary to see how Gandhi's arguments for *satyāgraha* and the universal claim depend on the unjustified factual assumption that non-violence is a "Law of Being".

Gandhi's final argument is that his ideological position expresses an ineradicable faith, so far substantiated in his own experiments sufficiently to "warrant" further experiments in that direction.

Gandhi considers direct logical arguments to the contrary to be indecisive. His claim is that in spiritual and moral scientific inquiry, just as in physical science, faith in previous experimental findings, and in one's speculations based on them, is needed to formulate concrete practical hypotheses and to carry out experiments based on them in the face of differing concepts of "correct" practice or direct theoretical opposition.

Parity of Reasoning: Counter Claims of Commonsense Faith. Gandhi intends by *satyāgraha* to explore in action the consequences for practice of a theory built on the assumptions and precepts of his ideology, his "faith".

It is necessary to remember how his experimental practice itself is based on false views, values and aims.

Gandhi's claim to the "warrant" of faith is especially "non-warranting" given the parity of reasoning in the counter claims of the orthodox Gītā position and common sense. Action can equally demonstrate the validity of loving use of violence in protection of justice and the good. One can have equal "faith" that *anāsakti* is a transcendent state which *does not* exclude *any* phenomenal quality or activity. And again, only by action based on *that* faith can the *non-identity* of violence with evil be proven and utilized for moral ends.

By parity of reasoning, though *satyāgraha* fails at the limits of the commonsense position and proves its falsity as an absolute factor, in the context of the new debate it may be paradoxically considered a *criterion* and *validation* of the last resort and necessity argument.

By parity, failure of *satyāgraha* only confirms that this necessity is not to be overridden by an ideologically defined faith, even one so supreme as Gandhi's. The real differences between the transcendent and the dual, the ideal and the practical cannot be expunged by that annulment of distinctions in moral consciousness which Gandhi does seem to prove possible by faith.

Gandhi expresses his faith through reasonings which have no independent claim. Repeatedly it is found that his arguments can be applied equally against his own position.

Gandhi's Key Admission: Argument Invalid if "Law of Love" Not the "Law of Our Being". Gandhi writes that the strongest argument

against his position on non-violence is the ". . . denial of non-violence /207
or love as the law of the human race. If love or non-violence is not the
law of our being, *the whole of my argument falls to pieces* and there is
no escape from the periodical recrudescence of war, each succeeding
one outdoing the preceding one in ferocity. . . ."[164]

On Gandhi's own admission, his argument against the justifiability
of any violence depends on the validity of his radical universal claims;
this in turn must rest on fact if it is to prove valid for *all practical* purposes in fulfillment of that claim.

Thus Gandhi translates the categorical homogeneity (deriving from
his dichotomous analysis) into a universalizing "scientific law" constitutive of the entire phenomenal and practical realm. His arguments for
the validity of this translation show already that it is only an expression of his moral presentiment and not the result of scientific and
philosophical inquiries. That 'if non-violence or love is not the law of
all being, then the "periodic recrudescence" of violence is the factual
situation,' says only that Gandhi would prefer a universe in which the
periodic recrudescence is not a fact. The argument makes no statement
demonstrating factual truth.

Gandhi defers giving a developed argument for his belief, but "ven-
ture(s) to make some relevant suggestions which may pave the way
for an understanding of the law."[165] He gives a list of brief arguments to outline more than to justify his views. Even so, one can readily see the essential predominance of ideological and rhetorical
elements. This is not excusable when it is in answer to what he admits
to be the strongest argument against him and therefore the logical test
of his own position.

Gandhi's Basic Arguments 1–8: Specific Criticisms.   A review of
Gandhi's points and their criticism based on the previous critical analysis will focus and complete the commonsense counter to the practical
component of his argument that *satyāgraha* is a universal sanction and
a sufficient substitute for the last resort to violence and force:

(1) All the teachers that ever lived have preached that law with more or
less vigour.
(2) If love was not the law of life, life would not have persisted in the
midst of death. Life is a perpetual triumph over the grave.
(3) If there is a fundamental distinction between man and beast, it is the

former's progressive recognition of the law and its application in practice in his own personal life. All the saints of the world, ancient or modern, were, each according to his light and capacity, a living illustration
of that supreme law of our Being. That the brute in us seems so often to
gain an easy triumph is true enough. That, however, does not disprove
the law. It shows the difficulty of practice. How should it be otherwise
with a law which is as high as Truth itself?

(4) When the practice of the law becomes universal, God will reign on
earth as He does in heaven. I need not be reminded that earth and
heaven are in us. We know the earth, we are strangers to the heaven
within us.

(5) If it is allowed that for some the practice of Love is possible, it is arrogance not to allow even the possibility of its practice in all the others.

(6) Not very remote ancestors of ours indulged in cannibalism and
many other practices which we would today call loathsome. No doubt
in those days too there were Dick Sheppards who must have been
laughed at and possibly pilloried for preaching the (to them) strange
doctrine of refusing to eat their fellow men.

(7) Modern science is replete with illustrations of the seemingly impossible having become possible within living memory. But victory of physical science would be nothing against the victory of the Science of Life,
which is summed up in love which is the Law of our Being.

(8) I know that it cannot be proved by argument. It shall be proved by
persons living it in their lives in utter disregard of consequences to themselves. There is no real gain without sacrifice. And since demonstration
of the Law of Love is the realest gain, sacrifice too must be the greatest
required.[166]

Here it is essential to see that each of Gandhi's points *assumes* the
law (and the law-likeness) that he is reportedly demonstrating, and
that the "law" is not demonstrated but only rhetorically expanded
upon and inculcated. The individual points of Gandhi's "brief" are
countered in the following enumeration:

(1) This point is argued previously with reference to Gandhi's textual and hagiographic arguments generally.

(2) This only asserts existence of a principle of life (spirit) not identical with the bodies through which it manifests. Aside from this life
element, the "law of decay, destruction, and death" is just as patent a
fact. Unless it is *assumed* that presence of spirit is equivalent to the existence of a constitutive law of material existence, there is no rule of
life conduct or law of action implied by this fact.

(3) Assuming the law is there waiting to be recognized as a moral datum, this argument trades on the commonsense distinction of man from beast by possession of distinctive faculties, e.g. scientific discernment and self-reference, self-culture and the moral presentiment on which our general commitment to non-violence is founded.

The ascription of "law" to make the generally acknowledged distinction, an exceptionless, objective condition, is wholly rhetorical.

The argument presenting saints as illustrations of this law likewise assumes that it is a "law" rather than, for example, a stage in spiritual evolution, or one line of practice leading to realization of that to which Gandhi ascribes "lawness" as in point 2. If all practicants were saints, still it would not prove it a "law". We call "saints" those who live by a rule something like Gandhi's law. They may conduct themselves with severe, circumspect, refined and studious attention to the general commitment, but not necessarily to the extreme applications implied in Gandhi's law-likeness.

If not all are such saints, then *a fortiori* non-violence as Gandhi conceives it is not the "law of our species". If all were saints, as Gandhi conceives them, then who would be there to protect the saints, and with what means would they protect them from the evil whose chief object is their destruction?

This distinction between brute and man (saint) confuses force and property. It is a further example of Gandhi's confusions of category created by misinterpretation of the micro-macro-cosm identity principle.

It has been repeatedly noted that Gandhi believes all force to be one continuum (on his *advaitic* principles). The translation of "contrariety of properties" to the "contradiction of substantial forces" in which they inhere makes the existential situation appear simply partible and analyzable by Gandhi's ideological dichotomies as a homogeneously moral reality. But the universal experience is a complex, constantly shifting and variously combining and recombining mix of even contradictory properties. Appearance structured by ideological categories and reified "law" does not speak to the reality confronted in experiential and existential life.

(4) This again assumes *that there is* a "law" that can become universal in practice and it trades rhetorically on the religious hope that such practice of God's law would win him to earth.

(5) This again assumes that there is a "law" which "some" do

practice, and it trades on the fear of being judged "arrogant". This has nothing to do with the "fact" of lawfulness of the precept of love as "non-violence".

It might be argued that to the contrary it is arrogance to assume that one can practice such an ultimate law or precept which does in fact translate the highest *advaitic* realization through its affective aspect of limitless love. There is no factual reason to assume that there must be a fundamental similarity of capability, shared by all, to manifest that aspect in its consummate form, any more than that all are incipiently about to achieve that supreme spiritual consummation of cognitive realization. There are obviously vast factual differences in spiritual and moral development that Gandhi's ideological homogenizing simply reads out.

(6) This shows an evolutionary tendency and does not demonstrate present validity of a law capable of superseding all evolutionary limitations "immediately". Again the presumption is in the direction of assuming law-likeness in challenge to the gradual pace and present incompleteness of that evolutionary tendency.

(7) This makes a double assertion of the presumed status of a "science" of life on the basis of the assumed "Law of our Being". It rhetorically sets Gandhi's ideological aspirations on an equal footing with established science, trading on the objective force and status of the physical sciences.

Even granted this status of established science, Gandhi gives no basis for believing that what is asserted of modern physical sciences ought to be and could be asserted of the putative "science" of life based on the "law" of *ahimsā*. Again it is assumed that *ahimsā* has already been discovered to be a "law" in the required formal and rigorous sense but it is this that is in question.

(8) This argument talks as if the demonstration "in lives" had already been given and need only be repeated, merely a multiplication of instances being needed to make the law self-evident to all.

But the main point at this stage in the critical examination of Gandhi's argument is that he has not produced this demonstration against the last resort argument of common sense in the unavoidably convincing way he believes and for which his entire science and practice of *satyāgraha* is intended.

The validity of *satyāgraha* as a
main component in Gandhi's mission depends on demonstration of its
universal applicability and practicability and its assured efficacy in all
contexts where violence might be suggested as a means.

Gandhi writes, "The usefulness of non-violent method seems to be
granted by all the critics. They gratuitously assume the impossibility of
human nature, as it is constituted, responding to the strain involved in
non-violent preparation. But that is begging the question. I say, 'you
have never tried the method on any scale. In so far as it has been tried,
it has shown promising results.' "[167]

The core of *satyāgraha* is the principle of self-suffering the logical
extreme and most potent practical form of which Gandhi claims to be
a form of non-retaliating self-immolation. He asserts that human nature, having the same soul or divine element in all, is "in its essence
one" and therefore everywhere, by nature and by law and "unfailingly
responsive to the advances of love"; therefore, a "Hitler and Mussolini" also are "not beyond redemption" and must finally succumb to
the "heat" generated by true non-violence of self-suffering.[168]

Gandhi expands, ". . . as a believer in non-violence I may not limit
its possibilities. Hitherto he (Hitler) and his likes have built upon their
invariable experience that men yield to force. Unarmed men, women
and children offering non-violent resistance without any bitterness in
them will be a novel experience for them. Who can dare say it is not in
their nature to respond to the higher and finer forces? They have the
same soul that I have."[169]

And also, ". . . It should be remembered that they have up to now
always found ready response to the violence that they have used.
Within their experience, they have not come across organized non-
violent resistance on an appreciable scale, if at all. Therefore it is not
only highly likely, but I hold it to be inevitable, that they would recognize the superiority of non-violent resistance over any display of violence that they may be capable of putting forth."[170]

Finally, Gandhi argues that such non-violent suffering, as Professor
Niemoeller's, failed to convert Hitler and had "not proved sufficient
for melting Herr Hitler's heart merely shows that it is made of harder
material than stone. But the hardest metal yields to sufficient heat.
Even so must the hardest heart melt before sufficiency of the heat of

non-violence. And there is no limit to the capacity of non-violence to generate heat."[171]

This again is an expression of faith, not an argument, demonstration or proof.

Asserting proof by analogy requires knowledge of both components. Gandhi admits a fundamental ignorance both on the ideal or spiritual side from which he derives his ultimate justification, and on the practical side where application meets an inherent recalcitrance of human action (especially non-violent action) to rational analysis: "Every action is a resultant of a multitude of forces even of contrary nature. There is no waste of energy. So we learn in books on mechanics. This is equally true of human actions. The difference is that in the one case we generally know the forces at work, and when we do, we can mathematically foretell the resultant. In the case of human actions, they result from a concurrence of forces, of most of which we have no knowledge."[172]

Gandhi then twists the argument: "But our ignorance must not be made to serve the cause of disbelief in the power of these forces. Rather is our ignorance a cause for greater faith. And non-violence being the mightiest force in the world, and also the most elusive in its working, it demands the greatest exercise of faith. Even as we believe in God in faith, so have we to believe in non-violence in faith."[173]

Though Gandhi's "faith" has demonstrably extended the scope of our general commitment with a clearer analysis and with more powerful methods than any previous conceptions of non-violence and pacifism, he trespasses his own limits when he applies the same analysis by faith across the categorical boundaries represented by the *prima facie* case and commonsense criteria.

Non-Universality of Satyāgraha: Principal Criticism of Gandhi's "Law of Being" Argument as Basis of Practical Methods and Argument (His Misanalysis of Human Rational and Moral Nature). In defense of his first premise, Gandhi tries to show the commonality between different parties of humanity, and against those who argue non-violence is no "Law of our Being", Gandhi writes,

The first argument (that there are some human beings who are incapable of responding to non-violence, and rather are provoked by it to greater violence), if it is valid, cuts at the very root of the anti-war movement, which is based on the assumption that it is possible to convert Fascists and Nazis. They belong to the same species as the so called democracies, or, better still, war resisters themselves. They show in their family circle the same tenderness, affection, consideration, and generosity that war resisters are likely to show even outside such circles. The difference is only of degree. Indeed Fascists and Nazis are a revised edition of the so-called democracies, if they are not an answer to the latter's misdeeds. . . . The late war has shown that both combatants were guilty of falsehoods, exaggerations, and inhumanities. The Versailles Treaty was a treaty of revenge against Germany by the victors. The so-called democracies have before now misappropriated other people's lands and have resorted to ruthless repression. What wonder if Messrs. Hitler & Co. have reduced to a science the unscientific violence their predecessors had developed for exploiting the so-called backward races for their own material gain? It is therefore a matter of the rule of three to find out the exact amount of non-violence required to melt the harder hearts of the Fascists and Nazis, if it is assumed, as it is, that the so-called democracies melt before a given amount of non-violence. Therefore we must eliminate from consideration the first argument, *which would be fatal if it could be proved to have any content in it.*[174]

This is a wonderful argument. But Gandhi has not proved anything. He only asserts an attitudinal condition of his method and outline of how he should like the universe to be *in fact,* for his argument to go through.

Further, it is ever an "open question" whether the violent opposition (or oneself) is in fact susceptible at the limit of argument. It is not in question whether, within the scope of normal or strained conditions, Gandhi is right that they may have similar behavior patterns and affections. It is the constitutive limits of these, and their factual recalcitrance or reactivity, that are in question. Reassertion of the facts of coincidence over a certain range is no proof of universality or even commonality.

These arguments therefore only reassert the conditions of faith that attach to Gandhi's methods.

It should be noted that Gandhi presents a second line of defense that is more promising (if not satisfying his radical claim). He argues that even if one may not reach a Hitler, the German or Japanese peoples, or any aggressor nation will undoubtedly in large measure respond to the "finer forces" of non-violence once the authoritarian oppression (which cannot last forever) is lifted;[175] or, in later generations, when the deeds of the present are seen for what they are;[176] the German nation, no less than any other, would not fail to respond to the human suffering of non-violence.[177]

Concluding this line, Gandhi argues that however hard-hearted the leaders and generals, the troops in the field could not long stand the sight of rows of innocent men, women, and children readily and without malice, but in gentle appeal, presenting themselves to sword and bullet—"The army would be brutal enough to walk over them, you might say . . . an army that dares to pass over the corpses of innocent men and women, would not be able to repeat that experiment."[178]

Rational Nature: Gandhi further delineates the form of the universality of non-violence asserting that human nature is instinct with reason, the spirit of accommodation and a basic moral discrimination and urge to non-violence.

Gandhi even argues that the essence of non-violence is the natural ascendancy and acceptance of reason to examine and adjust conflicting claims ("reason" being another name for non-violence as previously pointed out).

But Gandhi admits that reason is often rutted and mired in wrong belief and prejudice.

As part of his radical practical claim, Gandhi asserts that this unreason *can never* be beyond remedy by the *satyāgrahī's* self-suffering which reaches directly into the heart and touches the soul of the opponent, awakening and cleansing from within, straightening and rejuvenating the reasoning faculties distinctive of human nature. Soul-force alone has these capabilities.

This is Gandhi's reformulation and reassertion of his faith, in a more specific and detailed form. Connecting his view of human rational nature with the practical mechanism and operative factors postulated in his non-violent methods, Gandhi writes,

. . . in 1920, I became a rebel. Since then the conviction has been growing upon me, that things of fundamental importance to the people are not secured by reason alone but have to be purchased with their suffering. Suffering is the law of human beings; war is the law of the jungle. But suffering is infinitely more powerful than the law of the jungle for converting the opponent and opening his ears, which are otherwise shut, to the voice of reason . . . if you want something really important to be done you must not merely satisfy the reason, you must move the

heart also. The appeal of reason is more to the head but the penetration
of the heart comes from suffering. It opens up the inner understanding
in man. Suffering is the badge of the human race, not the sword.[179]

The fundamental question is whether all "human" *form* is constituted from human *nature,* or may be in fact (1) only an outer disguise
and deceit by a demonic being, intrinsic evil, or by an ordinary human
being who has given desire free reign and now suffers its tyranny, or
(2) only an outer biological form which covers a very large span of
spiritual evolution, including the very nearly brute and the very nearly
divine.

If Gandhi's characterization were meant to define "humanity" and
that range of rational faculties and moral consciousness generally covered by the term, the real target of Gandhi's methods, there would be
no argument. His methods may be accepted as the ideal means for exercising that human element and evolving "humanity" towards the
ideals of reason and graciousness.

Gandhi, however, insists that *all* human form (appearance) necessarily is possessed of this rational and moral responsiveness as human
content (reality). He does not believe himself to be merely recom-
mending a form of analysis to be investigated, but stating the factual
case. The factual situation, however, has a direct bearing on the adequacy of Gandhi's methodological reduction of his ideological axioms
and claims.

In fact, Gandhi contradicts himself. Though he discounts the "form/
content" distinction to explain his absolute and universal claim, he invokes it to explain the failures of non-violence that would limit his
claim. He phrases his recommendations with rhetorical condition.

Gandhi writes that if the world does not change its ways and Hitler
succeeds, "it will be one more proof that the law of the jungle is still a
great force in human affairs. It will be one more proof that though we
humans have changed form we have not changed the manners of the
beast."[180] And, "though we have the human form, without the attainment of the virtue of non-violence, we still share the qualities of
our remote ancestors, the orangoutang."[181]

*Gandhi Acknowledges Human Incorrigibility to Non-violence: De-
feat of His "Law of Being" Argument and therewith His Total Practical Position.* Behind such recommendations there is always the rhetorical force of judgment that "of course one wants to and could be

truly human and responsive to non-violence, if only one did (as one ought) choose to be so."

Gandhi's claims aside, his use of the term "humanity" is primarily commendatory and his admission that there are latent animal tendencies which may not respond to non-violence is all the commonsense view requires to counter those claims.

Gandhi, however, goes further: "I do not say that ("The August revolution caused a setback in the struggle for independence"). In the historical process the country will be found to have advanced towards freedom through every form of struggle, even through the August upheaval. All that I have said is that progress would have been much greater if we had shown the non-violent bravery of my conception."[182]

Gandhi even acknowledges that human beings may be irredeemable and require forceful or even violent means to curb their evil tendencies. Before beginning a fast unto death, he writes that he has ". . . rehearsed . . . the possibility of a wide fratricide" following his actions, just as in the Mahābhārata "the Yādavas had destroyed each other . . . if the people had become indolent and vicious like the Yādavas and God saw that there was *no way out but extermination,* he might make even an ordinary person like him, the instrument of such a catastrophe."[183]

This is acknowledgment that there may be cases of evil incorrigible to non-violence, in which violence does become justifiable by moral necessity. The method of such extermination may be to turn evil (as with the Yādavas) against itself.

Gandhi counters that God alone has moral right to destroy by violence what he has created and can recreate. His violent chastisement is in fact a process of recreating.

This theological argument need not be met. (Though one could argue that God's *avatāra,* not the saint, ought to be our exemplar.) All that is needed is the admission that *in fact* some things that look like human beings may not be so, or may be so little evolved, or so possessed of evil tendencies, that there is nothing in their constitution that can respond to soul-force in a non-violent way much less to reason and moral gesture, or non-violent action. These are empirical matters that cannot be discounted *ad hoc* by ideology. Such cases are met by the *prima facie* criteria for using violence as a last resort—when reason and moral sense have been probed, tested and cultivated beyond the point where even "unreasonable" doubt could hesitate.

Where that point lies depends very heavily on perceptions, particular circumstances and sensitivity of judgment. But the principle is clear,
and that is enough for the present argument.

Gandhi's claims that there is no creature irredeemable by non-violent force, and that precise means and degree of adequate self-suffering are merely a matter of discovery, are unjustified. His principles,
their advisability and the aspiration they represent are not in question,
but only the factual basis of their methodological reduction and application. Here, Gandhi's claims clearly fail, and hence his radical claim
and mission.

C. SATYĀGRAHA: A COERCIVE FORCE

Need for Positive Criticism: It may be admitted by the above critical
examination that *satyāgraha* does not solve the practical moral problem posed in the last resort argument.

This is a negative criticism of *satyāgraha* by a standard external to
it, expressing only what *satyāgraha* fails to do. It is necessary to give a
positive critique as well.

Satyāgraha, contrary to both Gandhi's analysis and the canons of
strict non-violence, is an essentially coercive force. But if its use is to be
recommended, as it will be under any but the strictest non-resistance
philosophy, its true nature and working should be known so that its
use would be accurate and effective, measured and predictable.

Methods, Claims and Facts: Gandhi's method of fasting provides a
focus for examining the coercive character of his principles.

Gandhi gives detailed analyses[184] and repeated warnings[185] that
fasting ought not to be taken up without careful elimination of all coercive intent, even what may be misinterpreted as coercive and so result in injury (insult) to one who feels the action offensive.

But Gandhi's method of fasting was continuously challenged as coercive. He repeatedly rejected those charges and attempted to refute
them by drawing distinctions based on the *satyāgraha* doctrine of self-
infliction. Nevertheless, Gandhi admits sizable coercive effects in his
own use of this, his most potent weapon[186] of non-violence. He notes
that fear of the beloved's fasting may provoke good actions.[187] His

fast against his colleagues' weakness in the untouchability campaign caused the "unintended consequences"[188] of pressure upon the government to release him from jail. Gandhi thought it unfortunate "that it went beyond the intention and coerced some people into giving a decision against their convictions."[189]

Gandhi believes, however, that he escapes the charge of coerciveness by arguments which emphasize the role of motive and intent. He writes that "in any examination of moral conduct, the intent is the chief ingredient,"[190] and that his intent was not to pressure government, or to compel agreement and assent against conviction. But disclaiming the coercive intent does not remove the coercive effects and repercussions. Again, Gandhi wishes to undo real results, present facts, with moral appeal based on ideological distinctions.

Gandhi's Displaced Onus for Coercive Effects: Methods Coercive in Principle and in Fact. First, Gandhi's use of fasting as non-violent weaponry in *satyāgraha* (as a *tapas*) is specifically intended to produce tangible effects and specific influences. He defines *"Satyāgrahic* fasting . . . (as) when you *seek* to influence people by fasting,"[191] and generally, "the fact is that all spiritual fasts always influence those who come within the zone of their influence. That is why spiritual fasting is described as *tapas*. And all *tapas* invariably exerts purifying influence on those in whose behalf it is undertaken."[192]

From the wider standpoint, all the force of Gandhi's reformist drive is behind its use. This "insistence" is built into the concept and principles of *satyāgrahic* action. Though Gandhi recognized the severity of the method and the imperative force produced, and though he admitted the harm done by its wrong use and the extreme, inadvertent effects of his own use, he nevertheless continued to assert that the method is non-coercive and legitimately non-violent.

Gandhi justifies these judgments by his principle of self-suffering. He claims that if properly motivated, initiated and guided, such fasting (or other non-violent action) can harm the user alone, if the cause turns out to have been an unjust one. He believes this is the unique characteristic that actually defines true non-violence and provides its ultimate justification in line with the strict non-injury criterion of *ahiṁsā*.

Gandhi therefore puts the onus of wrong use on society. In its weakness it succumbs to illegitimately conducted fasts for private or "unworthy" ends. He says that "such fasts will be robbed of the intent of coercive and undue influences and like all human institutions . . . can be both legitimately and illegitimately used."[193] But Gandhi's *ahiṁsā* is radically and forcibly heteronomous and *satyāgraha* is the practical expression of this heteronomy. The onus cannot be thus shifted.

Coercive in Effect; Coercive in Principle: Therefore, Coercive. Rhetorically, by means of irony, Gandhi asserts that his fasts were "coercive" only in the sense that action springing from love of parent, child or teacher might ever be considered "coercive".[194] His fasts were prompted only by such love.

But "love" does not conceptually rule out violence and coercion. Only Gandhi's ideological interpretation makes it seem so. In fact, his equation of the moral and the practical should imply that one is not morally excusable for results not comprehended in or contrary to the originating motive and intent.

Gandhi is made wary and his insistence, softened by the maxims "know them by their fruits," and "one cannot see one's own back". He does not deny coercive fruits, but he either relabels them in terms of non-violent motives and intentions or he falls back on the logical necessity that morally imperfect beings have only limited liability.

Even if his theory guaranteed a purely non-violent principle in the abstract, the application of the theory must also be governed by principles. It is these application principles and specific application conditions that ideology often overlooks in straining to make praxis and practice consistent with theory.

Gandhi, when faced with the problem of application, shifts to his theory of the ideal, and asserts that in fact it functions only as a regulative idea. This may protect the ideal, but it also renders it impotent. Faith may empower the ideal when it forms action on the ideal like a template. Gandhi's prescription of this "faith" is more an instinctive reaction and response to the problem than a theoretical reflection on it. The motive force of the reformist is deeply involved in insistence amounting to a coercion and his action is not rendered "non-coercive" by the theory and faith under which it is initiated and operated.

Insistence on Coercive Methods: Terrible Pressure of Reformist Ideology: Gandhi argues that "one ought not to be deterred from right action when one is sure of the rightness . . .",[195] and that "like everything that is good, fasts are abused. That is inevitable. One cannot forebear to do good, because sometimes evil is done under its cover,"[196] and though "ridiculous fasts (may) . . . spread like plague and are harmful, when fasting becomes a duty it cannot be given up . . . what I do myself, I cannot prevent others from doing under similar circumstances. It is common knowledge that the best of good things are often abused."[197]

Gandhi thus not only admits the critic's arguments, but, by universalizing, he seeks to enlist their sympathies. He argues a moral obligation not to deter others who feel as he does under compulsion of "duty". *Satyāgraha* postulates that one's primary duty is "insisting" on Truth and Goodness as one sees them as if they were Truth and the Good absolute.

Gandhi asks the central and fundamental question, "What is Truth? A difficult question; but I have solved it for myself by saying that it is what the voice within tells you. How then, you ask, different people think of different and contrary truths? Well, seeing that the human mind works through innumerable media and that the evolution of the human mind is not the same for all, it follows that what may be truth for one may be untruth for another."[198]

And, "Truth resides in every human heart, and one has to search for it there, and to be guided by truth as one sees it. But no one has a right to coerce others to act according to his own view of truth,"[199] and ". . . performance of one's duty should be independent of public opinion. I have all along held that one is bound to act according to what to one appears right, though it may appear wrong to others. And experience has shown that that is the only correct course."[200]

This "insistence" is the primary thing in coercion. Though Gandhi admits the relative nature of practical truth, his insistence is moralizing and absolute. In universalizing, he has used rhetorical devices, truisms, which can be enlisted on either side of the argument and which, therefore, can settle nothing. They merely give form to the generalized ideological insistence.

That the conditions of *satyāgraha* fasting (and all *satyāgraha* methods) are narrow and imperative does not change its coercive character and effects. The imperative force is undeniable.

(1) *Terrible Pressure of Reform*:   Argument and theory aside, the circumstance of the debate is that behind Gandhi's reasonings and practice is the constant and terrible pressure of reform.

It is argued that this is only "moral pressure" and in no way materially compelling. It is intended to carry only such force as does not change the quality or results of the force actually applied to any other than can be accurately described as "non-violent" in the strictest terms.

But given the average susceptibility to moral pressure, to moral praise and blame, and that this pressure is often more subversive of moral autonomy because of its patent moral intent and Gandhi's personal moral status, therefore, the pressure in fact involves very deeply and forcibly the "insistence" that "*āgraha*" translates. This cannot be described as "non-coercive" in ordinary terms.

(2) *Radical Heteronomy*:   Note how strong the pro *and* con reactions are. But Gandhi's *satyāgraha* is not felt to be in itself so greatly "coercive", but only adventitiously on account of the severe conditions in which he used it. Its coerciveness, however, stems from the radical heteronomy that Gandhi's philosophy of non-violence and *satyāgraha* forces on moral consciousness, not from the history of its application.

The heteronomous standard is so thoroughly defined ideologically and so well fortified by its congruity with the commonsense moral position that it compels self-judgment and moral self-condemnation. Gandhi's example becomes also an instrument of force self-applied. This is fundamentally contrary to Gandhi's own basic moral principles of autonomy and total moral responsibility.

(3) *Intent to Influence*:   The concept of *satyāgraha* includes the intent to influence and reform on the basis of a rational moral ideal. Influence designed in abstract and intended to apply generally can never address the individual qua individual; it must, in fact, coerce to conformity.

(4) *Ideological Posture*:   The theory of moral autonomy reflected in the spiritual aim of self-realization, and its moral and practical principle of *svadharma*, defines a human material absolutely individual and infinitely varied and rich. This moral and spiritual reality *ex hypothesi* cannot be encompassed by any narrow human concept and

ideal based on it. Hence coercion.

As has already been noted, Gandhi argues that his ideals are in themselves inexpressible. It is the ceaseless striving for the unrealizable ideal that confers spiritual force on one's thought and actions. One may be wrong in its translation to concept and practice. One may have a wrong belief and follow a wrong cause. The first rule of non-violence is thus tolerance and a willingness to suffer and to never inflict suffering in propagating the translation of one's ideal.

Gandhi alleges that this is the beauty of *satyāgraha,* its built-in safeguard—its wrong use and abuse recoil only on the user.[201] But there is already a strong coercive force in the very ideological posture that infects the gesture of exact conduct. There is a definite *a priori* limit and direction of what will be acceptable or exempt from judgment by the heteronomous standard.

In this way the reformist attitude itself constitutes a subtle judgment. It looks to more than the immediate practical need and to that extent supersedes that necessity. It thereby constitutes a coercive or arbitrary and ancillary force.

(5) *Moral Insistence:* The force of Gandhi's method is the more coercive if the opponent is a beloved or well-wisher. If the *satyāgrahī* is wrong, this opponent is all the more helpless.

The *satyāgrahī* is inflicting the suffering on himself and leaves no recourse to the wronged party who also does not want to yield to force, but now feels compelled to. The only alternative left him is to suffer quietly his misguided but sincere well-wisher's self-immolation. This is no "choice", but "coercion". His free reason would choose neither course, and in fact has already chosen, as the moral and right thing, what the *satyāgrahī* is forcing him to renounce.

The dilemma is magnified by the practicant's seemingly unassailable morality which makes it all the more difficult to defuse or defend against the wrong use of the method, whether that use is simply mistaken or purposefully abusive. The beloved in whose behalf the *satyāgraha* was undertaken is often the weakest and most abused, the least capable of resisting such pressures, especially since the suffering falling on the *satyāgrahī* is known to be needless. No wrong to admit and repent of has been done.

The "opponent" who could adopt the indifferent attitude recommended by Gandhi must be an advanced *satyāgrahī*. All others will suffer along with the erring *ahiṁsite.*

It simply is not true that the suffering falls only on the head of the *satyāgrahī* if he is wrong. The *satyāgrahī*'s love obviously cannot redeem the suffering and injury he is causing the beloved.

This limiting case shows clearly that the *satyāgrahī*'s love is misguided, however noble, when it replaces consideration of consequences with ideological attachment to means.

(6) *Conformism to Great Ideas and Great Actions*: Behind Gandhi's practice is the homogenizing force of propagation of and conformity to an idea implied in his ideology and methods. This required his constant defense and rationalization.

Gandhi is forced to argue on the offensive that "one may not be deflected from the right course for fear of possible but unintended consequences. If one were to be so deterred, it could be shown that hardly any great action could be undertaken."[202]

There is a presumption that such "great actions" are called for. There is a second presumption that the given ideal and reform are precisely the means required by most fundamental truth and by all historical forces.

The presumptions are justified by the manifest moral character and rational purity of an ultimate ideal which the ideologue believes himself to have captured and applied in his ideology and praxis. The logic of these justifications seems impeccable and is compelling. The programmatic translation is urgent. There is constant effort to force events and persons to conform to the ideal.

It is unlikely that any one man or group's ideology is adequate to analyze and control major historical processes and movements. Experience shows ideologies are invariably inadequate to understand and control large singular events. The single human being and his minor moral dilemmas seems far beyond ideological analysis. Yet this is the avowed intent and constant pressure involved in the ideological posture.

The moral onus added by the direct appeal to moral instead of only practical and political consciousness is even more radically imposing and distorting.

(7) *Social Norms*: A condition Gandhi brings to insure his methods against coerciveness is that there should be no penance for inferential guilt.

Gandhi writes that "There should be no room for doubt as regards the fault . . . one should not do penance for an act which he alone regards as wrong . . . the wrong must be one that is accepted as such by society . . . (that) is not penance but coercion where the wrong doer is not conscious of having done anything wrong."[203]

This "wrong" is relativized to social norms. Social validity is insured since the society must go on, and standards of behavior must be maintained. But it is intrinsically a coercive mode of control if measured against the standard of moral autonomy and by Gandhi's own absolute standard defining fundamental violence as the soul's registration of "tearing".

(8) *Public Opinion*:   The mechanism of enlisting public opinion, a large element in Gandhi's *satyāgraha,* directly appeals as a mode of fundamental coercion.

Ascetic Roots of Satyāgraha Coercion: In theory and intent some of Gandhi's fasts were instruments of self-purification with no ulterior motive that could possibly be a lever of coercion.

But it has been shown that Gandhi models his methods on ascetic tradition, practice and ideals.[204] He says that as such they are direct appeals to God[205] and, in fact, are meant to compel His assistance.[206]

This is the same attitude found in strikes and other *satyāgraha* non-cooperation methods. The object is coercion, whatever the disclaimer of intent or explanation of the operative mechanism. The principal motive is to have one's way. The particular force enlisted is totally adventitious, whether materially so or spiritually.

If Gandhi holds consistently his belief that all spirit is material and all material spirit, and all force a continuum, then any use of force at all and to any purpose and intent (even to force divine succour) is the basic unavoidable fact. This constitutes coercion.

Gandhi writes that ". . . just as there is identity of spirit, so is there identity of matter and in essence the two are inseparable. Spirit is matter rarefied to the utmost limit. Hence, whatever happens to the body must touch the spirit and whatever happens to one body must affect the whole matter and the whole spirit."[207]

Therefore, the *nature of such method and attitude* is necessarily to draw *equal and opposite reaction.*

The coercer, by definition, must become the coerced. The chain of violence is assured at whatever level the coercion occurs.

This is the fundamental critique of Gandhi's entire non-violence.

If Bengal proves injustice, it will be an exception. In no case was there
any idea of exercising coercion on any one. Indeed, I think that the
word coercion would be a misnomer for the influence that was exerted
by the fasts under criticism. Coercion means some harmful force used
against a person who is expected to do something desired by the user of
the force. In the fasts in question, the force was used against myself.
Surely, force of self-suffering cannot be put in the same category as the
force of suffering caused to the party sought to be influenced. If I fast
in order to awaken the conscience of an erring friend whose error is
beyond question, I am not coercing him in the ordinary sense of the
word.[208]

This again is to reassert Gandhi's ideology in terms of a definition
and it does not answer the question raised.

The ordinary sense of the word "coercion" merely says that the person is to be influenced against his will, restrained or compelled to do
something or forego something. Any idea of harm in it is there implicitly in the self-centered nature of the motive that informs the coercive
use of force.

Ordinarily there need not be any active intent to harm. Gandhi defines his *satyāgraha* to obviate this condition. The idea of "using the
force only against himself" clearly has no place in the analysis of the
ordinary term. The categorical question Gandhi asks in relation to it is
only rhetorical, depending for its content and sense on the ideology he
imports into his definition.

Gandhi assimilates "harm" and "coercion", "violence" and
"force", and then creates the distinction between force used "*against*
others" vs. "*against* himself". Out of this distinction he constructs his
definition of "coercion".

On the basis of *this* definition or recommendation, Gandhi may not
be "coercing". In the ordinary sense he certainly is, despite his claim
for support from the ordinary sense and definition.

Gandhi's stipulative or commendatory definition needs to be examined in light of the ordinary usage and commonsense sensitivities and
understanding, just as earlier it was acknowledged that the ordinary
usage needs to be widened and adjusted in light of Gandhi's work, if it
is to guide scientific investigation into the constitutive facts of human
action and the debate on justifiability.

Is it possible to restrict suffering and harm to oneself as Gandhi avers? Certainly not if he maintains his own rigorous definitions. If suffering and harm are measured by the absolute standard of the soul's perception, affections, moral career and spiritual evolution, then Gandhi's stipulative definition of coercion fails. The force that communicates itself, whether produced by directing suffering against oneself or others, is an externally impinging factor.

If it is argued that in *satyāgraha* the impelling force comes from within the wrong doer and therefore constitutes a moral force, the reply is that this is not the autonomous response or direction of soul-force but only the reactive response of moral or practical consciousness under pressure from the *satyāgrahī*'s forceful constrainings.

In consonance with Gandhi's definition, it may be recommended that "coercive" force has been used when the resulting transaction satisfies the statement "the coercer is coerced"—positive proof that the transaction is amongst material forces, all external to and binding on each other. In that case there is no need to elaborate the concepts and application of "violence", "force" or "harm".

In the language of the Gītā, the reformer, attached to his ideology and reform, is caught and compelled by the reactions of *prakṛti* to his personalized actions upon it. The moral ideology, praxis and program of reform actions are constituted of *guṇas*, not *guṇātīta*, so their actions will bind by reaction and the coercer will be coerced by attachment to his own ideas and efforts at purity. The standard under which he propagates his forces will be external to the *svadharma* of every other.

Gandhi takes the "superior" position of "correction of the wrongdoer"—the "erring friend" will see that his error is beyond question. But that it is "error" is determined beforehand by ideology. Actions based on that judgment will constitute coercion even if possibly mitigable by the benefit brought to the wrongdoer, who may be in fact influenced to change his ways and does in fact make amends for a real wrong.

But this puts Gandhi's analysis in line with that of commonsense justification allowing otherwise wholly evil coercion to be somewhat redeemable by beneficent use and results. There seems to be no justification for differentiating the pressure created by *satyāgraha* from that denoted by the ordinary use of the term "coercion".

Gandhi opposes his fasts to hunger strikes. The difference between penitential and purificatory fasting on the one hand and self-starvation for personal gain on the other lies wholly in the motive. The essential factor in the analysis is supposed to be selfish vs. unselfish intent.

But the moral point of view is supposed rather to separate categories of substantially differentiable forces and not merely to make indifferent and adventitious ascriptions. Gandhi writes,

> Of course, it is not to be denied that fasts can really be coercive. Such are fasts to attain a selfish object. A fast undertaken to wring money from a person or for fulfilling some such personal end would amount to the exercise of coercion or undue influence. I would unhesitatingly advocate resistance to such undue influence . . . And if it is argued that the dividing line between a selfish and an unselfish end is often very thin, I would urge that a person who regards the end of a fast to be selfish or otherwise base should resolutely refuse to yield to it, even though the refusal may result in the death of the fasting person.[209]

Such advice looks harsh. A fast is a terrible weapon for coercion generally, for all the reasons given above and extremely so if the fast is "unto death". The supposed wrongdoer may be right and is yet defenseless against the fast—forced to watch the beloved die or to use counterforce and force-feed him. Nothing in the dialectic of these considerations can be considered innocent of coercive force.

In sum, Truth as Freedom, the avowed aim of *satyāgraha,* cannot be realized or advanced by methods of action built on essentially coercive principles that are applied with essentially coercive intent. The good intent does not compensate for the bad effects. (Much more is involved compared to which the dynamics of the consciously formulated intent are of very small order and consequence.)[210]

It remains to pull together the elements of the exposition and critical analysis of Gandhi's philosophy of non-violent action and to examine its application in the present world situation in terms of the debate it was created to close.

It is suggested that while Gandhi's practical claim fails and he does not close the debate over the justifiability of violence, his work may be a key factor in averting large scale violence and even nuclear conflict, if it is adapted (1) on the personal level as an objective method of moral self-culture and sensitizing, basic to all other search and struggle for Truth and Justice; and (2) on the social level as a technique and tactic on a par and in conjunction with all other practical methods that may naturally present themselves.

The situation to be met is a plural world struggling towards justice, freedom and peace as best it can by all feasible and promising means— a world not so nearly ideal as Gandhi's methods would require were they unmodified and solitarily to hold the field and advance the struggle.

A. SUMMARY: ANALYSIS, ASSESSMENT, APPLICATION

Objective Analysis and Assessment: In assessing the validity and application of an ideal, a clear and objective perception is wanted.

Categories must not be confused or used to restrict reality *a priori* to any ideal element. Judgment must be provisional and experimental. The conceptual apparatus tied to its hypothesis and specific objectives, is meant to generalize and to infer from particulars; but the natural growth of empirical consciousness on the whole is inconstant, alternatively restricting or advancing through particulars.

Any mental formulation forces on understanding a limited and single-appertured view of reality. Action based on that understanding and conceptual structure must be coercive to the degree attention is focussed on the possession and propagation of that formation or ideal as the legitimizing standard for reality to match.

Gandhi claims to have discovered non-violence in his search for Truth, while truthfulness came to him naturally. But his ideal of Truth is also an *a priori* formation—he assumes the moral necessity of making external conformity to the ideal the realization and criterion of it. *Satyāgrahic*, non-violent, exact conduct constitutes that realization and criterion. His practical claim is its ideological expression and logical outcome.

According to the analysis presented in this study, Gandhi's methods have a definite power, scope and viability. They have great utility in raising issues of reform and redress, defining claims and defusing conflict. They greatly refine the last resort criterion. They offer a set of new procedures to extend every encouragement and impetus to latent good and reason in the opponent. They give a new weaponry to meet the limiting case of incorrigible evil.

Gandhi's methods are nevertheless wrong in ascribing to soul-force an absolute latitude and potency justified only by ideological presumptions, and in making his practical claim absolute and definitive of his philosophy and methods of non-violence. The invalidity of this claim distracts but does not detract from the valid core of his analysis and application.

If the analysis presented here is correct, a definite type of necessity and limiting case *satyāgraha* may prove to be a viable substitute (sometimes no less coercive) for physical violence, but where violence (or forceful *satyāgraha*) is justifiable it is *also* required.

If non-violence is not known *a priori* to be *always* the right and practical means, and violence is not known *a priori* to be *always* a wrong and inadmissible means, then there is need to ask where, when, how, for what purposes and with what concomitants in mind, either force ought to be used.

What is morally required is a reasonable assessment of need in place of doctrinal *a priorisms*.

Justice and Truth in Today's World; Justice the Condition of Peace. The present world situation is morally extremely complex. Even such a standout case as South Africa cannot be summarily addressed.

Today, behind every just claim against an oppressor there is a partisan self-interest which itself brings incipient injustice into consideration. All interactions have a history and a future that are a morass of partially justified claims and counter-claims with no discernible beginning and self-evidently equitable resolution.

Truth of the claims of justice is not absolutely clear on any side and the price paid for direct action of a severe sort, non-violent or violent, is great. In either case, equally exacting consideration and care are needed as to both method and strategy, and as to how most generously and objectively to fulfill the last resort criterion—to give every benefit of doubt to non-violent strategies to clarify that limit, to make clearly manifest that that limit has been reached and still to make effort at that limit to elicit latent good, and as long as possible, to keep open the possibility of inspiring reasonable response. Once decided on, however, violence requires equal all-out commitment to its methods, tactics, and strategies.

Even in South Africa, one cannot say *a priori* the oppressing white regime and population will never respond or that the oppressed are perfectly free from taint against others. The oppressed will likely have malice in the heart and to that extent cannot satisfy Gandhi's criteria of non-violence. Whatever justification there is for direct action to alleviate an unjust situation or redress an acknowledged wrong, that evil would remain.

Of course the victim always has the presumption of innocence on his side, and the first claim to moral approval and support—but only for the moment and only relatively to the present unjust circumstances in which he is the "victim".

Gandhi is correct in maintaining the severity of his ideal to keep moral perception clear, whatever may be the decision on morally justifiable action. But appeals and methods on a wide spectrum are required to give the assessment of necessity a demonstrated content. Injustice and harm cannot be wished away or their effects undone. But short of war, sincere will to make amends and reparation may well excite in the abused party benevolence and forgiveness sufficient to cancel claims and to redefine the "justice" sought in the flexible human terms of effort and sincerity rather than moral and absolute or mathematical ones of exact material compensations.

The problem of non-violence is not peace as Gandhi argues, but justice.

Because of his overemphasis on the external aspect of the moral (by the prescription of moral convertibility of substance and appearance, ends and means), Gandhi makes life the highest value. This places a premium on a symptom rather than on the causes of the distemper.

Besides, as we noted, there are things one would die for, and Gandhi many times undertook a fast unto death. He thought the essence of *ahiṁsā* to be voluntary choice of dignified death — the only human answer to the insolent and inhumane demand for submission and servility.[211]

It is part of everyone's experience that there are things without which life would be rendered more than meaningless — a burden or a positive evil.

It is a separate question whether one can at the critical moment live up to one's values and self-expectations. But it is nearly universal human experience that often men respond as moral heros, and nobly, even cheerfully, suffer or die for values they had never consciously cultivated or reflected on. This un-self-consciousness almost defines true bravery.

Gandhi writes against superficial pacifist programs denying conscription or calling for mere disarmament:

To refuse to render military service when the particular time arrives is to do the thing after all the time for combating the evil is practically gone. Military service is only a symptom of the disease which is deeper. I suggest to you that those who are not on the register of military service are equally participating in the crime if they support the State otherwise . . .participates in the sin. . .I said to myself during the war that, so long as I ate wheat supported by the army whilst I was doing everything short of being a soldier, it was best for me to enlist in the army and be shot. . .Therefore all those who want to stop military service can do so by withdrawing all cooperation. Refusal of military service is much more superficial than non-co-operation with the whole system which supports the State. But then one's opposition becomes so swift and so effective. . .[212]

Satyāgrahic non-violence is conceived as a practical moral instrument. It aims at achieving tangible, predictable, moral practical results and must therefore look for real causes.

Gandhi writes, "all activity for stopping war must prove fruitless so long as the causes of war are not understood and radically dealt with.

Is not the prime cause of modern wars the inhuman race for exploitation of the so-called weaker races of the earth?"[213]

It has been noted that Gandhi considers justice the condition of non-violence. He writes that the present ". . .war is showing the futility of violence" to establish justice. Should Hitler win, another, larger war is inevitable. But also, "Supposing the Allies are victorious, the world will fare no better. They will be more polite but not less ruthless, unless they learn the lesson of non-violence during the war and unless they shed the gains they have made through violence. *The first condition of non-violence is justice all round in every department of life.*"[214]

The terrorism that was rife in his time, and that is more widespread today, has its roots in territorial, ethnic and economic domination, oppression and exploitation. Even when these are not its direct causes in particular cases they provide the covering justification. Gandhi noted that colonialism and neo-colonialism are but armed robbery, and "War is a respectable term for goondaism practiced on a mass or national scale."[215] Peace treaties concluded after these conflicts only document the split of the spoils.

Such war aims, victory and treaty, only sow the seed of future uprisings by those still oppressed. They initiate competition and nurture malice among the victors.

Gandhi notes,

> During the War of 1914–18 the declared war aims were the preservation of democracy, self-determination, and the freedom of small nations, and yet the very governments which solemnly proclaimed these aims entered into secret treaties embodying imperialist designs for the carving up of the Ottoman Empire. . .While stating that they did not want any acquisition of territory, the victorious Powers added largely to their colonial domains. The present European war itself signifies the abject failure of the Treaty of Versailles and of its makers, who broke their pledged word and imposed an imperialist peace on the defeated nations.[216]

Gandhi calls exploitation the "essence of violence".[217] Gandhi writes that "I have no doubt that unless the big nations shed their desire of exploitation and the spirit of violence of which war is the natural expression and atom bomb the inevitable consequence, there is no hope for peace in the world."[218]

Gandhi calls peace based on force and suppression a "peace of the grave."[219] He considered mass rioting in resurgent India better than the morally stagnant, debilitating and unnatural condition that had prevailed in its recent colonial period. And he believed that in peace based on superior force, the hatred and bitterness could only go deeper, with the eventual violence all the more vehement and vile.[220]

Peace is a definite state, but justice is almost by definition a matter of balances. In the question of justice one is free to ask which means, violent or non-violent, will in the given case be most likely to overwhelm evil, undermine it or actively defuse it. If the resultant really is justice, then the oppression half of the problem of peace is solved.

It is Gandhi's overemphasis on the outer form of action and resultant that leads him to reversing the formula; he makes peace the condition of justice rather than justice the condition of peace.

If justice is worth dying for then killing for it is a greater value than peace.

The ideal peace and justice would mean an awake fellow-feeling and mutuality which needs only pure non-violent means to readily correct discovered imbalances. But the ideal does not exist in a vacuum and need not be "pure" in the sense of isolation as Gandhi takes it. Limited realization is not a defect.

What does one do in the complex given political reality?

Gandhi makes of the maxim, "Render unto Caesar what is Caesar's," a pacifist's weapon of non-violence—give to surfeit in order to disarm.

Unless one attaches Gandhi's ideological interpretation of non-violent non-cooperation, this maxim is a counsel of pure practical non-resistance. One tactically maintains a low profile and gives what is required to reach the balance represented by common sense and the *prima facie* criteria. Life should go on non-violently until an unconscionable and unavoidable limit is reached.

Complicity with evil through compromise with the State is not the simple evil thing that Gandhi asserts. It does not unconditionally obligate all to dissociation and non-cooperation. Duty is something deeper and more complex, having reference to the wider spiritual reality and growth, not merely the moral.

But at the level of tactics the obligation is questionable. To Gandhi the ever-active evil principle requires ever-active striving against it.

But it is precisely this direct engagement upon which evil thrives and which would drain all but the staunchest ideological upholder of non-violence.

Gandhi equates action with evil and arrives at a pervasive moral asceticism. This is insupportable by any but the most advanced of moral practitioners.

B. OPERATIVE CORE

Critique of Gandhi's Analysis of the Operative Core of All Struggle for Justice and Truth:　　With Gandhi it can be said that the operative core of all struggle for Truth and justice is self-sacrifice and renunciation or self-purification.[221]

But this needn't bear the puritan and ascetic interpretation that Gandhi gives them. His refined and forceful puritanism leads him to a wrong theory of *karma*, a fundamentally punitive and "miserly" theory of reality that is sparse and ungiving.

Gandhi's entire translation in the practical sphere, of non-violence as non-exploitation, rests on the proposition that ". . .the Divine Law . . .gives to man from day to day his daily bread and no more,"[222]— exactly the opposite of the conception of God and reality as creative and abundant, full and gracious.

Also, though Gandhi believes in an all good, loving and gracious God, his theory identifies divinity with law and law with punishment. In the logic of Gandhi's concepts God figures as a punitive meter of just deserts, and "just" has a hard negative tone. One must beware what one sows because one will have to reap its consequences, or one should not complain because one is only receiving the fruits of one's own actions. These are negative readings of moral and practical law connecting action and reaction, fruits and actions, as if on a business ledger.

Contrary to this reading it may be asserted that desire and joy are not evil in themselves. Only the ill will, gross negligence and gross dereliction of duty constitute evil because of the needless harm they inflict. These clear evils *in fact* produce more pain than joy. They *in fact* are self-defeating (against reason, common sense and simple delight). And because of these *facts* one is cautioned against them.

Theologically, the implication should be a God who is wrathful and punishes. Being constantly in a state of sin, one is constantly under penalty of punishment and of liability to transmigrate in order to receive the fruits of one's actions to pay the penalty of sin.

But the Upaniṣads make joy and bliss of existence and creation the basis of life. The *abhiniveśa* (tenacity to life survival, will to live) of Patañjali that Gandhi interprets as a fundamental selfishness and violence, the radical source of sin, points rather to joyous and precious empirical existence and embodiment—or why would all so tenaciously refuse to give it up? The suffering aspect must not be the reality that really moves one. That is the exception; and the result is then not "clinging to life" but clearly the reverse—suicide.

Gandhi's analysis puts emphasis and weight on suffering that the facts do not merit.

A loving critic summed up this aspect of Gandhi and said simply that "Gandhiji is allergic to pleasure."

Need the theory be accepted if the conclusion seems so plainly to contradict the facts? It is on such a contradictory theory that Gandhi believes violence can be ruled out even for extreme cases of evil and injustice. But can violence be absolutely ruled out by a theory that is invalid *a priori* in its evaluations of life and existence, upon which its concepts, aims and methods are founded?

To common sense there seems nothing intrinsically wrong with enjoyment on the one hand, or killing on the other. One may be called upon to renounce possessions and consumption in non-violent methods, to kill in violent methods—both in defense of justice, protection of the weak and redress and reparation of wrong; and one may enjoy the fruits of a just life. The struggle needn't constantly be sought out and "Caesar" constantly challenged.

Gandhi's negative valuation of life and consequent determination that the aim of life is its negation in a supra-empirical concept of liberation and salvation, *mokṣa*, and his negative conception of the conditions of spiritual growth as a process of moral austerity, all overemphasize evil and its evasion.

Finally, does not the human respond more readily to joy rather than the call to suffering?

Suffering of non-violence may make its deep appeal to the human moral consciousness, its nobility and dignity; but joy of existence, of fullness of being and activity, even in the form of war and fight for noble causes, makes its effective appeal also. This experience has been known often to go deeper and to sober and inspire more even than moral suffering.

There is no *a priori* way to rule out either nobility of suffering or joy of action as the appropriate and effective inspiration in any given case. Only on the basis of such an unbalanced and skewed view, as represented in Gandhi's radical claim and morally purist ideology, can one make sense of the proposition that "it is not right to kill evil but it is right to kill yourself instead."

Though Gandhi's aim is the salvation of all, his fundamental method of non-violence must be seen *de facto* to counsel and achieve only personal purity and salvation.

Thus a wrong theory of action (*karma*), of divine inspiration and of liberation leads to a wrong theory of moral and practical political responsibility and reform, and to the unbalanced methods of putatively practicable, but presently untenable, mass asceticism.

The operative core common to all struggle for Truth and justice need not have the exclusively ascetic orientation and puritanistic basis that Gandhi makes its prerequisite.

C. TRUTH AND PRACTICE

Gandhi is correct that in deriving and applying practical moral methods the first requisite is Truth—what exists and how it works.

The objective analysis of reality must precede all ideology, praxis and practice. But it is evident that Gandhi does not realize in his ideology and methods the objective ideal of Truth that he sincerely avowed, and that is called for in practical ethics.

Practicability and practical efficacy are essential and not ancillary aspects of moral inquiry. Here it is asked: How do Gandhi's ideology and inquiry answer to these criteria of Truth and practice? How far is it a valid (practical and scientific) translation of the moral principles of sacrifice and renunciation? Where do his methods stand both in practice and in his own estimate? How does his work structure the new debate on the justifiability and use of violence?

Inadequacy of Ideology: If the ideal of objective Truth is to guide inquiry, then categorical realities having fixed status and implications
within a given ideological framework must be respected and must be
tested in their own right independently of the ideological parameters
that are brought to interpret them. They must be examined as they
function in experience, common sense and ordinary reflective consciousness, if inquiry is to progressively realize Truth in the practical
sphere.

Gandhi fully acknowledges his failure to realize the true method of
non-violence, and the full practical program to which he aspired. His
own failure, as its originator and most accurate and intense practicant
and investigator, is the best argument against the radical viability and
practicability that he claimed for his ideology and praxis.

Gandhi is unlikely to have an equal in his experiments, and "1,000
years hence" he will scarce be believed to have walked this earth, as
Einstein is often quoted about him. It is almost impossible to imagine
an equal, much less a more thorough effort.

Gandhi's "practical idealism" of non-violence is an intense but limited investigation of the practical potential of only one ideal conception. Any such ideology can open only one aperture on the moral reality and the nature of moral, practical action—the reaction of these
under practice in accord with its leading ideal.

Great as Gandhi's application was, it had these inherent limitations
of the ideological inquiry, and it too fixed on its own terms and ex-
plored only the scope of its own practical concept.

It must not be missed that the greatness of Gandhi's philosophy and
methods of non-violent action is largely the result of the greatness, the
extensity, of his application and exploration of it. Its proper study
must be as much a matter of hagiography as of logical and technical
investigation.

The vastness of Gandhi's efforts and results with the general moral
commitment to non-violence and aspiration to peace is itself a certifi-
cate of the work's value. Even its failure in its extreme form and effort
has the character of a success. But the failure is assured by the self-
limiting nature of the mode of analysis and experiment employed.

Limit of Gandhi's Self-Evaluations: Admission of Failure Also Needs

Analysis and Qualification. Gandhi's self-evaluations are significant on this point.

The last two years of his life Gandhi tried to face massive inter-religious and fraternal violence with his techniques of non-violence in Noakhali, Calcutta and Delhi. Without a study of historical records and firsthand accounts, it is hard to grasp the magnitudes of the violence and to gauge the dimensions of his efforts and comparative success.

Gandhi's own assessment of these campaigns was failure of his technique and insufficiency of his own spiritual evolution and purity (innocence) measured in terms of *ahiṁsā*. Applied to the problem of criteria and mass application, he writes, "that art of true self-defense by means of which man gained his life by losing it, had been mastered and exemplified in the history of individuals. The method had not been perfected for application by large masses of mankind and India's *satyāgraha* was a very imperfect experiment in that direction. Hence, during the Hindu-Muslim quarrel it proved a failure on the whole."[223]

In one of his last self-evaluations, Gandhi writes, "Whatever I have said does not refer in any way to the failure of *Ahiṁsā*, but it refers to my failure to recognize, until it was too late, that what I had mistaken for *Ahiṁsā* was not *Ahiṁsā* but passive resistance of the weak, which can never be called *Ahiṁsā* even in the remotest sense . . . the proper way to view the present outburst of violence throughout the world is to recognize that the technique of unconquerable non-violence of the strong has not been at all finally discovered as yet."[224]

In spite of his extraordinary concept and the enormous thought and work he applied to give it substance, Gandhi could not help but find it to fail in the end because the claim he sought to vindicate was *ab initio* false; a limitless claim about limited reality is impossible to support.

An empirical test of an ideology provides a powerful tool for exploring a certain moral point of view and basis of action, but it *cannot* test the interpretive framework that it presupposes in every self-evaluation.

If Gandhi's own austerity (*tapas*) of *ahiṁsā* and asceticism of his *satyāgraha* way of life and social action could not succeed as projected, there seems little reason to think that the mass application of his methods is a tenable, practical position.

Paradoxically, Gandhi acknowledges that violence and evil have equal place in God's plan and that God kept him blinded to the violence in his own mass application of *satyāgraha*. He confessed he had "all along laboured under an illusion. But he was never sorry for it. He realized that if his vision were not covered by that illusion, India would never have reached the point which it had today."[225]

This is tantamount to admitting that in fact moral progress proceeds by means of violence as well as non-violence as a practical rule. This directly contradicts the absolute prescription and proscriptive force of Gandhi's ideological claims and injunction.

It is concluded that as a general analysis of the working of moral consciousness and of the general commitment to non-violence in practical action, Gandhi's *ahiṁsā* and *satyāgraha* are a valid and important contribution to the philosophy and practice of non-violence—for their clarity, thoroughness and range of real application and cases.

However, the same clarity, intensity and vigor in its absolute and universal application, respecting no limitations, render it invalid so far as these radical aspects are allowed to distort the theory and application as a whole.

Gandhi's work fails on both logical and practical grounds to prove its practical claim and to make good its absolute case against the justifiability of violence.

The critical question now becomes what is the role of Gandhi's philosophy in that debate and what is its relevance for present, moral-political practice?

Gandhi's basically sound and generally applicable analysis should be rendered a powerful, practical aid once its limitations are recognized. The practicant may assume that not ideal purity, but the need and aim in the total situation and the total projected outcome, must determine the correct action.

"Correct action" is constituted simply by judicious and intelligent use of the forces at one's disposal. "Intelligent use" is that acknowledged by common sense—balanced, objective, based on clear perception, reasonable, geared to the aim and given context, independent of *a priori* limitations, and having adequate theoretic perspective, knowledge and analytic acumen.

Nuclear Context: The new debate on the justifiability and use of violence and practical uses of non-violence is set by both the advent of nuclear arms and the advent of Gandhi's *satyāgraha*.

The atom bomb and the new generations of other mass-destruction weaponry make direct engagement with evil and old methods of direct revolution on a popular scale obsolete. Local insurgency may go on, but anything on a larger scale, or in strategic positions (e.g. Palestine and South Africa), has direct implications for the nuclear powers. But for the balance and deterrent fear among them, their nuclear self-annihilation, from even minor misreadings of intent and resolve—or of a faulty surveillance system, is a strong possibility—some say inevitability.

All conflict must be seen in the light of escalation to nuclear conflagration, mostly an unthinkable event. However, the magnitude and *sui generis* moral dimension of these powers, and scenarios of such an escalation, raises the issues of peace and conflict with a new vividness, force and urgency. This debate is further sharpened by the contrast with Gandhi's non-violence, his own example against the British Rāj and his work in South Africa, and by efforts of proponents in various parts of the world—notably Nehru in his non-alignment movement, Martin Luther King's civil rights movements in the United States and various South African congresses in coalition campaigns against apartheid.

Gandhi's *satyāgraha* has been the chief resource in studies of non-violent change, conflict resolution and the new branch of sociology, peace science (irenology).

It may be found by future historians that Gandhi's ideas of and faith in his practical non-violence have forestalled nuclear confrontation by the stark contrast they give to atomic warfare and the hope they offer to emerging peoples and nations who might otherwise have precipitously or more concertedly engaged oppressive powers with violent means where the net effect might have been rapid nuclear escalation—weak peoples or sectors of larger nations also have then a means of engagement.

Plural Nations and Histories: But it seems that violence cannot be
ruled out in today's world where the current is so manifestly towards
decolonization, self-determination, freedom and self-development,
and where rife injustice is no longer tolerable. The aim and moral
thrust of historical and social forces seem to be justice and freedom.
There has been in this century a swelling refusal on the part of smaller
nations to accept the oppressive debilitating peace of the *status quo*.
The proclaimed aim is also evolution of a "family of nations" as an
"organic unit", where only non-violent methods are naturally and reasonably chosen to adjust claims, as between states within a nation.

But though the *aim* is an ideal community of nations, the *starting
place* is a complex plurality of peoples, histories, and aspirations, and
a conflicting array of claims rising out of the unchastened plurality
that has not yet found its equilibrium. What will work to gain justice
and freedom? There are many perceptions and claims, none wholly
true and none purely justified, yet all largely valid also. There are great
bulwarks of historical inertia to overcome.

The question is not so much the final empirical form that the ideal
may take but how best to struggle towards that ideal without destroying the conditions of its manifestation and operation by a choice of invalid means. What will work in a factually fractured, plural world
where this organic sense of cooperation is the exception, and exists
only within nation-states, not between them; when materialism is the
ruling outlook, and its natural concommitants of greed and competition the ruling international motives—for both haves and have-nots?
What means can be used where the established oppressive and exploiting states have the monopoly on police technology and non-nu-
clear military power?

The question must be what, in such a world, will move humanity,
and each nation's humanity, towards the goals of justice and freedom?
If there is no automatic universal, non-violent method always available and *a priori* guaranteed to succeed in realizing justice and freedom regardless of material circumstances as Gandhi claimed, and if
the fight must progress somehow (if the world socio-economic situation is admittedly intolerable on any moral reading), then there must
be some other way than the restricted choice of either purely violent
weaponry or Gandhian non-violence—plural methods, not chosen

through any monolithic value system and adapted to specific situations and occasion.

Violent methods must be equally acceptable when, to their sincere practicants, intelligent use seems justified. Tolerance of all methods to advance the historical current is a natural corollary to the new debate.

This intelligent use of force implies the same careful regard for Truth in both violence and in non-violence as Gandhi required for *ahiṁsā* and *satyāgraha*. By the previous analysis, the truth would seem to be that non-violence is not the weapon of the strong in Gandhi's sense; that was the weapon of a Gandhi. As a technique it must be regarded as a weapon of the materially weak. Gandhi may have wielded that weapon with the extraordinary strength derived from his own spiritual resources, but generally, as a socio-political technique, it is a *strategic instrument* whose effective operation varies with the degree of soul-force or moral strength brought to bear by the individual presiding over its use. Soul-force has its necessary place in the fight for justice. But it is not the universal, spiritual weapon Gandhi conceived it to be.

Gandhi must be considered the individual and initiatory force behind his techniques and campaigns. The forces released by use of the technique must be carefully distinguished from those conferred by the presiding practicant and also from those released by the method when used by such an individually inspired force. It is the personal factor, the extraordinary access to supra-phenomenal force, and the will and wisdom to apply it in practical terms, that gave his methods the potency witnessed. Analysis of his methods and practice, as such, must be accurate, must proceed with this acknowledgement.

It is common knowledge that at the Calcutta and Delhi riots of 1947–48, Gandhi's mere presence had the electric and stilling effect that he had claimed was the final criterion of the active working of the force of *ahiṁsā*—"Enmity vanished in his neighborhood,"[226] and shooting stopped wherever he passed by. His presence stilled large crowds.

It need not be denied that superior force can be drawn upon and brought to bear on material reality in manifestly moral and practical terms. But the ultimate limiting factor is always there in the nature of the medium through which that force must act to express the ideal of the agent of that force.

Analysis of Gandhi's methods, and practice meant to follow his lead, both fail to achieve his results because of inappropriate or inadequate empirical analysis. Empirical or scientific analysis generally fails to take into account the factor of personality and hagiography. The spiritual and moral facts cannot be discounted from the total problem any more than the empirical ones. Gandhi's work has given ample justification for study in these directions.

What methods are finally enlisted is a matter of intelligent study and decision.

Some advocates of violence claim it necessary to awaken the really oppressed from an inertia and irresponsive torpor.

But violence also does not always work either. Gandhi did awaken India with non-violent means. That India did not retain the impetus and momentum only verifies the importance of the presiding personality in such methods. That the methods do work under given person-oriented conditions is a practical fact like any other.

On the other hand, it is a question whether even Gandhi's non-violence could have removed British colonial rule except for Hitler's violence and the momentum of historical trends. It is difficult to imagine non-violence, even with such as Gandhi leading, working today in South Africa, just as it was repeatedly questioned how a Gandhi could do anything to overcome the evil of a Hitler. In a plural world such as ours, all these forces seem to work only in combination—not necessarily a rationally analyzable combination.

Disarmament and Conversion of the Heart: Localized conflict, however approached, exists against the background of the large nuclear dilemma, the pervasive materialistic value system and surging technological advance. Can unilateral disarmament solve that dilemma? No, because if the will is there (motive to dominate and accumulate, hegemony and greed), the arms will be rebuilt or surreptitiously built all along—cyclically dismantled in show of trust, and cyclically reassembled in feigned pique. Error is bound to occur in a world so technologically sophisticated, so morally cavalier and so politically irresponsible and unreflective. The cycles could not be perpetual and the breakthrough could come only by sincere change of heart, accident, or miscalculation inevitable to perception governed by ill will, mistrust and fear.

The moral climate is not such that unilateral show of trust and good faith could be met by its like. Among the superpowers, both sides do not make that move because each really does not want to give up its will to world-domination, material or ideological—the latter perhaps the more subversive, whether by feigned democracy or feigned communism, feigned capitalism or feigned socialism, all abused in the interests of feigned nationalism. All sides recognize their image in the others and see behind this feigning behavior the real intent and motive forces. Sincerity and Truth stand out in this climate, as did Gandhi's. A slight shift in the adversary posture is the more noticeable.

Negotiation in such a climate and among such adversaries is only a "gamble" to win without paying even the price of honest war. Its mechanism is deceit and shrewdness, so its operative principles are untruth and violence. It is hard to understand how Gandhi could conceive the conversion of this willfully demonic (glorified and magnified ego in the guise of national interests) posturing and manipulating or gaming, by means of unilateral application of just the principle that all other sides hope to prey upon.

Where there is no real basis for moral regret there is no leverage for moral force. Unless possessed of Gandhi's faith in the force and truth of an opposing moral ideology there is no point arguing for unilateralism aside from naiveté or deceit and ploy. Unilateralism would invite attack because the real will and motive is to win, not to settle justly and amicably.

The *chief cause* of unrest and lack of peace is injustice and exploitation, taking without paying; of these, greed; of this, the materialist outlook and value system.

Gandhi was correct in his last assessments that the solution must lie with the individual. Only if greed is eradicated from the heart and mind can there be naturally that organic unity and family relations and feelings among masses and nations of men.

Unilateralism is in that context not a mere principle, technique or doctrine, but the natural opening move by one side in a negotiation of like-minded parties, faithfully entering a mutual decision procedure. It is not a calculating gamble seeking unearned return at high risk. It is a gesture of good will and surety.

Without this change of heart, will, outlook and values, nuclear disarmament talks can only be either "endless" unto exhaustion of all en-

ergy and resources, or end in mutual suicide. So long as material values and aspirations of aggrandizement and hegemony govern human
relations, so long will "today's" local revolutionaries continue to be
tomorrow's reactionaries.

The change of heart, outlook and values itself requires opening to
and receiving from a source of satisfaction and fulfillment that is not
hostage to the transient phenomenal conditions and necessarily limited and unpossessable materials. This is what Gandhi refers to as the
necessity to recognize the permanent element in oneself, recognition of
which itself is a delight and quenching that cannot be accomplished by
the self-re-stimulating sense and mental life.

The real peace, that which is substantive and effective, which creates that external climate in which negotiation and unilateralism become effective gestures and procedures, is an inner state and modulation of the subjective being. Being itself fulfillment, it does not seek
and exploit or harm for gain. Rather it gives by nature because its reality is wider than that of empirical individuality, and because relative to
material nature, its nature and activity are abundance and accommodation. This feeling and fullness alone can create the true, just conditions in which external peace is possible — and negotiation and unilateralism and disarmament meaningful. If the aim of all powers
involved is external claim of right to possession and domination, there
can be no justice, no real peace. How to pursue that aim in the midst
of unrest and in the effort to surmount possession and domination is
the question of the new debate.

On this reading, Gandhi's radical claim commends what must be
pointless suicide. It cannot be the noble and generous death or self-
immolation that is ultimately justified by its practical efficacy. Without the actual efficacious resultant, the noble must look foolish and
the virtuous just full of bravado. As a personal act, if it is authentic,
the suicide may lead to personal salvation. But as an element in the
practical social ethic that Gandhi's claim is meant to realize, self-immolation of *satyāgraha* may often be a mistake, and often a positive
harm to the cause one wants to build up.

Individual salvation correctly is not the point. But individual realization is a large and fundamental part of the solution. Social wisdom
and practical accuracy are required rather than ideological commitment; and individual responsibility, decision and action are finally the
point and the means. Means, in a situation that is too complex to be

comprehended in any ideology, too rich to be accurately depicted in black and white dichotomies, must be determined in full cognizance of and humility before the fact that no simple rule or conceptual reduction can do justice to the reality faced and the action and commitment required.

Whichever method is decided on as the intelligent choice—the one according best with the historical current towards justice and liberty, the one matching the corrigibility or its lack in the opponent, the one respecting the state and history of the oppressed (as also that of the oppressor who also has his point and his truth), the one respecting and building on one's own evolutionary stage, spiritual status, socio-economic role, and present state—Gandhi is correct in that mass methods have their dramatic appeal and large effects, but that their basis and purpose is always the individual's conversion, purification, training, preparation and growth. The basis of intelligent struggle, violent or non-violent, is the purification of *one's own* heart and mind of greed, anger and hate, i.e. ego and desire, attachment and aversion, attraction and repulsion. Gandhi is correct that this has its practical, just as its spiritual and moral, bearing and aim.

The objectivity necessary for any practical endeavor, and more so for moral struggle, is impossible if clarity, balance, and authenticity are not there. It is the distorted and highly modulated subjective states of greed, anger and hate that destroy inner peace and objectivity. It should be noted again that common to both violent and non-violent struggle are the self-sacrifice and renunciation or purification Gandhi required of the *satyāgrahī*.

Non-violent methods especially, require patience, detachment, non-possession and willingness to suffer, not merely to convert the opponent as a spiritual principle, as Gandhi believed, but simply as a practical matter to outlast the evil whose will is attached to desire and circumstance more transient and less sustaining than motivation by the higher ideals of justice and freedom that sustain the oppressed in his struggle.

Sacrifice and renunciation are the operative factors in all struggle, material as well as moral and spiritual, because what one wants determines the dimensions and particulars of what will be given up and what suffering sustained to achieve one's objective.

Adapting Non-violence: The efficacy of Gandhi's non-violent non-   /247
cooperation and civil disobedience needn't be underestimated. In principle there is no reason why such large and complex state mechanisms
as the USSR and the US should not succumb if adequately paralyzed
from within. But this is not a problem of soul-force. It is a problem of
material reality and strategy.

It may equally be said that without soul-force being active in the
people such corporate renunciation is unlikely. What would replace
the joys given up and where would strength come from to sustain the
suffering implied in the renunciation required by the methods—
whether used on spiritual principle or principles of practical strategy?
This is a problem for experimental non-violence and historical and social studies of a deep and specific kind to discover: What spiritual and
moral resources may be tapped by a given population and how, in a
given circumstance and historical context?

Gandhi suggested the non-violent method to Europe for "deliver-
ance" of its masses.

Asked how the masses exploited by the ruling classes might use
non-violent methods to attain justice, Gandhi replied specifically to
the European circumstances:

> Violence on the part of the masses will never remove the disease. . .
> sooner or later the European masses will have to take to non-violence, if
> they are to find their deliverance. . .someone has to make a beginning
> with a faith that will not flinch. I doubt not that the masses, even of Eu-
> rope, will respond, but what is more emergent in point of time is not so
> much a large experiment in non-violence as a precise grasp of the mean-
> ing of deliverance. From what will the masses be delivered? It will not
> do to have a vague generalization and to answer: 'from exploitation and
> degradation'. Is not the answer this that they want to occupy the status
> that capital does today? If so, it can be attained only by violence. But if
> they want to shun the evils of capital, in other words, if they would re-
> vise the viewpoint of capital, then they would strive to attain a juster
> distribution of the products of labour. This immediately takes us to con-
> tentment and simplicity, voluntarily adopted. Under the new outlook
> multiplicity of material wants will not be the aim of life, the aim will
> be rather their restriction consistently with comfort. We shall cease to
> think of getting what we can, but we shall decline to receive what all
> cannot get. It occurs to me that it ought not to be difficult to make a

successful appeal to the masses of Europe in terms of economics, and a fairly successful working of such an experiment must lead to immense and unconscious spiritual results. I do not believe that the spiritual law works on a field of its own. On the contrary, it expresses itself only through the ordinary activities of life. It thus affects the economic, the social and the political fields. If the masses of Europe can be persuaded to adopt the view I have suggested, it will be found that violence will be wholly unnecessary to attain the aim, and that they can easily come into their own by following out the obvious corollaries of non-violence. It may even be that what seems to me to be so natural and feasible for India may take longer to permeate the inert Indian masses than the active European.[227]

Gandhi writes that in methods of non-violence, generally, "the policy would vary with different countries, but sacrifice and self-denial are the essential points."[228]

Gandhi gives the scientific evidence of the potency of congregational chanting of the Name of Rāma—not a difficult efficacy to understand for gaining corporate strength and power. One can see the same essential spiritual character exhibited (in a far less refined form) in the contemporary rock concert. He advocated "simple living and high thinking", for hygiene and health reasons as also for strategic reasons—to have one less point of leverage for the exploiting powers to gain power through. This translates easily to the rising environmental movements for simplifying life, returning to natural foods, cooking one's own meals, natural shelter and clothing, minimal furniture and technological independence.

These are signs of a bloated material culture feeling the need to look deeper and to free itself of reliances that are not only unhealthy but the mechanisms of mass subjugation on an unheard-of scale and of terrible subtlety.

Renunciation as mass non-consumerism would be a contemporary translation of Gandhi's non-cooperation and economic boycott. Choice of a consistent life-routine based on values not susceptible to market pressures and marketing manipulations, adopted and sustained against consumer indoctrination, is itself a manner of spiritual or moral battle, translating the principles of self-sacrifice, purification and renunciation. But these are hardly felt as renunciation when there is recognition of the material dependence, subservience and supportless non-routine, that are "renounced" simply as a consequence of

adopting some healthier, saner, stronger, clearer, more life-giving /249
modes and values of life. One has been and is constantly being conditioned to believe there would be a great loss in this simple return to
sane and healthy life.

The chief need is to realize the non-identity of evil and violence, the
focal point of all questions of means in this debate and to remember
that the main problem is inner growth.

The larger social methods must accord first with these demands. In
these terms, does non-violence of the extreme form represented in
Gandhi's practical claim interfere by requiring too much attention to
outer purity and technique, presenting a heteronomous "goodness" as
the aim rather than realization of self and spirit? Gandhi *in fact*, however, never lost sight of this aim and requirement.

The success of any of these means therefore will not be the organi-
zation structures or corporate fashions they instigate, but the effect of
these on the individual in substantially changing his vision and values
and his way of living and relating.

Any mass methods may at times be antagonistic to this aim if they
prove to be only further "trends" and "diversions". Only if the main
aim is kept clear can the main basis be worked towards, the individual—that strength of character, potency and clarity of love that are
necessary to recognize the Truth of complex claims of justice, to gra-
ciously accommodate and adjust oneself to them in personal and corporate life, and, if necessary, to maintain them in the midst of the
fight.

Whether one has chosen the non-violent means of direct resistance
or violent means of forceful attack, it is necessary to see clearly in the
midst of the fight when the opposite means may be required.

Gandhi's *sādhana* of non-violence is one such preparation and
cleansing of moral and practical consciousness. Its application in daily
life and domestic relations is the moral prerequisite for developing
that non-retaliatory, non-hating moral consciousness and spiritual
poise that is capable of sustaining Love and Truth in either method.

Gandhi stresses this point:

Last week I wrote about three fields for the operation of *Ahiṁsā*
(against illegitimate constituted authority, to quell communal dissen-
sions, and to meet external aggression). I propose to invite attention today to the fourth and the best field for the operation of non-violence.

This is the family field, in a wider sense than the ordinary. The members of an institution should be regarded as a family. Non-violence between members of such families should be easy to practice. If that fails, it means that we have not developed the capacity for pure non-violence. For the love we have to practice towards our relatives and colleagues in our family or institution, we have to practice towards our foes, dacoits, etc. If we fail in one case, success in the other is a chimera.

We have generally assumed that, though it may not be possible to exercise non-violence in the domestic field, it is possible to do so in the political fields. This has proved a pure delusion. We have chosen to describe our methods adopted so far as non-violence, and thus caricatured non-violence itself. If non-violence it was, it was such poor stuff that it proved useless at the critical moment. The alphabet of *Ahiṁsā* is best learnt in the domestic school, and I can say from experience that, if we secure success there, we are sure to do so everywhere. For a non-violent person the whole world is one family.[229]

This last is a reiteration of the chief difficulty in Gandhian studies. His assumption that such a morally desirable and seemingly unexceptional state of affairs exists—that success is easy "there" in the family, and, therefore, everywhere, if *ex hypothesi* all is one family. But it *is not* easy in the family, and the oneness in the world cannot be familial until it is an effective reality in the primary family. This is all a matter still to be evolved and not the "matter of fact" state of things, '. . .if only we would.' There appears to be an historical distance to be covered before that stage is a factual reality. We can, of course, work towards this wider family ideal now, in our own lives and relations.

With regard to the path through that historical distance, the problem of means, Gandhi writes further:

I have not concentrated upon it [the question of developing pure *ahiṁsā* of the strong, the domestic and basic *ahiṁsā*], or given it the weight I might have. This was all right while I was devoting all my energy to forging means to give battle to the government. But it had the result of retarding the growth of pure *Ahiṁsā* of the strong. If we now want to advance further, we ought at least for some time, to completely forget the idea of offering non-violent resistance to constituted authority. If non-violence in the domestic field is successfully achieved, we shall surely see the non-violence against constituted authority revived in its purified form, and it will be irresistible. . .those who may want to join the non-violent force of my conception should not entertain any immediate prospect of civil disobedience. They should understand that,

so long as they have not realized *Ahiṁsā* in their own person in its pure
form, there can be no civil disobedience for them.[230]

When peace is in a substantial majority of hearts, then the organic unity of family life will be the natural mode of institutional and international interaction, and non-violence and public opinion will operate as Gandhi has prophesied—as gentle loving prods to momentarily obstinate or blind but willing conscience and intent. In this sense Gandhi is more a visionary and forerunner of an ideal state than the model for contemporary practical reform. His work will likely be found to have greatly accelerated the advent of that ideal state and given its basic shape. But until then Gandhi's methods and example must be objects of empirical study and of spiritual study, for how in fact they may best work as weapons of the weak in the overall struggle for Justice.

As often is the case in socio-political-moral debate, the end sought is not open to much objection. The problem is of means and the route traveled to reach it. Gandhi's position is abundantly clear. Only it must be balanced.

For the present and for the purpose of this study, it is important to remember that the choice and use of means must be objective, not biased by ideological presentiments of any sort, if that state is to be accurately and effectively pursued. It is nevertheless necessary, while acknowledging that violence is in itself always and positively wrong, to propagate the injunction that if necessary, "Strike with open heart!"

There should be pure tolerance which expresses itself in joy of plurality, even of vital and moral opposition, of all doing as they see fit and timely, with no condescending "allowance" and tacit moral judgment, as is implicit in *programs* for moral heteronomy.

If use of, or non-obstruction of, violence is believed necessary, it must not be unreflectively denied only because of one-sided faith and moral ideology.

As Gandhi rightly insisted, fear too easily misuses this proscription for self-deception. But by parity of reasoning the merely ideological character of this position can be seen, remembered and respectfully balanced. It may be that violence does not necessarily bring more evil into the world. It may be that Love, clarity and Truth, at least non-hate and non-anger, can be maintained while force and violence are resorted to in both love and outrage, and embraced as noble, moral, just and justified means.

By parity of reasoning, so what if there is no historical precedent? It does not matter if it is more difficult of practice than even "pure" non-violence; by parity of reasoning, is it not then more worthy to strive after and in fact morally called for? By parity of reasoning, what does it matter if good and right are always abused and the whole world stands against the choice of means—if conscience, duty and unencumbered reason dictate it?

All of Gandhi's arguments can be exactly countered by their opposite in parity of reasoning so far as they take rhetorical form and express only moral preference.

If violence is not the believed decisive means, and opposing powers too large and unavoidable (nuclear force its all-embracing limit), the way may be *pure* (more strictly so than even Gandhi's) non-resistance—pursuit of simple, straight, independent life, with no confrontation with "Caesar," no fear or guilt at complicity or default in obligations of love—but inheritance of the earth by meekness when strategically the large powers have been left to destroy themselves, as inherent evil in time must, by nuclear suicide.

The role one plays and advocates or propagates in the wider society must be a matter of individual free inquiry, self-examination and responsible choice. The above argument is intended only to clarify the issues that must be faced in making that decision and in pursuing its implications in personal and social life by examining what is acknowledged to be the most intense and far-ranging practical thought and experience in this area—Gandhi's advocacy of absolute non-violence and his mission against the justifiability of all violence. Gandhi's ideal solution embodies the fullest aspiration of the general commitment to non-violence and must be a point of constant reference, if also at times of certain and unregretting departure.

Final Value and Critique: It must be noted that Gandhi's final value is *not* non-violence. Whatever his disclaimer and arguments, he in fact always preferred violence to cowardice—without exception.

Gandhi writes, "I would rather risk violence a thousand times than the emasculation of a whole race."[231]

We have no better indicator of real values than where one feels compelled to draw the line in practical fact, and Gandhi writes that "My nonviolence does not admit of running away from danger and leaving dear ones unprotected. *Between violence and cowardly flight,*

I can only prefer violence to cowardice. I can no more preach non-
violence to a coward than I can tempt a blind man to enjoy healthy
scenes. Nonviolence is the summit of bravery,"[232] and, "Nonviolence cannot be taught to a person who fears to die and has no power
of resistance."[233] He concludes that "I do believe that, *where there is
only a choice between cowardice and violence, I would advise violence.*"[234]

Finally, it should be reiterated that though the position argued for
in the present study is admittedly a reassertion of a widely-held, commonsense one of a general commitment to non-violence which nevertheless can and ought to be set aside when overriding moral considerations require it, still it must again be recognized that Gandhi, by his
absolute views and application, has shown the political importance
and power of non-violence and its practical validity as no one else has.

It must be reiterated that Gandhi is therefore a resource that should
be a constant reference in self-reflection and in debate on these fundamental issues; he should be studied in a way that most illumines the
practical, commonsense position as it is relevant to both the daily life
and the present world political situation of nuclear threat, emergent
national pluralism and the need of complex adjustment where justice
has had no powerful international advocate and little local consti-
tuency.

It is thus important to see how Gandhi's methods and practical success depend upon his metaphysical position, the limits of those views
and methods, when and how they need to be modified for a wider
practical outcome and a more realistic, commonsense political view
and relevance.

To this purpose, it has been necessary to see how inextricably Gandhi's ideological interpretation of his classical metaphysical roots and
fundamental spiritual facts are bound up in his conception of non-
violence, how these *a priorisms* directed and informed his practical application of these ideas in the methods of *satyāgraha*, and how they
affected his personal assessment of his practical success and of the viability of these methods.

Though the conclusions of this book look like only common sense,
they are greatly indebted to Gandhi's metaphysics and ethics, and even
to his ideology. A much richer and more sensitive application of these
conclusions is made possible and fostered by the study of Gandhi's
investigations.

20. Hingorani, . . . *Truth,* pp. 79–80, (*Bapu's Letters to Mira,* p. 268).

21. Mohandas K. Gandhi, *Gītā—My Mother,* ("*Gītā* . . .") Anand T. Hingorani, comp. (Bombay: Bharatiya Vidya Bhavan, 1965), Chapt. X, esp. identity of the "ideal of a *Sthitaprajña*" as a *Satyāgrahī*; p. 70, (H 4/14/46).

22. Hingorani, . . . *Love,* p. 22, (YI 6/24/26).

23. Kher, III, p. 219, (YI 6/8/31; *Anāsaktiyoga,* Intro. to Gandhi's translation and commentary on the Gītā).

24. *Ibid.,* II. p. 54, (YI 24/9/25, p. 327).

25. Kripalani, p. 85, IV:34 (An Autobiography).

26. Kher, II, p. 52, (YI 19/3/25, p. 98).

27. *Ibid.*

28. N.V.:I, p. 268, (H 6/1/40).

29. *Ibid.,* p. 183, (H 24/12/38).

Chapter 2

30. Kher, I, p. 196, ("AOA", Edition 1959, Chapter II).

31. *Bhagavadgītā,* (Gorakhpur: Gita Press, 1968, p. 73).

32. Hingorani, *Gītā.* . . , p. 189, (from the *Gītā Discourses,* YI 1930).

33. *Ibid.*

34. *Ibid.*

35. *Ibid.,* p. 38, (*Diary of Mahadev Desai,* "DMD", p. 105).

36. *Ibid.*

Chapter 3

37. Mohandas K. Gandhi, *An Autobiography: The Story of My Experiments with Truth,* (1st paperback ed.: Boston: Beacon Press, 1957, p. 35).

38. Hingorani, *Gītā.* . . , p. 62, (YI Nov. 12, 1925).

39. *Ibid.,* p. 62.

40. Mohandas K. Gandhi, *The Science of Satyāgraha* (". . . *Satyāgraha*"), Anand T. Hingorani, comp. (3rd ed.; "Pocket Gandhi Series"; Bombay: Bharatiya Vidya Bhavan, 1970), No. 4, pp. 129–30, (H 7/20/47).

41. Hingorani, . . . *Satyāgraha,* p. 28, (YI Nov. 5, 1919).

42. *Ibid.,* p. 122, (H March 31, 1946).

43. *Ibid.,* p. 7, (*Hind Swarāj,* "HS", 1908).

44. Iyer, Raghavan N., *The Moral and Political Thought of Mahatma Gandhi,* (New York: Oxford University Press, 1973), pp. 50–51, (YI Jan. 1920).

45. Kher, II, p. 17, (H Feb. 22, 1942, p. 45 at p. 47).

46. *Ibid.*

47. See *Rāmanāma,* Bharatan Kumarappa, comp. (2nd ed.; Ahmedabad: Navajivan Publishing House, 1949).

48. Letter to Amiya Chakravarty, *A Saint at Work: A View of Gandhi's Work and Message* (pamphlet; William Penn Lecture, 1950; Philadelphia: Young Friends Movement of the Philadelphia Yearly Meeting, 1950, p. 20. Cited: Gene Sharp, *Gandhi as a Political Strategist* (Boston: Porter Sargent Pub., Inc., 1979), p. 110.

49. N.V.:II, p. 327, (H 14/12/47).

Preface

1. Mohandas K. Gandhi, *In Search of the Supreme*, V.B. Kher, comp. (3 vols., 1st ed.; Ahmedabad: The Navajivan Publishing House, 1961); II, p. 36, (*Harijan*, "H" 4/28/46).

PART I

Chapter 1

2. Mohandas K. Gandhi, *The Law of Love*, (". . . *Love*") Anand T. Hingorani, comp. (2nd ed.; "Pocket Gandhi Series"; Bombay: Bharatiya Vidya Bhavan, 1962), No. 3, p. 11, (H 3/14/36).

3. *Ibid.*, p. 69, (H 14/3/36); also, pp. 83-84, (H 5/13/39).

4. Mohandas K. Gandhi, *Non-violence in Peace & War*, Vol. I, Mahadev Desai, comp. Vol. II, Bharatan Kumarappa, comp. (from here on, noted "N.V., I or II"), (2 vols.; Ahmedabad: Navajivan Publishing House, 1942), I, pp. 121–22, (H 14/3/36).

5. This is the basis of Gandhi's philosophy and method of non-retaliation; see Hingorani, . . . *Love*, p. 54, (*Young India*, "YI", 8/12/26), p. 21, (YI 3/9/20), and p. 22, (YI 6/24/26).

6. N.V.:I, p. 107, (YI 30/1/30).

7. See Kher, II, p. 23, (H 13/5/39, p. 121 and p. 122).

8. Hingorani, . . . *Love*, p. 38, (YI 5/21/25).

9. See Kher, II, p. 275, (YI 2/7/25, p. 232).

10. Mohandas K. Gandhi, *God Is Truth*, (". . . *Truth*"), Anand T. Hingorani, comp. (2nd ed.; "Pocket Gandhi Series"; Bombay: Bharatiya Vidya Bhavan, 1962), pp. 4–5 (H 2/22/42).

11. *Ibid.*, p. 5, fn. #1, (YI 6/4/25).

12. See Hingorani, . . . *Love*, pp. 35–39, (YI 5/21/25), and pp. 28–33, (*Āśrama Observances in Action*, "AOA", p. 30).

13. Hingorani, . . . *Truth*, pp. 9–10, (YI 1/21/26).

14. *Ibid.*, p. 9, fn. #1, (*Conversations of Gandhiji*, "COG", p. 37).

15. Kher, II, p. 279, (H 8/29/36, p. 226).

16. *Ibid.*, (*Gandhiji's View of Life*, "GVL", p. 57).

17. See Kher, I, Sections 2 and 3.

18. Kripalani, I:9, p. 52, (YI 10/11/28).

19. *Ibid.*, II:51, p. 62, (An Autobiography).

50. *Ibid.,* I, p. 119, (H 12/10/35).
51. Mohandas K. Gandhi, *The Selected Works of Mahatma Gandhi,* ed. Shriman Narayana, (Vol. 5, *Selected Letters*; Ahmedabad: Navajivan Pub. House, 1968), p. 31, (Col. Works of M.G., V.XIII, pp. 37–39; ltr. to Maganlal Gandhi, 3/14/15).
52. Hingorani, . . . *Satyāgraha,* pp. 29–30, (YI 11/5/19).
53. Mohandas K. Gandhi, *Non-violent Resistance (Satyāgraha),* ed. Bharatan Kumarappa (1st Schocken edn., 1961; New York: Schocken Books, 1961), p. 199, (YI 24/9/25).

Chapter 4

54. Kher, III, p. 86, (H 30/11/47, p. 442 at p. 446).
55. Kher, I, p. 92, (YI 5/1/21, p. 4).
56. *Ibid.,* II, p. 16, (H 27/11/49, p. 340).

PART II
Chapter 5

57. Kripalani, IV:43, p. 87, (YI 3/17/27).
58. *Ibid.,* V:5, p. 99, (YI 7/2/25).
59. *Ibid.,* IV:77, p. 96, (*Mahatma,* "M", V; H 1/13/40).
60. Ellul, Jacques, *Violence: Reflections from a Christian Perspective,* trans. Cecilia Gaul Kings, (New York: The Seabury Press, 1969), p. 6.
61. Hingorani, *Gītā. . . ,* p. 53, (H 1/9/36).
62. Wittner, Lawrence S., *Rebels against War: The American Peace Movement, 1941–1960,* (Contemporary American History Series, Wm. E. Leuchtenburg, gen. ed., New York: Columbia University Press, 1969), pp. 282–83; (in conclusion). . . "by 1960 two fresh developments gave mankind's age-old struggle against war a new perspective—the creation of alternative forms of social conflict and overarching disaster awaiting humanity should it fail to adopt these . . . The new peace movement had begun to develop a political as well as a moral relevance. It sought to grapple in the political arena with two of the most perplexing problems of the twentieth century: how to secure a large measure of justice without betraying human values; and how to avoid the mass slaughter which advances in science and technology portended."
63. N.V.: II, p. 55, (Poona, 3/3/46; H 10/3/46); also, p. 157, (H 7/4/46), and p. 237, (H 20/4/47).
64. See Wittner, pp. 18–19: Pacifists saw horrors of fascism but they saw in modern warfare only its perpetuation under other names; Hitler dead, Hitlerism would continue in the victor's own breast. Ellul makes the "fourth law of violence . . . not a moral judgement . . . but a factual experimental judgement based on experience. Wherever a violent movement has seized power, it has made violence the law of power. The only thing that has changed is the power who exercises violence . . . captured by the very thing it fights. To combat communist propaganda by 'good propaganda' is in fact to fall victim to the psychological violence of the enemy. The violent struggle against racism at first against Hitler's racism . . . has caused the development of racism throughout the world . . . violence can never realize a noble aim, can never create lib-

erty or justice, I repeat once more that the end does not justify the means, that, on the contrary, evil means corrupt good ends!" pp. 101–102.

65. N.V.: II, p. 137, (New Delhi 7/11/47; H 16/11/47).

66. *Ibid.*, p. 90, (H 10/2/46).

67. *Ibid.*, p. 247, (New Delhi, 25/5/47; H 1/6/47).

68. Kripalani, XIII:41, p. 158; "No action which is not voluntary can be called moral. So long as we act like machines, there can be no question of morality. If we want to call an action moral, it should have been done consciously and as a matter of duty. Any action that is dictated by fear or by coercion of any kind ceases to be moral." (*Ethical Religion*, 1930).

69. *Ibid.*, VI:18, p. 111, (H 5/10/36).

70. For an extensive cataloging of types and forms of violence, see Ellul, pp. 97–99, where he makes it a law of violence that every violence is identical with every other violence, and produces the same moral and practical results, brutalization, debility and destruction or harm.

71. Nirmal Kumar Bose, *Selections from Gandhi,* (Ahmedabad: Navajivan Publishing House, 1947), p. 146, #391, YI 5 Nov., 1931. Italics mine. See also: N.V.:II, p. 89, (Simla, 2/5/46; H 12/5/46).

72. Judith M. Brown, *Gandhi and Civil Disobedience: The Mahatma in Indian Politics, 1928–34,* (Cambridge: Cambridge University Press, 1977), pp. 27, 29.

73. N.V.:I, pp. 417–19, (On the train to Wardha, 5/4/42; H 12/4/42).

74. Naess, p. 20; "When judging Gandhi's influence by the standards he himself set for empirical inquiry we must subject it to the same rigorous critical scrutiny that we apply to any piece of social research. But we should note too the enormous complexity of Gandhi's experiments compared with ordinary experiments in say, social psychology. The number of unknown, or insufficiently known quantities is overwhelming; so much so in fact that no conclusion can really claim the title of 'scientific'. Nevertheless, not all worthwhile research need culminate in well-founded scientific conclusions, nor need the unavoidable uncertainty of a conclusion cause us to regret it." Also see Gandhi's disclaimer, N.V.:I, p. 36: "I am in the position of a scientist who is in the midst of a very incomplete experiment and who therefore is unable to forecast large results and large corollaries . . ." (YI 17/9/25). Also, Kher, I, p. 283: "I for one believe that spiritual acts have clearly defined results precisely like combinations or processes in the natural sciences. Only as we have no such means of measurement in the former case as in the latter . . . untruth gets a long lease on life." (AOA, pp. 13–22). See also, Kher, I, p. 313, (H 8/7/33, p.4) on the intangible nature of spiritual results, and Gandhi's repeated allusions to the incalculable factor of faith at the root of *satyāgraha* action.

Chapter 6

75. Ellul, p. 6. His summary is from what he considers the theological view. Actually, Ellul's analysis, similarly to Gandhi's, is ideological, while the theologians actually only modify the commonsense position of fundamental moral experience and judgment.

76. *Ibid.,* pp. 5–6.

77. *The Upanishads,* trans. Max Muller, (The Sacred Books of the East, Vol.
XV, 1879; New York: Dover Publications, 1962), pp. 68–69. It is evident
that here Gandhi is more influenced by Jaina and Christian thought.
78. He makes an exception for spiritual surgery, in which "taking of life" to
relieve the soul of suffering where no other means is possible, is like amputa-
ting a limb to relieve the whole body. Still, the physical result is the ending of
life, which is all that is needed in the present argument.
79. N.V.:II, p. 140, (New Delhi, 2/9/46; H 8/9/46).
80. N.V.:I, p. 265, (Sevagram, 5/12/39; H 9/12/39).
81. See Desai, *The Gita According to Gandhi,* p. 196; comment on IV:8;
also, Hingorani, . . . *Gītā,* p. 152, (DG 8–44; comment on IV:7–8).
82. Hingorani, . . . *Gītā,* p. 30, (YI Dec. 1, 1921).
83. Kher, I, p. 264 (H 11/3/33, p. 2).

Chapter 7
84. N.V.:II, p. 372, (Birla House, New Delhi, 29/1/48; H 8/2/48).
85. *Ibid.,* p. 308, (Birla House, New Delhi, 1/10/47; H 12/10/47).
86. *Ibid.,* p. 308, (Birla House, New Delhi, 29/9/47; H 12/10/47).
87. *Ibid.,* p. 306, (Birla House, New Delhi, 26/9/47; H 5/10/47). Italics mine.
88. *Ibid.,* pp. 306–7.
89. *Ibid.,* pp. 307–8.
90. N.V.:I, p. 135, (H 17/10/36).
91. *Ibid.,* p. 106, (30/1/30).
92. *Ibid.,* pp. 132–33, (H 3/10/36).
93. *Ibid.,* p. 287, (Sevagram, 4/6/40; H 8/6/40); also see, p. 80 (YI 13/9/28).
94. *Ibid.,* p. 171, (26/11/38).
95. *Ibid.,* p. 30, (YI 11/12/24).
96. *Ibid.,* p. 176, (H 10/12/38).
97. *Ibid.,* p. 297, from an open letter "To Every Briton", (New Delhi, 2/7/40;
H 6/7/40). Italics mine.
98. N.V.:II, pp. 92–3, (Poona, 1/7/46; H 7/7/46).
99. *Ibid.,* p. 94, (New Delhi, 24/9/46; H 29/9/46).
100. *Ibid.,* p. 90, (H 10/2/46).
101. *Ibid.,* p. 10, (Sevagram, 9/2/46; H 17/12/46).
102. N.V.:I, p. 78, (YI 13/9/28).
103. *Ibid.,* pp. 53–54, (YI 5/11/25).
104. *Ibid.,* p. 78, (YI 13/9/28).
105. *Ibid.,* pp. 86–7, (YI 7/2/29).
106. *Ibid.,* p. 78, (YI 13/9/28).
107. *Ibid.,* p. 86, (YI 7/2/29).
108. *Ibid.,* p. 92, (YI 7/5/29); also see, p. 80, (YI 13/9/28).
109. *Ibid.,* pp. 76–7, (YI 15/3/28).
110. *Ibid.,* p. 78, (YI 13/9/28).
111. *Ibid.,* p. 77, (YI 15/3/28); also see, p. 74, (YI 8/3/28).
112. *Ibid.,* p. 77, (YI 15/3/18); also see, p. 79, (YI 13/9/28).
113. *Ibid.,* p. 87, (YI 7/2/29); also see, p. 93, (YI 9/5/29).
114. Hingorani, *Gītā* . . . , p. 30, (YI Dec. 1, 1921).
115. *Ibid.,* p. 29, (YI 2/23/21).

260/ 116. *Ibid.*, p. 29, (YI 5/25/21).

117. *Ibid.*, p. 33, (YI 5/21/25); p. 34, (YI 12/15/27); p. 30, (YI 12/1/21).

118. *Ibid.*, p. 36, (DD p. 93).

119. *Ibid.*, p. 29, (YI 2/23/21).

120. *Ibid.*, pp. 64–5, (YI 11/12/25).

121. *Ibid.*, pp. 55–6. Italics mine.

122. See N.V.:I, p. 359, (Sevagram, 2/9/40; H 8/9/40).

123. Referring to France's surrender to Hitler, Gandhi wrote, "I think French statesmen have shown rare courage . . . refusing to be party to senseless mutual slaughter . . . The cause of liberty becomes a mockery if the price to be paid is wholesale destruction of those who are to enjoy liberty." *Ibid.*, p. 289, (Sevagram, 18/6/40; H 23/6/40).

124. See Kher, II, p. 299, (YI 17/6/26, p. 215); also note that Gandhi treads a fine line and maintains a keen balance between the claims of reason, faith and guidance. But finally, in opposition to the requirements of his basic epistemology and logic, he gives an unjustified status and role to reason in its ordinary exercise as if it were already the pure reason that answers to and reveals true precepts in the ideal state. While correctly insisting on its purity and urging constant self-purification, disclaiming pure reason for himself, Gandhi yet theorizes, judges, applies and evaluates dogmatically with it.

125. For example, N.V.:II, 106–7; "Independence must begin at the bottom. Thus, every village will be a republic or *panchāyat* having full powers. It follows, therefore, that every village has to be self-sustained and capable of managing its affairs even to the extent of defending itself against the whole world. It will be trained and prepared to perish in the attempt to defend itself against any onslaught from without. Thus, ultimately, it is the individual who is the unit. This does not exclude dependence on and willing help from neighbours or from the world. It will be free and voluntary play of mutual force . . . In this structure composed of innumerable villages, there will be ever widening, never ascending circles. Life will not be a pyramid with the apex sustained by the bottom. But it will be an oceanic circle whose centre will be the individual always ready to perish for the village, the latter ready to perish for the circle of villages, till at last the whole becomes one life composed of individuals, never aggressive in their arrogance but ever humble, sharing the majesty of the oceanic circle of which they are integral units . . . I may be taunted with the retort that this is all Utopian and, therefore, not worth a single thought. If Euclid's point, though incapable of being drawn by human agency, has an imperishable value, my picture has its own for mankind to live. Let India live for this true picture though never realizable in its completeness. We must have a proper picture of what we want . . . in which the last is equal to the first, or, in other words, no one is to be the first and none the last." (Panchgani, 21/7/46; H 28/7/46); also see two articles on his ideal socialism, pp. 265–67, July 1947, in which he claims that true socialism cannot be attained without Truth and non-violence as he conceived and practiced them.

126. N.V.:I, p. 136, (H 17/10/36).

127. Kripalani, IV:34, p. 85.

128. *Ibid.*, IV:64, p. 91, (M:VII, 1946).

129. *Ibid.*, IV:63, p. 91, (H 6/22/35).

130. N.V.:I, p. 128, (H 26/9/31).

131. *Ibid.*, pp. 138–40, (H 20/3/37).

132. *Ibid.*, p. 287, (Sevagram 4/6/40; H 8/6/40).

133. *Ibid.*, p. 116, (YI 31/12/31); also see, pp. 395–96, (Train to Calcutta, 17/2/42; H 22/2/42).

134. *Ibid.*, p. 130–31, (H 26/9/36).

135. *Ibid.*, p. 283, (Sevagram 30/4/40; H 4/5/40). Italics mine.

136. *Ibid.*, p. 30, (YI 11/12/24).

137. *Ibid.*, p. 334, (Sevagram 12/8/40; H 18/8/40).

138. *Ibid.*, p. 252, (Sevagram 16/10/39; H 21/10/31). Thus Gandhi sided with the allies against the axis powers though noting Britain's own questionable war aims so far as justice and democracy were concerned in her own colonies.

139. Hingorani, *Gītā*. . . , p. 192, (*Gītā Discourses*, Chapt. XXI, pp. 8–44; see also pp. 147, 150), and p. 122, (*Āśrama Sisters*, p. 112).

140. *Ibid.*, p. 55, (H 9/1/40).

141. *Ibid.*, p. 64, (YI 11/12/25).

142. *Ibid.* , p. 49, (YI 8/8/31).

143. *Ibid.*, p. 39, (DMD p. 105).

144. *Ibid.* Italics mine.

145. *Ibid.*, p. 30, (YI 5/25/21). Italics mine.

146. *Ibid.*, p. 39, (H 1/21/39), and p. 50, (*Āśrama Sisters*, p. 53).

147. *Ibid.*, p. 64, (YI 11/12/25).

148. *Ibid.*, p. 30, (YI 12/1/21) Italics mine; and p. 39, Gandhi writing about the description of *Sthitaprajña* (Gītā II:54–72) says that "these verses show that the fight Krishna speaks of is a *spiritual fight*." (H 1/21/39). Italics mine.

149. *Ibid.*, p. 152, (DG 8–44, comments on Chapt. III).

150. *Ibid.*, p. 189, (comments on Chapt. XVIII). Italics mine.

151. *Ibid.*, p. 90, (H 7/8/33); also pp. 91–92, (DMD p. 250).

152. *Ibid.*, p. 30, (YI 12/1/21).

153. *Ibid.*, p. 31, (YI 5/29/24).

154. *Ibid.*, p. 142, commentary introduction (DG, 8–44).

155. *Ibid.*, p. 145, Chapt. II (DG, 8–44).

156. *Ibid.*, p. 151, Chapt. III:36–43 (DG, 8–44).

157. E.g., Śrī Rāma calls anger to service in battle against demonic forces (Vālmīki, Rāmāyaṇa, Araṇyakāṇḍa, Canto 26:12:5); Śrī Rāma, whom Gandhi looked upon as the personification of Truth and non-violence. Gandhi reads such references as this and the Bāli incident referred to previously as interpolations, or, acknowledging a limited understanding, he excuses himself from judging but maintains his views "on faith".

Chapter 8

158. N.V.:I, pp. 229–30, (Sevagram 11/9/33; H 4/5/40).

159. See *ibid.*, p. 283, (Sevagram 30/4/40; H 4/5/40).

160. Hingorani, *Gītā*. . . , p. 52, (H 9/5/36).

161. N.V.:I, p. 225, (Sevagram 28/2/39; H 2/9/39).

162. N.V.: II, p. 153, (New Delhi 27/10/46; H 3/11/46).

163. N.V.:I, p. 130, (H 26/6/36).

164. *Ibid.* Italics mine.

165. *Ibid.*

166. *Ibid.*, (numeration not in original).

262/   167. *Ibid.*, pp. 312–13, (Sevagram 17/7/40).

168. *Ibid.*, p. 186, (Sevagram 12/12/38; H 24/12/28).

169. *Ibid.*, p. 163, (Peshawar 6/10/38).

170. *Ibid.*, p. 186, (Sevagram 12/12/38; H 24/12/28).

171. *Ibid.*, p. 191, (train to Bardoli, 2/1/39; H 7/1/39).

172. *Ibid.*

173. *Ibid.*

174. *Ibid.*, p. 216, (Rajkot 9/4/31; H 15/4/39). Parentheses mine.

175. *Ibid.*, p. 339, (Sevagram 6/8/40; H 18/8/40).

176. *Ibid.*, pp. 429–30, ltr. "To Every Japanese", (Sevagram 18/7/42; H 26/7/42).

177. *Ibid.*, p. 191, (train to Bardoli, 2/1/39; H 7/1/39).

178. *Ibid.*, p. 117, (YI 31/12/31; and p. 417, train to Wardha, 5/4/42; H 12/4/42).

179. Kripalani, p. 82, IV:20.

180. N.V.:I, p. 230, (Sevagram 11/9/39; H 16/9/39).

181. *Ibid.*, p. 160, (H 8/10/38).

182. N.V.:II, p. 5, (on train to Madura, 2/2/46; H 10/2/46).

183. Mohandas K. Gandhi, *Delhi Diary,* (Ahmedabad: Navajivan Publishing House, 1948), p. 364, (21/1/48). Italics mine.

184. Kher, I, p. 285, (AOA, Chapt. I, ed., 1959, pp. 13–22).

185. *Ibid.*, p. 297, (YI 30/9/26, p. 342).

186. *Ibid.*, p. 279, (H 18/2/39, p. 36—to be used only as a last resort). Also, p. 321, (H 21/4/46, p. 93; 310, H 4/3/33).

187. *Ibid.*, p. 284, (AOA pp. 13–22).

188. *Ibid.*, pp. 316–17, (H 9/9/33).

189. *Ibid.*, p. 317.

190. *Ibid.*, p. 316.

191. *Ibid.*, p. 280, (YI 28/10/26, p. 342).

192. *Ibid.*, p. 318, (H 9/9/33, p. 4).

193. *Ibid.*, p. 319, (H 9/9/33, p. 4).

194. *Ibid.*, p. 307, (H 11/2/33, p. 2).

195. *Ibid.*, p. 278, (H 24/12/47, p. 476).

196. *Ibid.*, p. 331, (H 15/4/33, p. 4).

197. *Ibid.*, p. 321, (H 21/4/46).

198. Kripalani, II:61, pp. 64–5, (YI 10/27/21).

199. *Ibid.*, II:62, p. 65, (H 11/24/33).

200. *Ibid.*, I:130, p. 37, ("The Fiery Ordeal", YI 1928).

201. Hingorani, . . . *Satyāgraha,* p. 45, (H 8/18/40).

202. Kher, I, p. 317, (H 7/9/33, p. 4).

203. *Ibid.*, p. 286, (AOA, I, 13–22).

204. *Ibid.*, p. 278, (H 18/3/39); also, pp. 330–32, (H 15/4/33, p.4).

205. *Ibid.*, p. 278, (H 24/12/47, p. 476); also, p. 300, (YI 25/9/24, p. 319).

206. *Ibid.*, p. 310, (H 4/3/33, p. 7).

207. *Ibid.*, p. 291, (H 5/8/33, p. 4).

208. *Ibid.*, p. 318, (H 9/9/33, p. 4).

209. *Ibid.*

210. N.B.—In the theory of *karma,* factual or material liability and ethical responsibility include a component of the degree of self-consciousness of the

factors involved; but that is a more conditioning than determining component
in the total complex outcome.

Gandhi takes account of this when he insists on the course of self-purification required for all efficacy shown in his *satyāgraha*.

The difficulty for his analysis is that intent on propagating his ideology, constraining all use of force, his concepts of force and coercion are left at the level of categorical difference defined by the dichotomy "violence/nonviolence", while the whole theory (and Gandhi's loving personal application of it) operates at the *advaitic* level of metaphysical oneness and spiritually informed or divine love.

At this most fundamental level, non-violence is not an imposing ideational form constraining all use of force, but the spontaneous result of any force used in service of that divine element.

Chapter 9

211. Kripalani, I:131, pp. 38–9, ("The Fiery Ordeal", YI 1938).

212. N.V.:I, pp. 114–16, (YI 31/12/31).

213. *Ibid.,* p. 94, (YI 9/5/29).

214. *Ibid.,* p. 283, (Sevagram 30/4/40, H 4/5/40). Italics mine.

215. N.V.:II, p. 143, (New Delhi 9/9/46; H 15/9/46).

216. N.V.:I, p. 233, (Working Committee's Manifesto, Wardha 14/9/39).

217. *Ibid.,* p. 258, (Sevagram 29/10/39; H 4/11/39).

218. N.V.:II, p. 157, (Sodepur 30/10/46; H 10/11/46).

219. *Ibid.,* p. 233, (H 6/4/47); also, pp. 230–31, (H 30/3/47).

220. *Ibid.,* pp. 230–31, (H 30/3/47).

221. Hingorani, . . . *Satyāgraha,* p. 86, (YI 4/3/30).

222. Kripalani, p. 119, VIII:6; (YM 1935).

223. N.V.:II, p. 279, (Calcutta 20/8/47; H 31/8/47).

224. *Ibid.,* pp. 316–17, (New Delhi 1/1/48; H 11/1/48); also, p. 314, (New Delhi 29/11/47; H 7/12/47).

225. *Ibid.,* pp. 279–80, (Calcutta 20/8/47; H 31/8/47).

226. *Ibid.,* p. 327, (N.D. 8/12/47; H 14/12/47); also, pp. 199–200, (28/12/46; H 26/1/47), and p. 219, (H 9/3/47).

227. N.V.:I, pp. 33–34, (YI 3/9/25).

228. *Ibid.,* p. 115, (YI 31/12/31).

229. *Ibid.,* p. 315, (Sevagram 15/7/40; H 21/7/40). Parentheses mine.

230. *Ibid.,* p. 317, (Sevagram 16/7/40; H 21/7/40). Parentheses mine.

231. Kripalani, IV:71, p. 93, (YI 8/4/20).

232. *Ibid.,* IV:72, p. 93, (YI 5/28/24). Italics mine.

233. *Ibid.,* IV:73, p. 93, (YI 7/20/35).

234. *Ibid.,* IV:76, p. 94, (M:II YI 8/11/20). Italics mine.

Note to the Reader

There are three sections to the Bibliography which follows: (A) Primary Sources: by M. K. Gandhi, and Compilations of His Writings, (B) Secondary Sources and Studies of M. K. Gandhi, and, (C) Other Works on Related Topics. These have been separated for convenient reference.

The reader will find Gandhi's own words in Section (A), studies about Gandhi, his life, thought and work in Section (B), and studies of subjects related to the inquiry of this book, e.g. on violence, civil disobedience, philosophy of action, pacifist writings and Indian philosophy, in Section (C).

For the student who wants to go more deeply into Gandhi's ideas, he will do well first to master his autobiography *The Story of My Experiments with Truth, Satyāgraha in South Africa* and *Hind Swaraj*. He should then study Gandhi on the Gītā. These will ground the reader well in Gandhi's life and the basis of his thought and methods. He should then look into the Complete Works. The reader will understand why when he has done so.

Thorough and ample compilations which stand repeated study are the three volumes of Kher, *In Search of the Supreme,* and the two volumes by Desai and Kumarappa, *Non-Violence in Peace and War.* Hingorani's "Gandhi Pocket Series", Bharatiya Vidya Bhavan, is very good for extended well-chosen, well-organized selections on specific topics. Gandhi said the one volume *Selections from Gandhi* by Bose was the best of that sort. The later UNESCO selection by Kripalani, *All Men Are Brothers,* is also very good. *Non-Violent Resistance (Satyāgraha),* is a specially good collection on that topic by Kumarappa.

Of scholarly and philosophical secondary studies, those by Arne Naess are to be most highly recommended. Datta's little book *The Philosophy of Mahatma Gandhi,* is brief but beautifully done. Iyer's study is the most comprehensive and a model of Gandhian scholarship. Leo Kuper's chapter on *Satyāgraha* in his *Passive Resistance in South Africa* is a model for sociological studies.

Louis Fischer's *Life of Mahatma Gandhi* is almost a classic of biography; the recent Harper & Row reissue is very nicely done. Tendulkar's eight volume *Mahatma* and Pyarelal's four volumes (projected six volumes) are epic in scope and character, well worth the effort and enjoyable as well. One gets from these a sense of the grandeur and sheer vastness of Gandhi's life.

There are many wonderful memoirs. The recent memoir by Shirer is very good. The half-memoir, half-biographical *Gandhi through Western Eyes* by Horace Alexander is also an excellent book, recently reissued by New Movement Press. The early "biographical" editing and reflections of C. F. Andrews are probably the best of these writings. The earliest biography, somewhat informal, by Rev. Doke in South Africa, has a special place and interest in works on Gandhi.

For those particularly interested in the larger question of this book—non-violence and the justifiability of violence—*The Riddle of Violence,* by Kenneth Kaunda, President of Zambia, will be very helpful. He is a great disciple of Gandhi, but as a leader in the political field in an African nation emerging from colonialism, he found he could not for all his efforts follow Gandhi's non-violence to the end. He comes to many of the same conclusions as the present book, but with fifteen years and a life of struggle and questioning behind his arguments.

For those interested in non-violence, generally, the writings and biographies of A.J. Muste and of Bayard Rustin will be found to have a special importance.

Finally, the writings of Nehru will have special interest for students of non-violence in international affairs. Jawaharlal Nehru was one of the closest colleagues of Gandhi in the Indian Freedom Movement; as a national leader he could not escape the claims of violence, domestically or internationally. Einstein told Nehru that the development of *satyāgraha* had been exactly parallel to that of the atomic bomb, that Gandhi alone was responsible for restraining it, and that, with Gandhi's assassination, the mantle of that responsibility had fallen on Nehru. The principle of non-alignment and the five principles of international peaceful co-existence were Nehru's contribution to world peace.

(A) PRIMARY SOURCES: BY M. K. GANDHI, AND COMPILATIONS OF HIS WRITINGS

All Men Are Brothers; Autobiographical Reflections. Krishna Kripalani (com. & ed.). New York: The Continuum Publishing Corp., 1980.

An Autobiography: The Story of My Experiments with Truth. Mahadev Desai (trans.). Authorized Ed.; Boston: Beacon Press, 1957. (Originally published in two volumes; Vol. I, in 1927, and Vol. II in 1929, in Gujarati; translation, revised by M. K. Gandhi, appeared serially in *Young India,* issued as a single volume in 1940, under the editorship of Mahadev Desai.)

Ashram Observances in Action. V. G. Desai (trans.). Ahmedabad: Navajivan Press, 1932, 1955.

Bapu's Letters to Mira (1924—48). Mirabehn (Margaret Slade), (selected & ed.). Ahmedabad: Navajivan Publishing House, 1949.

Christian Missions. Ahmedabad: Navajivan Publishing House, 1941.

The Collected Works of Mahatma Gandhi. New Delhi: The Publications Division, Ministry of Information and Broadcasting, Government of India, Vol. I was published in January 1958; still under publication, projected 85-100 vols.

Constructive Program. Ahmedabad: Navajivan Press, 1941.

Conversations of Gandhiji. Chandrashankar Shukla (ed.). Bombay: Vora,
1949.

More Conversations of Gandhiji. Chandrashankar Shukla (ed.). Bombay: Vora, 1949.

Delhi Diary (Prayer Speeches from 10-9-47 to 30-1-48). Ahmedabad: Navajivan Publishing House, 1948.

The Diary of Mahadev Desai. V. G. Desai (trans.). Ahmedabad: Navajivan Press, 1953, Vol. I.

Discourses on the Gītā. Ahmedabad: Navajivan Publishing House, 1960. (See *Gita—My Mother,* Hingorani, and *Selected Works,* Narayan, below).

Ethical Religion (Niti Dharma). Madras: Ganesan, 1922.

For Pacifists. Ahmedabad: Navajivan Publishing House, 1949.

From Yaravda Mandir. Ahmedabad: Navajivan Press, 1945.

Gandhiji's Correspondence with the Government. Vol. I, 1942–44. Ahmedabad: Navajivan Press, 1945; Vol. II, 1944–47; Pyarelal (ed.). Ahmedabad: Navajivan Publishing House, 1959.

The Gita According to Gandhi: The Gospel of Selfless Action (Translation of the original in Gujarati, with an additional introduction and commentary). By Mahadev Desai, with M. K. Gandhi, and collaboration of Pyarelal. Ahmedabad: Navajivan Publishing House, 1946.

Gita—My Mother. Anand T. Hingorani (comp.). Bombay: Bharatiya Vidya Bhavan, 1965.

God Is Truth. Anand T. Hingorani (comp.). Second Ed.; "Pocket Gandhi Series", No. 1; Bombay: Bharatiya Vidya Bhavan, 1962.

Hind Swarāj, or Indian Home Rule. (Revised New Ed.). Ahmedabad: Navajivan Press, 1939.

Hindu Dharma. Ahmedabad: Navajivan Press, 1953.

In Search of the Supreme, Vols. I, II, and III. V. B. Kher (comp. & ed.). First Ed.; Ahmedabad: Navajivan Publishing House, 1961.

The Law of Love. Anand T. Hingorani (comp.). Second Ed.; "Pocket Gandhi Series", No. 3; Bombay: Bharatiya Vidya Bhavan, 1962.

Non-violence in Peace and War, Vols. I & II. Vol. I, Mahadev Desai (comp.); Ahmedabad: Navajivan Press, 1945. Vol. II, Bharatan Kumarappa (comp.); Ahmedabad: Navajivan Press, 1945, (Navajivan Publishing House, 1960).

Non-violent Resistance (Satyāgraha). Bharatan Kumarappa (comp.). New York: Schocken Books, 1961. (Originally published as *Satyāgraha*; Ahmedabad: Navajivan Press, 1951.)

Sarvodaya (The Welfare of All). Bharatan Kumarappa (comp.). Ahmedabad: Navajivan Press, 1954.

Satyagraha in South Africa. Ahmedabad: Navajivan Press, 1951.

The Science of Satyagraha. Anand T. Hingorani (comp.). Third Ed.; "Pocket Gandhi Series", No. 4; Bombay: Bharatiya Vidya Bhavan, 1970.

Selected Letters. V. G. Desai (trans. & ed.). Vol. I, with foreword by Gandhiji, 1949; Vol. II, 1962. Ahmedabad: Navajivan Publishing House, 1962.

The Selected Works of Mahatma Gandhi. Vols. I-VI. Shriman Narayan (ed.). Ahmedabad: Navajivan Publishing House, 1968. (Note esp. Vol. IV, "Basic Works", including Gandhi's paraphrase of Ruskin's

Unto This Last, and *Discourses on the Gita*; and Vol. V, "Selected Letters".)

Selections From Gandhi. Nirmal Kumar Bose (comp.). Ahmedabad: Navajivan Publishing House, 1947.

Self-Restraint v. Self-Indulgence. Ahmedabad: Navajivan Publishing House, 1947.

Songs from Prison. The *Āśrama Bhajanāvali,* selected hymns and devotional songs used in common or congregational prayer by Gandhi's co-workers in their *āśrama* and on campaign, adapted by John S. Hoyland. London: Allen & Unwin, 1934. (Original Bhajanāvali published by Navajivan, Sanskrit, Hindi, etc., 1961.)

The Speeches and Writings of Mahatma Gandhi. Madras: Natesan, 2nd Ed., 1918; 4th Ed., 1934.

Young India. Vol. I, 1919–22, Vol. II, 1924–26, and Vol. III, 1927–28. Madras: S. Ganesan. (Gandhi's early Indian Journal, in English; complete 1919–32, published by Navajivan Publishing House.)

(B) SECONDARY SOURCES AND STUDIES OF M. K. GANDHI

Alexander, Horace, *Gandhi through Western Eyes.* Philadelphia: New Society Publishers, 1984.

Birla, G. D. *In the Shadow of the Mahatma, A Personal Memoir.* Bombay: Orient Longmans Ltd., 1953.

Brown, Judith M. *Gandhi and Civil Disobedience: The Mahatma and Indian Politics, 1928–34.* Cambridge: Cambridge University Press, 1977.

———. *Gandhi's Rise to Power: Indian Politics 1915–1922.* Cambridge: Cambridge University Press, 1972.

Case, Clarence Marsh. *Non-violent Coercion: A Study in Methods of Social Pressure.* New York: The Century Co., 1923.

Datta, D. M. *The Philosophy of Mahatma Gandhi.* Madison: University of Wisconsin Press, 1953.

Dhawan, G. *The Political Philosophy of Mahatma Gandhi.* Ahmedabad: Navajivan Publishing House, 1951.

Diwakar, R. R. *Satyagraha—Its Technique and History.* Bombay: Hind Kitabs, 1946.

Doke, J. J. M. *Gandhi—An Indian Patriot.* Madras: Natesan, 1909.

Einstein, Albert. *Einstein on Peace.* Otto Nathan, Heinz Norden (eds.). (Preface by Bertrand Russell). New York: Schocken Books, 1960.

Fischer, Louis. *Gandhi: His Life and Message for the World.* New York: New Directions Library, 1964.

———. *Gandhi and Stalin.* New York: Harper, 1927.

———. *The Life of Mahatma Gandhi.* New York: Collier Books, 1950, 1973.

Fulop-Miller, Rene. *Lenin & Gandhi.* F. S. Flint, and D. F. Tait (trans.). London: G. P. Putnam's Sons, 1927.

Gandhi, Manubehn, *Bapu—My Mother.* Ahmedabad: Navajivan Publishing House, 1949.

George, S. K. *Gandhi's Challenge to Christianity, An Essay in Appreciation.* Ahmedabad: Navajivan Publishing House, 1947.

Government of Bombay State. *Source Material for a History of the Free-*
dom Movement in India. Vol. III, Parts II, Mahatma Gandhi 1922–
29; III, 1929–31; IV, 1931–32. Bombay: Government Central Press,
1968–73.

Government of India. *Gandhian Outlook and Techniques.* UNESCO. (An
International Symposium, in cooperation with the United Nations.)
Delhi: Ministry of Education, 1953.

Hancock, W. K. *Four Studies of War & Peace in This Century.* (Wills Lec-
tures 1960–61). Cambridge: Cambridge University Press, 1961.

Horsburg, H.J.N. *Nonviolence and Aggression: A Study of Gandhi's Moral
Equivalent of War.* New York: Oxford University Press, 1968.

Husain, S. Abid. *The Way of Gandhi and Nehru.* London: Asia Publishing
House, 1959.

Iyer, Raghavan N. *The Moral and Political Thought of Mahatma Gandhi.*
Oxford: Oxford University Press, 1973; First Paper ed., New York,
1978

Jaspers, Karl. *The Future of Mankind.* E. B. Ashton (trans.). Chicago:
University of Chicago Press, 1961. (Originally published, R. Piper &
Co., Munich, 1958, as *Die Atombombe und die Zukunft des
Menschen.*)

Jesudasan, Ignatius, S.J. *A Gandhian Theology of Liberation.* Maryknoll,
N.Y.: Orbis Books, 1984.

Karanjia, R. K. *The Mind of Mr. Nehru* (*As Revealed in a Series of Intimate
Talks with Him*). London: George Allen & Unwin, 1960.

Klitgaard, Robert E. "Gandhi's Non-violence as a Tactic," *Journal of Peace
Research,* International Peace Research Assoc., Groningen, No. 2
(1971), p. 143.

Kotturan, George. *Ahiṁsā: Gautama to Gandhi.* New Delhi: Sterling Publishers Pvt. Ltd., 1973.

Kripalani, Krishna. *Gandhi: A Life.* New Delhi: Orient Longmans Ltd.,
1968.

Kumar, Ravindra, (ed.). *Essays on Gandhian Politics; The Rowlatt Satyāgraha of 1919.* Oxford: Clarendon Press, 1971. (Seminar under the
aegis of the Dept. of History, Australian National University, Nov.
1966.)

Kuper, Leo. *Passive Resistance in South Africa.* New Haven: Yale University
Press, 1957. (See also his "Nonviolence Revisited", in Rotberg and
Mazrui, *Protest and Power in Black Africa*; Oxford: Oxford University Press, 1970, for his reconsiderations of few but significant
points.)

Lester, Muriel. *Entertaining Gandhi.* London: Ivor Nicholson & Watson,
1972.

Mahadevan, T. K., and G. Ramchandran (eds.). *Gandhi, His Relevance for
Our Times.* Berkeley: World Without War Council, 1971.

Mahendra Kumar. *Current Peace Research and India.* Varanasi: Gandhian
Institute of Studies, 1968.

———. *Violence and Nonviolence in International Relations.* Delhi: Thom-
son Press, 1975.

Maritain, Jacques. *Freedom in the Modern World.* Richard O'Sullivan (trans.). New York: Scribner's, 1936.

———. *Man and the State*. Chicago: University of Chicago Press, 1962.

Mashruwala, Kishorlal G. *Gandhi and Marx*. First Ed.; Ahmedabad: Navajivan Publishing House, 1951; with Introduction by Vinoba Bhave.

———. *Practical Non-violence*. Ahmedabad: Navajivan, 1941.

Maurer, Herrymon. *Great Soul*. New York: Doubleday, 1948.

Merton, Thomas (ed. and introductory essay). *Gandhi on Non-violence*: Selected Texts from M. K. Gandhi's *Non-violence in Peace and War*. New York: New Directions, 1964.

Mirabehn. *Gleanings*. Ahmedabad: Navajivan Publishing House, 1949.

Naess, Arne. *Gandhi and Group Conflict; An Exploration of Satyagraha— Theoretical Background*. Oslo: Universitetsforlaget, 1974.

———. *Gandhi and the Nuclear Age*. Totowa, N.J.: The Bedminster Press, 1967.

Narasinhaiah, C. D. (ed.). *Gandhi and the West*. Mysore: University of Mysore Press, 1969.

Nehru, Jawaharlal. *An Autobiography*. London: John Lane, 1936.

———. *Bunch of Old Letters: Written Mostly to Jawaharlal Nehru and Some Written by Him*. New York: Asia Publishing House, 1960.

———. *The Discovery of India*. Calcutta: Signet Press, 1941.

———. *Mahatma Gandhi*. Calcutta: Signet Press, 1949.

Niebuhr, Reinhold. *Moral Man in Immoral Society*. New York: Scribner's, 1934.

Orwell, George, from his *Collected Essays,* Vols. I–IV, especially "Reflections on Gandhi". The Collected Essays, Journalism and Letters of George Orwell. New York: Harcourt, Brace & World, 1968.

Power, Paul F. *Gandhi on World Affairs*. Washington, D.C.: Public Affairs Press, 1960.

———. (ed.). *The Meanings of Gandhi*. Honolulu: An East-West Center Book, 1971.

Prabhu, R. K., and U. R. Rao. *The Mind of Mahatma Gandhi*. Ahmedabad: Navajivan Publishing House, 1967.

Prasad, Rajendra. *At the Feet of Mahatma Gandhi*. Bombay: Hind Kitabs, 1955.

———. *Mahatma Gandhi in Bihar*. Bombay: Hind Kitabs, 1949.

Pyarelal. *The Epic Fast*. Ahmedabad: Navajivan Press, 1932.

———. *Mahatma Gandhi, The Last Phase*, 2 Vols. Ahmedabad: Navajivan Press, 1958.

———. *Mahatma Gandhi, The Early Phase*. Ahmedabad: Navajivan Press, 1965.

Radhakrishnan, S. (ed.). *Mahatma Gandhi: Essays and Reflections on His Life and Work*. London: Allen & Unwin, 1949. 2nd Enl. Ed.

———. *Mahatma Gandhi—100 Years*. New Delhi: Gandhi Peace Foundation, 1968.

Ramana Murti, V. V. "Influence of the Western Tradition on Gandhian Doctrine", *Philosophy East and West,* 18:1&2 (Jan.-Ap. '68), pp. 55–65.

Ranade, R. D. *The Conception of Spiritual Life in Mahatma Gandhi and Hindi Saints*. Ahmedabad: Gujarat Vidya Sabha, 1956.

Ray, Shibnarayan (ed.). *Gandhi, India and the World*. Philadelphia: Temple University Press, 1970.

Reynolds, Reginald, *A Quest For Gandhi: An Anecdotal Biography Based upon Personal Acquaintance*. Garden City, N.J.: Doubleday & Co., 1952.

Richards, Glyn. *The Philosophy of Mahatma Gandhi*. Totowa, N.J.: Barnes and Noble, 1982.

Rolland, Romain. *Mahatma Gandhi*. London: Allen & Unwin, 1924.

Saxena, K. D. (ed.). *Gandhi Centenary Papers*. Bhopal: Council of Oriental Research, 1972.

Schechter, Betty. *Peaceable Revolution*. Cambridge, Mass.: Houghton Mifflin Co., The Riverside Press, 1963.

Sharp, Gene. *Gandhi as a Political Strategist*. Boston: Porter Sargent Publishers, 1979.

Sheean, Vincent. *Lead Kindly Light*. New York: Random House, 1949.

Shridharani, Krishnalal. *The Mahatma and the World*. New York: Duell, Sloan and Pearce, 1946.

———. *War Without Violence: A Study of Gandhi's Method and Its Accomplishments*. New York: Harcourt, Brace & Co., 1939.

Shukla, Chandrashankar. *Gandhi's View of Life*. Bombay: Bharatiya Vidya Bhavan, 1956.

Tara Chand. *History of the Freedom Movement in India*, Vol. III, Foreword by Humayun Kabir. Delhi: The Publications Division, Ministry of Information and Broadcasting, 1961.

Tendulkar, D. G. *Mahatma: Life of Mohandas Karamchand Gandhi*. 8 vols. Bombay: V. K. Jhaveri and D. G. Tendulkar, 1951–54.

Unnithan, Dr. T. K. N. *Gandhi and Free India*. Groningen, Netherlands: J. B. Wolters, 1956.

Verma, Surendra. *Metaphysical Foundation of Gandhi's Thought*. New Delhi: Orient Longmans, on behalf of Gandhi Peace Foundation, 1970.

Watson, Francis, and Maurice Brown (eds.). *Talking of Gandhiji*. Calcutta: Orient Longmans, 1957.

Woodcock, George. *Mohandas Gandhi*. New York: Viking Press, 1971.

(C) OTHER WORKS ON RELATED TOPICS

Aiyar, S. P. (ed.). *The Politics of Mass Violence in India*. Bombay: Mandantalas, 1967.

Arendt, Hannah. *On Violence*. New York: Harcourt, Brace & World, Inc., 1970.

Bachrach, Peter, and Morton Baratz. "The Two Faces of Power," *American Political Science Review*, 56(Nov. 62) 947–52.

Bay, Christian. "Civil Disobedience," *International Encyclopaedia of Social Science*, David Sills (ed.). Vol. II. New York: Macmillan & Co., 1968.

Bedau, Hugo Adam (ed.). *Civil Disobedience: Theory & Practice*. Indianapolis: Pegasus, Div. Bobbs-Merrill Co., Inc., 1969.

———. "On Civil Disobedience," *Journal of Philosophy* (Oct., 1961).

272 /   Bernstein, Richard J., *Praxis & Action*. Philadelphia: University of Pennsylvania Press, 1972.

Bienen, Henry. *Violence and Social Change: A Review of the Current Literature*. Chicago: University of Chicago Press, 1968.

Blumenthal, Monica D. *Justifying Violence*. Ann Arbor: Ann Arbor Institute of Social Research, University of Michigan Press, 1972.

Cameron, J. M. "On Violence," *New York Review of Books* (July, 1970), p. 30.

Charner, Perry. "Violence—Visible and Invisible," *Ethics*, 81 (1970).

Chatterjee, B. B., and S. S. Bhattacharjee. "Meanings of Non-violence," *Journal of Peace Research*, 2 (1971), 153–61.

Chatterjee, S., and D. Datta. *An Introduction to Indian Philosophy*. Calcutta: University of Calcutta Press, 1950.

Cohen, Marshall. "Liberalism and Disobedience," *Philosophy and Public Affairs*, Vol. I, 3 (Spring, 1972) p. 283.

Das, M. N. *The Political Philosophy of Jawaharlal Nehru*. New York: The John Day Co., 1961.

Dasgupta, Surama. *Development of Moral Philosophy in India*. New York: Frederick Ungar Publishing Co., 1961.

Dasgupta, Surendra Nath. *A History of Indian Philosophy*. 5 vols. Cambridge: Cambridge University Press, 1922–55.

Deming, Barbara. *Revolution and Equilibrium*. New York: Grossman Publishers, 1971.

Dick, James C. *Violence and Oppression*. Athens, Georgia: University of Georgia Press, 1979.

Edwards, Paul (ed.). *The Encyclopedia of Philosophy*. New York: Macmillan Co., 1967. (Especially articles on theory of action, motives, reasons, and cause.)

Ellul, J. *Violence: Reflections from a Christian Perspective*. Cecelia Gaul Kings, (trans.). New York: Seabury Press, 1969.

Fanon, Franz. *The Wretched of the Earth*. New York: Grove Press, 1961.

Freeman, Harrop. *Civil Disobedience*. Santa Barbara: 1966. N. P.

Gandhi, Virchand R. *The Karma Philosophy*. Speeches and Writings of Virchand R. Gandhi, No. 3; 2nd Ed.; Bombay: Coll. Bahagu F. Karbhari, 1924.

Graham, Hugh, and Ted R. Gurr. *Violence in America: Historical and Comparative Perspectives* (A Report to the National Commission on the Causes and Prevention of Violence). New York: Bantam Books, 1969.

Gray, J. Glenn. *On Understanding Violence Philosophically, and Other Essays*. New York: Harper, 1970.

Grundy, Kenneth W., and Michael A. Weinstein. *The Ideologies of Violence*. Columbus, Ohio: Charles E. Merrill Publishing Co., 1974.

Gupta, Ram Kishore. *Political Thought in the Smṛti Literature*. Allahabad: The Leader Press, 1952, Thesis.

Habermas, Jurgen. "Hannah Arendt's Communications Concept of Power," *Sociological Research* 44 (Spring, 1977), 3–24.

Hampshire, Stuart. *Freedom of the Individual*. London: Chatto & Windus Ltd., 1965.

——. *Thought and Action*. London: Chatto & Windus Ltd., 1959.

Haring, Bernhard. *A Theology of Protest*. New York: Farrar, Strauss, and Giroux, 1970.

Heimann, Betty. *Indian and Western Philosophy: A Study in Contrasts*. London: George Allen & Unwin Ltd., 1937. (See also the posthumous collection of her essays, *Facets of Indian Thought,* and her studies in philosophical linguistics.)

Held, Virginia, Sydney Morgenbesser, Thomas Nagel (eds.). *Philosophy, Morality, and International Affairs*. New York: Oxford University Press, 1974.

Held, Virginia, Kai Nielson, Charles Parsons (eds.). *Philosophy and Political Action*. New York: Oxford University Press, 1972.

Hentoff, Nat, *Peace Agitator: The Story of A. J. Muste*. New York: A. J. Muste Memorial Institute, 1982.

Hofstadter, Richard, and Michael Wallace (eds.). *American Violence: A Documentary History*. New York: Random House, 1971.

Hubert, Henri, and Marcel Mauss. *Sacrifice: Its Nature and Function.* W. D. Halls (trans.). From *Essai sur la Nature et la Fonction du Sacrifice, L'Annee Sociologique,* 1898. Chicago: University of Chicago Press, 1964.

Huxley, Aldous. *Ends and Means*. New York: Harper & Bros., 1937.

Iglitzin, Lynne B. *Violent Conflict in American Society*. San Francisco: Chandler Publishing Co., 1972.

Jaini, J. *Outlines of Jainism*. Cambridge: Cambridge University Press, 1916.

James, William. *Varieties of Religious Experience*. New York: New American Library, Mentor ed., 1962.

Kaunda, Kenneth, *The Riddle of Violence,* San Francisco: Harper & Row, 1980.

Landesman, Charles. "The New Dualism in the Philosophy of Mind," *Review of Metaphysics* 19, (Dec., 1965).

Landesman, Charles, and Norman S. Care. *Readings in the Theory of Action*. Bloomington, Indiana: Indiana University Press, 1968.

Lang, Berel. "Civil Disobedience and Nonviolence," *Ethics,* (July, 1970), 156–59.

Langford, Glenn. *Human Action*. New York: Doubleday, 1971.

Lynd, Staughton (ed.). *Non-violence in America: A Documentary History*. Indianapolis: Bobbs-Merrill, 1966.

Maitra, Sushil Kumar. *The Ethics of the Hindus*. Calcutta: University of Calcutta Press, 1925.

Mayer, Peter (ed.). *The Pacifist Conscience*. New York: Holt, Rinehart and Winston, 1966.

Murphy, Jeffrie (ed.). *Civil Disobedience and Violence*. Belmont, California: Wadsworth Publishing Co., 1971.

Neiburg, H. L. "Uses of Violence," *Journal of Conflict Resolution* 7(1963), 43–52.

Nelson, Keith, and Olin Spencer. *Why War? Ideology, Theory, and History*. Berkeley: University of California Press, 1979.

Nomos XIV, *Coercion*. James Roland Pennock, and John W. Chapman (eds.). Yearbook of the American Society for Political and Legal Philosophy; Chicago: Aldine Atherton, 1972.

Radhakrishnan, S. *The Bhagavad Gītā*. London: George Allen & Unwin Ltd., 1958.

———. *The Hindu View of Life*. London: George Allen & Unwin Ltd., 1954.

———, (ed.). *History of Philosophy, Eastern and Western*. London: George Allen & Unwin Ltd., 1952.

———. *Indian Philosophy*. Two Vols. London: George Allen & Unwin Ltd., 1948.

———, (ed.). *The Principal Upanishads*. London: George Allen & Unwin Ltd., 1953.

———. *Religion and Society*. London: George Allen & Unwin Ltd., 1953.

———, and J. H. Muirhead (eds.). *Contemporary Indian Philosophy*. London: George Allen & Unwin Ltd., 1952.

Raju, P. T. *Idealistic Thought in India*. London: George Allen & Unwin Ltd., 1953.

———. *Structural Depths of Indian Thought*. Albany: State University of New York Press, 1985.

Ranade, R. D. *The Bhagavad Gita as a Philosophy of God-Realization*. (Nagpur: Nagpur University) Bombay: Bhavan's Book University Series; Bharatiya Vidya Bhavan, 1959.

———. *Essays and Reflections*. Bombay: Bharatiya Vidya Bhavan, 1964.

———. *History of Indian Philosophy Volume II: The Creative Period* (in collaboration with Dr. S.K. Belvalkar). Poona: Bilvakunja Publishing House, 1927.

———. *Mysticism in Maharashtra,* 1st ed. Poona: Bilvakunja Publishing House, 1933; *Pathway to God in Marathi Literature,* 2nd ed. Bombay: Bharatiya Vidya Bhavan, 1961; *Mysticism in India: The Poet-Saints of Maharashtra,* reprint with new Pref. and Foreword. Albany: State University of New York Press, 1983.

———. *Pathway to God in Hindi Literature*. Sangli: Adhyatma Vidya Mandir, 1954.

———. *Pathway to God in Kannada Literature*. Bombay: Bharatiya Vidya Bhavan, 1960.

———. *Philosophical and Other Essays*. Jamkhandi: Shri Gurudeo Ranade Satkara Samiti, 1956.

———. *The Vedanta as a Culmination of Indian Thought*. Bombay: Bharatiya Vidya Bhavan, N. D.

Rawls, John. *A Theory of Justice*. Cambridge: Harvard University Press, 1971.

Rose, Thomas (ed.). *Violence in America: A Historical and Contemporary Reader*. New York: Vintage Books, 1970.

Roy, S. S. *The Heritage of Śaṅkara,* Allahabad: Udayana Press, 1965.

Ruskin, John. *Unto This Last: Four Essays on the First Principles of Political Economy*. Lloyd J. Hubenka (ed.). Lincoln, Nebraska: University of Nebraska Press, 1967.

Russell, Bertrand. *Common Sense and Nuclear Warfare*. New York: Simon & Schuster, Inc., 1959.

————. *Power, A New Social Analysis*. London: George Allen & Unwin, Ltd. 1938.

Saksena, Shri Krishna. *Nature of Consciousness in Hindu Philosophy*. Benares: Nand Kishore & Bros., 1944.

Schweitzer, Albert, *Indian Thought and Its Development*. Mrs. C. E. B. Russell (trans.). New York: Henry Holt & Co., 1936.

Shaffer, Jerome A. (ed.). *Violence*. New York: David McKay, Inc., 1971.

Short, James F. (ed.). *Collective Violence*. Chicago: Aldine Atherton, 1972.

Simpson, Evan. "Social Norms & Aberrations: Violence and Some Related Social Facts," *Ethics* 81(1970), 22–35.

Singer, Peter. *Democracy and Disobedience*. Oxford: Oxford University Press, 1973.

Skolnick, Jerome H. *The Politics of Protest*. New York: Simon & Schuster, 1969. (Report of the Task Force for Demonstrations, Protest, and Group Violence to the Nat'l Commission of Causes and Prevention of Violence.)

Unnithan, Dr. T. K. N., and Yogendra Singh. *Traditions of Non-violence*. New Delhi: Arnold-Heinemann India, 1973 (for UNESCO). (Companion work, *Sociology of Non-violence and Peace*, same authors; New Delhi: Research Council for Cultural Relations, 1969.)

Walter, E. V. "Power and Violence," *American Political Science Review* 58(June 64), 350–60.

Weiner, Philip, and J. Fisher (eds.). *Violence and Aggression in the History of Ideas*. New Brunswick, N.Y.: Rutgers University Press, 1974.

White, Alan R. (ed.). *The Philosophy of Action*. London: Oxford University Press, 1968.

Woodcock, George. *Civil Disobedience*. Toronto: Canadian Broadcasting Company, 1966.

Wrong, Dennis H. *Power: Its Forms, Bases, and Uses*. New York: Harper & Row, 1980.

Zinn, Howard. *Disobedience and Democracy: Nine Fallacies on Law and Order*. New York: Random House, 1968.

TEXTS

The Bhagavadgītā, or The Song Divine. Gorakhpur: Gita Press, 1943, 1968.

The Ramayana of Tulsidas, Rendered into English Verse by the Rev. A. G. Atkins. 2 Vols. New Delhi: The Hindustan Times, 1954.

The Upanishads. F. Max Muller (trans.). Two Parts: New York: Dover Publications, Inc., 1962. (Originally published as Vols. I and XV, in "The Sacred Books of the East," Clarendon Press, Oxford, 1879, and 1884.)

abhiniveśa, 9, 12, 101, 104, 235
abhyāsa, 44, 45, 72
Absolute, 26–27
Action(s) 9, 10, 27, 33, 34, 38–46, 68, 71, 82, 90, 109–10, 143, 155, 172, 226–27; equated with evil, 234; moral, if voluntary, N68
advaita, 5, 108, 154, 192
Agency, 51, 82, 143–44, 148, 154–55, 184
Agent, 137; changed by exact conduct, 105
Aggression, 162, 163, 249
āgraha, 221
ahankāra, 28
ahimsā, 11, 17, 51, 59, 93, 110, 161, 167, 175, 176, 210, 238, 242, 250; means to *anāsakti*, 194; core, superior force, 15; enmity vanishes before, 77, 242; and compromise, 172–73, 185; deduced, 5; vs. *himsā*, 186, support defender, 191; domestic, best school, 249–50; I, the failure, 238; is God, 110; forcibly heteronomous, 219; infallible, 110; invalid in radical aspects, 239; makes life impossible, 9; is love, 185–86; is *moksa*, 176; others' good, only motive, 186; strict noninjury criterion, 218; individual is basis, 250; religion of, 172; must incarnate as socialism, 61; soul of Truth, 59; unifying force, 59
akrasia, 11
Allies, 81, 158, 201, 232, N138
Analogy, 28, 50, 148, 180, 186, 190, 212; across categorical boundaries, 29

anāsakti, 8, 35, 42, 44–49, 51, 53, 54, 81, 92, 102, 103, 178, 179, 195–96, 206; transcends *ahimsā*, 194; interprets *ātmic* state, 201; G's interpretation self-contradictory, 192, 194–95; basis of human nature, 111–12; only universal obligation, 111; transcends all material states, 197
anāsaktiyoga, 46–47, 51
anekāntavādi, 5
Anger, 8, 13, 40, 44, 45, 62, 64, 68, 103, 159, 162, 172, 194–98, 246; *anāsakti* excludes, 198
Anti-untouchability, 90
Anti-war movement, 212–13
aparigraha, 93
Apartheid, 240
Appearance, 131, 167, 188, 190, 209
Arjuna, 36, 137, 175–76, 201
Arms Act, 172
Army, 101, 214
asat, 27, 65
Asceticism, 224, 238
āśrama, 94
asteya, 93
ātmabrahma, 26–28, 34
ātman, 8, 26, 40, 48, 79, 90, 101, 178, 201; laws of humanity derive from, 111
ātmānātma-viveka, 44
Atom bomb, 58, 122, 126, 170–71, 232, 240; absolute evil, 126; Einstein on, NTR; useless against N.V., 127
Attachment, 28, 45, 226, 246
Attitude, 10, 17, 37, 46–47, 74, 79, 91, 133, 222; changed by exact conduct, 23; self-modifying, 48

August Revolution, 216
Authenticity, 4, 63, 93, 155, 171, 246
Authority, 25, 70, 250
Autonomy, 221
avatāra, 198, 216
avyakta, 43, 50
Axiology, 105, 170, 203
Axis powers, N138

Bāli, 149–51
Bardoli, 98
Beauty, 49, 59, 74, 80, 205, 222
Beliefs, 6, 66, 79, 80, 62–83, 106; to change old, 60
Bengal, 225
Bhagavad Gītā. *See* Gītā
bhajan, 72–73
Bible, 195
Bihar, 74, 76, 77
Boer War, 171
Bondage, 40, 62
Boycott, 81–86, 248
brahma, 37, 43
brahmacarya, 93
brahman, 26, 28, 48, 66, 138, 178
brahmasamārpaṇa, 46, 51, 92, 102
brahmasatyam jagan mithyā, 28, 30, 107
Bravery, 189, 216, 231
British Rāj, 107, 240
Brute-force, 14, 21, 25, 57, 64, 66, 70, 76, 96, 99, 149, 151, 154, 202
Buddha, Mahātmā, 59
buddhi, 28, 45
Buddhistic "Conquer with Truth", 65, 68

Caesar, not confront, 235, 252
Calculations, 109, 149, 152, 178
Calcutta, 74, 132, 238, 242
Calculus, relating categories, 29
Campaigning, *satyāgrahic*, 90–92, 107, 112, 238, 242
Capitalism, 244, 247
Casuistry, 50, 128
Champaran, 98
Chāndogya Upaniṣad, 195
Character, 156, 249; state, 76
Christian peace witness, 125
Circular analyses, 5, 123, 162, 182, 199

Civil disobedience, 86, 88, 91–92, 247, 250–51
Civil rights movement, 240
Codes of conduct, 34, 51, 63
Coercion, 16, 64, 67, 79, 85, 91, 92, 106, 220, 224, 225–26, 228–29, N68, N210
Colonialism, 13, 232, NTR
Common sense, 146, 237
Communism, 244
Community of Nations, 241
Compassion, 185
Competition, cause of conflict, 197
Competitiveness, 55, 232
Conflict resolution, 240
Conformism, 85, 223, 229
Confusion, 38, 139, 152, 160, 162, 165, 166–67, 179, 182, 190, 192, 196–97, 200, 202, 209
Congregational chant, 72–75, 132, 248
Conscience, 84–85, 87, 93, 225, 248, 251, 252. *See also*, Inner voice & Voice within
Consciousness, 7, 9, 17, 21, 23, 28, 32, 38, 43, 46, 76, 85, 90, 101, 108, 109, 131, 133, 177, 226, 237; and matter, 6nb, 50
Consequences, unintended, 70–71, 91
Constructive program, 13, 80, 96, 132
Consumption, renounce, 235
Contentment, 79, 247
Contradiction, 27, 65, 154, 165, 188, 209, 235; of means and ends, 203
Conversion, 77, 78, 83, 103, 106, 123, 197, 243, 244, 246; as *karmic* transaction; 70–71; material process, 69, 81; progressive, 105
Correct action, 239
Courage, 68, 189
Courtesy, substitution ethics, 68
Cowardice, 55, 172, 175; G. prefers violence, 99, 176, 252
Criteria, 14, 30, 35, 59, 60, 76, 85, 90, 99, 100, 102, 103, 104, 121, 124, 125, 127, 129, 136, 137, 147, 157, 159, 185, 195, 205, 216, 218, 229, 230, 238; "good of all", 16; part of methods, 95; Patañjali's, 59, 74, 77;

stilling of masses, 242; universalizability, 138–39, 204

Damage, 141, 145, 149, 152, 154, 157
Dandi Salt March, 99
Daniel, 205
Death, 32, 102, 227
Deceit, 149–52, 244
Decolonization, 241
Defense, 25, 99–102, 203
Delhi, 60, 73, 93, 238, 242
Democracy, 92, 213, 232
Desire, 45, 70, 103, 113, 197, 264; cause of sin, 28, 45; escalation, 65; not itself evil, 234
Desirelessness, obligatory, 54
Deterrence, 129
dharma, 176
dharmayuddha, 36
Direct action, 68, 80, 81, 85, 105, 230
Disarmament, 197, 231, 243, 245
"Doer" and "Deed", 16, 64
Domestic model, 64, 179, 181
Duty, 36, 38, 47, 80, 86, 91, 96, 97, 175, 176, 179, 193, 220, 233, 234, 252; conflicts of, 172, 175; eradicates evil, 197; of one's station, 178; universal, 46
dvaitism, 5
dvandvabandha, 40
dveśa, 44

Economics, 38, 56, 232, 248
Education, 66, 92, 106
Ego, 38, 40, 43, 47, 69, 71, 81, 84, 103, 109, 112, 113, 150; cause of action, 41, 44; in whom destroyed, called "God", 111
Egotism, opposite religion, 102
Einstein, Albert, 237, NTR
Ellul, Jacques, 136–37, N64
Empirical consciousness, 12, 27, 29, 80, 86–87, 89, 108, 228
Empiricism, 97
Ends & means, 29, 30, 44, 59, 96, 145, 184, 192, 203; convertibility, 13, 18, 138, 231. *See also* Means & ends
Environmental movements, 248
Epistemology, 6nb, N124
Escalation, 45, 58, 67, 134, 166, 240

Ethics, 8, 95, 140
Europe, mass N.V. for, 247
Evil, 3, 7, 9, 10, 11, 13, 17, 37, 50, 55, 56, 72, 75, 88, 109, 110, 126, 133, 138, 141, 148, 150, 151, 153, 154, 158, 169, 174, 185, 216, 233, 234, 249, N64; atom bomb, 126; equated with violence, 4; isolated by *satyāgraha*, 81; essence, self-destruction, 123, 145, 252; not self-sustained, 69, 110, 151, 152
Exact conduct, 19, 22, 23, 24, 26, 30, 65, 68, 76, 78, 80–84, 94, 125, 133, 134, 194, 197, 222, 229; deduced, 63, 68; right action, 105
Expansionism, 13
Experience, 35, 144, 154, 191
Experiments, 5, 11, 15, 24, 26, 51, 132, 183, 188, 205, 206, 248
Exploitation, 13, 55, 92, 244, 247, 248; essence of violence, 232; cause of war, 231–32

Faith, 7, 14, 20–21, 22, 29, 34, 40, 46, 73, 87–88, 113, 142, 155, 205, 212, 219, 251, N74, N157; basis of *satyāgraha*, 62; "sixth sense", 21
Family, 31, 36, 57, 63, 64, 91, 110, 178, 244, 250; of nations, 241, 250
Fascists & Nazis, 213, N64
Fasts, 60, 79, 86, 132, 216–17, 218, 231
Fate, 22, 42
Fear, 13, 162, 177, 251
Force, 46, 56, 61, 64, 65, 204, 209, 227, 239, 242, 243, N210; of N.V., 3, 4, 14, 16, 59, 61, 126–27, 242, 250; spiritual, 11, 84, 120, 154
Forgiveness, 114, 230
Fratricide, 164, 174, 178, 216
Freedom, 9, 15, 16, 22, 41–42, 50, 85, 128, 151, 179, 193, 202, 216, 227, 232, 241, 246; of speech, 91

Galileo, Galilei, 101
Gandhi, Mohandas K.: chief arguments, 153, 206–208; allergic to pleasure, 235; models on ascetic tradition, 224; judges his campaigns, 99, 107; contradicts himself, 148, 188, 215; confusions, 190, 201; key

criticism of, 199, 224; experiments, 205; Naess on, N74; failures, 237, 239; claims fasts non-coercive, 218–20; on Gītā, 37, 50; ideologue, 52, 181; inconsistency patent, 165; votary of knowledge, 48; magnitude of work, 238; misinterprets both realities, 192; mission, 26, 85, 97, 121–22; on N.V., 57, 99–102, 217, 229, 238; troubled pacifists, 171–72; on peace movement, 146–47, 172; key to philosophy, 8; politics, spiritual, 25, 56; defends radical practical claim, 108, 110, 115; Rāmanāma, final solution, 72–75; learned Rāmanāma as child, 72; turns from reason to action, 130; arguments against him, 206–10, 252; G's. rhetoric, 196, 207, 220, 252; on right action, 105; on satyāgraha, 22, 33, 91–92, 125; ceaseless self-examination, 188; scientist, 51–52, N74; socio-political ideal, N125; sources, 25; prefers violence to cowardice, 172, 174, 252–53; prefers war to injustice, 164; visionary, 251; against all war, 164, 172–74; value of writings, 84; wrong theories, 236

Germany, 168, 170, 201, 213

Gītā, 30, 34, 39, 69, 86, 90, 103, 149, 163, 165, 168, 171, 174, 178, 193, 195, 201, 204, 226, NTR; argument of, 36–37; G. interprets, 204; "gospel" of non-cooperation, 81; locus classicus, 166

God, 5, 6, 7, 13, 18, 21, 22, 31, 42, 73, 81, 149, 208, 216, 224, 234, 235; as ahiṁsā, 110; described, 21, 22, 61; a "force," 61; one with His Name, 74; realized man called, 111; in satyāgraha, 82, 89, 113; inner voice, 90

God-realization, 7, 9, 56. See also, Realization

Good, 27, 105, 108, 150, 154, 162, 184, 191, 220, 244; "—of all", 14, 16, 42

"Goods" and "Benefits", 150

Government, 70, 173, 218, 250

Grace, 49, 69, 73, 89, 107, 132

Greed, 13, 44, 55, 62, 81, 241, 243, 244, 246

Guerilla insurgency, 126

Gujarat, 76

guṇaprakṛti, 41

guṇas, 32, 37, 40, 45, 194, 196, 226

guṇātīta, 41, 195, 198, 204

guruvāda, 180

Habit, 45, 62, 75, 81, 94

Hagiography, 205, 208, 237, 243

Hate, 13, 105, 152, 159, 162, 186, 194, 195, 233, 246; counter by love, 170

Hatred. See Hate

Hegemony 13, 243, 245

Heroism, 189

Heteronomy, 138, 192, 221–22

hijrat, 86, 88

hiṁsā, 5, 9, 11, 185, 186, 194, 195, 204

Hinduism, 102

Hindu-Muslim conflict, 23, 55, 60, 73, 74, 77, 80, 107, 163, 238

Hiroshima, 170

Hitler, Adolph, 155–56, 168, 169, 201, 211, 213, 215, 232, 243, N64, N123

Human action, 8, 24, 74, 108, 212, 225

Human condition, 31–33, 38–44

Human nature, 124, 129, 173, 211, 214, 215; good & evil, 151, 189, 201

Human relations, 11, 22, 53, 60, 67, 91, 97, 103, 111, 140, 245

Humility, 68, 246

Hunger strike, 226–27

"I" & "mine", root of conflict, 197

Ideal, 8, 10, 19, 22, 24, 44, 56, 61, 63, 68, 78, 79, 84, 86, 87, 90, 91, 102, 106, 108, 135, 167, 174, 179, 180, 181, 182, 183, 186, 190, 205, 219, 221, 222, 223, 224, 228, 229, 233, 237, 241, 242, 246; Equality, Fraternity, Liberty, 54, 92; evolving toward, 217; unrealizable, 9, 71, 88, 222

Ideal observer, 12

Ideological characteristics, 4

Ideology, 48, 91, 133–34, 135, 146,

180, 223, 236, 237, 238, 246;
"Gandhite", 4
Ignorance, 8, 24, 31–33, 37, 38, 40,
41, 44, 54, 55, 65, 82, 109, 179, 212
Illusion, 28, 32, 33, 58, 108, 110, 239
Imagination, 109, 179, 195–196
Imperialism, 13, 171; peace, 232
Independence, 76, 98, 99, 216, N125
India, 55, 81, 125, 147, 164, 172, 233,
239, 248; Freedom Movement,
NTR; government, 164; masses, 248
indriyas, 45
Inference, scientific, 28–29
Injury, 16, 65, 70, 93, 112, 145, 174,
217
Injustice, 230; G. prefers war, 164;
chief cause of unpeace, 244
Inner voice, 85, 86, 90, 186; God, 90.
See also Conscience & Voice within
Insistence, 66, 87, 178, 218, 219, 220
Institutional relations, 111
Insurgency, 240
Intentions, 3, 6, 13, 47, 63, 70, 166,
167, 218, 227, 240
Intolerance, 13
Introspection, 133
Intuition, 7, 146, 147, 165
Īśa Upaniṣad, 31, 34, 39, 47, 64, 179
Īśvara, 21, 31, 41, 43, 45, 46, 48

Jaina ideal, 69
Jaina metaphysics, 68, 69, N77
Japan, 170; invasion, 132; peoples,
213
Jesus, 10, 205
jīva, 50
jīvātmā, 16, 43, 193
jñānendriya, 28
Joseph, George, 93
Just war criteria, 137, 190
Justice, 13, 14, 36, 201, 228, 230, 233,
241, 246, 249, 253, N62, N64,
N138; condition of N.V., 190, 232;
of peace, 204, 230
Justifiability, 119, 122, 123, 136, 204,
228, 239
Justification, 4, 5, 66, 145, 159, 181,
204, 226, 232; logic of, 223; by results, 186–88; self-deception, 66
kāma, 44

karma, 22, 27, 32–33, 40, 42, 66, 69,
70, 72, 93, 99, 105, 191, 202, 234,
236, N210
karmasaṅskāra, 32, 48
karmayoga, 79
karmendriya, 28
karmic adjustment, 154–55
Kashmir, Pref.
Kaṭha Upaniṣad, 195
Kaunda, Kenneth, NTR
khaddar, 96
Killing, 12, 36, 104, 174, 176, 195,
196
King, Martin Luther, 240
kisan, 55
Knowledge, 20, 25, 28, 30, 32, 35, 38,
39, 41, 45, 47, 50, 180, 239; in renunciation, 39, 71, 87, 114
Krishna. See Kṛṣṇa
krodha, 44
Kṛṣṇa, 35, 175, 178, 201, 205, N148.
See also Yogeśvara Kṛṣṇa
kṣatriya, 174
kṣetra, 43, 46, 49, 67
kṣetra-kṣetrajña, 42–43
Kurukṣetra, 197

Labor strike, 90
Last resort argument, 62, 124–25,
216
Liberation, 32, 38, 40
Liberty, 246, N64, N123
Life, 12, 80, 94, 137–38, 186, 231,
248, 249
Logical principles, 26–29
Logico-metaphysical analysis, 27–31
Love, 10, 17–18, 59, 64, 68, 77, 84,
99, 100, 104, 110, 114, 133, 182,
219, 249, 251, N210

Macrocosm, 16
Mahābhārata, 35, 166, 175, 201, 216
Maheśvara, 49
Majority, 251; principle, 14
Man, 59, 87, 111; distinct from beast,
207, 208, 209
manas, 28, 45
mārga-viveka, 44
Mass methods, 246, 249
Mass movements, 85, 112
Material, 6nb, 11, 224

Material existence, 11, 12, 14, 23, 29, 46
Material reality, 34, 132, 194, 242, 247
Material relations 178
Material transactions, 67
Materialism, 82, 92, 97, 241
Materialist, 30, 117, 243, 244
Matter, 50, 224
māyā, 41, 43, 53, 59
Means, 23–24, 61, 152, 192, 203, 223, 245, 249, 251
Means & ends, 40, 50, 76, 97, 190–91, N64; convertible, 5, 23, 47
Metaphysics, 5, 6nb, 10, 62, 124, 125; "of—", 6, 9, 15, 73, 163
Methodological reduction, 215, 217
Methods, 10, 11, 81, 82, 86, 88–89; 92, 215, 222, 224, 229, 238–39, 241–42, 243, 246, 249, 251, 253; contradict aim, 201; mass *bhajan* as, 72–74; change beliefs and motives, 80; faith not optional, 73; cases of self-defense, 99–102; types, 86–93
Microcosm & macrocosm, 28, 59, 146, 183
Might is right, 14
Military power, monopoly on, 241
Mind, 7, 28; and body, 6nb
Mirabai, 205
Miracles, 187
Mission, Gandhi's, 4, 24, 60, 119, 122, 131, 200, 252; fails, 217; teach the masses, 26, 74
Mistrust, 243
Model, 63, 181, 251; on self, 60
mokṣa, 9, 21, 32, 72, 176, 179, 235
Moral action, 5, 6, 143, 146, 162, 195
Moral authenticity, 121
Moral autonomy, 221, 224
Moral consciousness, 17, 58, 102, 104, 129, 186, 206, 215, 221, 235, 239, 249; categories which function in, 193; non-retaliation reconstitutes, 133
Moral dilemmas, 223
Moral force, 10, 92, 226, 244
Moral ideal, 23, 181, 192, 199; paradox of, 183
Moral imagination, 7, 123, 195

Moral "physics", 187, 191
Moral psychology, 11, 45, 69, 73
Moral rules, 156, 163
Moral sense, 35, 101, 153, 216
Moral will, 128, 133, 146, 157
Motives, 6nb, 12, 13, 66, 70, 80, 91, 102, 105, 106, 148, 163, 166, 167, 169, 172, 178, 183, 184, 185, 186, 187, 188, 191, 198, 204, 218, 224, 227, 241, 244
Mussolini, 169, 211
Muste, A.J., NTR

Naess, Arne, N74, NTR
Name of God (*Rāmanāma*), 72–75, 248
Nature cure, 80
Nazis & Nazism, 170
Necessity, 141–44, 156–60, 161; mathematical, 150
Negotiation, 67, 244, 245
Nehru, Jawaharlal, 240, NTR
Neo-colonialism, 126, 232
neti, neti, 27
New debate, 125–30, 170, 236, 240, 242, 245
New Testament, 57
Newton, Sir Isaac, 101
Niemoeller, Professor, 211
nirdvandva, 40
Noakhali, 60, 73, 74, 77, 132, 238
Non-alignment, 13, NTR; movement, 240
Non-conformist, 125
Non-cooperation, 43, 73, 76, 81, 88, 151, 152, 224, 231, 233, 248
Non-doership (Gītā), 40–43, 56, 94
Non-resistance, 17, 233, 252; philosophy, 217
Non-retaliation, 10, 17, 75, 77, 87, 88, 100, 133, 140, 162, 163; perfect state, 51; core of *satyāgraha*, 24
Non-violence, 10, 15, 17, 24, 56, 59, 68, 70, 72, 75, 78, 93, 96, 104, 112, 134, 142, 158, 168, 169, 171, 184, 187, 198, 222, 241–42, 247, 248, 253, N210, NTR; alone superior to the atom bomb, 126–127, 170; axioms, 77; fatal challenge, 211–14; G. coined term, 3; defined, 3, 13, 59, 85, 153; key distinction, 76; new ele-

ments, 53; equated with Truth, 4, 58; N.V. for Europe, 247; a spiritual force, 3, 16, 64, 103, 170–71; mass means in *Rāmanāma*, 72–75; works mysteriously, 172; as non-exploitation, 234; expression of omnipotence, 14; originality, 7–8; essence is reason, 214, transforms relationships, 66; basis of true socialism, N125; transcends time & space, 3

Non-violence of the strong, 74, 77, 88, 99, 103, 106, 114, 146–47

Non-violence of the weak, 107

Non-violent army, 92

Non-violent resistance, 25, 80, 88, 125, 173, 250; three-fourths invisible, 187

Nuclear conflict, 228

Nuclear confrontation, 88, 240

Obligation, 46, 56, 176, 233; *anāsakti*, only universal, 111

Objective perception, 179, 228

Objectivity, 66, 158–59, 246

Open question, 129, 143, 213

Ordinary usage, 225, 26

Organic unity, 241, 244, 251

Ottoman Empire, 232

Ought, 119, 181

Outlook, 33, 245, 247

Pacifism, 163, 168, 176, 192, 202, 212

Pacifist arguments, 177–83

Pacifists, 171, N64

Pakistan, 164

Palestine, 240

panchāyat (village republic), N125

Paramātman, 43

parabrahman, 48

Parity of reasoning, contra G., 206, 251–52

Passions, 13

Passive resistance, 76, 131, 187

Patañjali, 59, 68, 74, 235

Patience, 113, 158, 246

Peace, 38, 64, 128, 137, 159, 168, 169, 172, 199, 228, 230, 233, 240, 246, 251; external, created by internal, 245; justice its condition, 190, 204, 244; inner, only from renunciation of fruits of action, 175

Peace Churches, 122

Peace movement, 122, 147; new, N62

Penance, 72, 223–24

Personality, 32, 243

Phenomenal field, 79, 81, 100

Phenomenal reality, 33, 167, 194, 200

Philosophy, 8, 237; of N.V., 192, 205, 221

Picketing, 83, 98–99

Pleasure, 21, 36, 40, 42, 147, 235

Plural methods, 241

Plural nations & histories, 241

Plural world, 228, 243

Plurality, joy of, 251

Polis, 111

Political consciousness, 223

Political ethics, G's, 70

Political life, 56; economic & social, 97

Politics, G's, 25, 56

Power, 11, 22, 23, 30, 43, 49, 55, 56, 66, 70, 76, 86, 90, 111, 114, 147, 171, 248; of God, basis of *satyāgraha*, 69; of God, helplessness condition of receiving, 115; of God, *Rāmanāma* the key, 73; of ideal, 186; of reality, 33, 58, 65

Practical idealism, G's, 237

Pragmatism, spiritual, 30

Prahlāda, 205

prakṛti, 40, 43, 49, 196, 226

prakṛti/guṇabandha, 40

Praxis, 131, 132, 142, 180, 198, 219, 223, 226, 236, 237; problem of, 181

Prayer, 67, 72, 89

prima facie case, 123, 125, 127, 147, 155, 158, 159, 165, 203–204, 212, G. adds dimension not covered by, 108

Progress, 50, 65

Psychology, group, social, political, 111

Public opinion, 220, 251; coercion, 224; N.V. weapon, 92

Puritanism, 234

puruṣa, 41, 49, 50

puruṣakāra, 69, 76, 114; & theory of *karma*, 72

puruṣakāra-karma, 45

Puruṣottama, 43

284/

Quaker activism, 122
"Quality" vs "quantity", 18
Races, oppressed, 171
Racism, N64
Rāma, 149–150, 205, N157
Rāmanāma, 72–75
Rāmāyaṇa, 149
Radical practical claim, 11, 95, 120, 121, 128, 130–32, 199, 214; *differentia* of G's methods, 24, 121, 205
rāga, 44
rajas, 194
Rajkot, 60
rajoguṇa, 196
Reaction, 40, 47, 66, 76, 82, 86, 110, 126, 154, 219, 224, 237, action binds by, 226; coercion brings, 224; equal & opposite action, 150; root fact of violence, 169
Real, the, in Upaniṣads, 26–28
Real & unreal, Jaina view, 5
Reality, 5, 7, 21–22, 26–28, 41, 45, 48, 51, 58, 108, 144, 155, 178, 180, 234
Realization, 6, 17, 27, 31, 33, 34, 45, 48, 71, 210, 245; contents, 7, 27; defined, 7, 21–22; external counterpart & exact conduct, 21, 229; eschatological problem, 21, 23; inherent urge for, 54; obligatory, 54; *Rāmanāma*, principle means, 72–74. *See also*, God-realization, Self-realization & Spiritual Realization
Reason, 7, 35, 38, 60, 66, 84, 85, 110, 140, 151, 162, 173, 179, 214–15, 252, N124: name for N.V., 202, 214; pure, N124; reached by self-suffering, 214
Rebirth, spiritual, 31, 71
reductio ad absurdum, 58, 203
Reform, 19, 98; attitude of, 222; pressure of, 219
Relations, 13, 18, 25, 104, 122, 178; transformation of, 66–69, 77, 104
Religious movement, 24
Religion, 48, 59, 61, 82, 168; of *ahiṁsā*, 172; common principles, 24, 51; equated with expediency, 53, 95;

to spiritualize the mundane, 49; summarized by Tūlsīdās, 102
Remembrance, 45, 46, 48, 67, 72–74; training for *satyāgraha*, 132
Renunciation, 31, 43, 71, 99, 103, 114, 179; contemporary, 248–49; corporate, 247; effectiveness & knowledge, 39, 163; as non-consumerism, 248; of fruits of action, 46–47
Repression, 12
Return of good for evil, 15, 17, 57, 68, 69
Revolution, 240
Revolutionaries & reactionaries, 245
Right action, 37, 105, 175, 220
Right effort, 72, 179
"Right-making" act, 105
Rightness, 120, 122, 141, 143, 144, 201, 220; of action, 193; & necessity, 140–42; outcome, 148
Rights, 37, 63, 66, 70, 97, 191, 220
ṛta, 138
Rules, 182, 247; *a priori*, 166, 179
Ruskin, John, 56, 97
Rustin, Bayard, NTR
Sacrifice, 46, 47, 48, 208, 246, 248; core of religion, 49
sādhana, 37, 54, 56, 58, 80, 84, 86, 249; social life as, 79
sādhanā, 22, 94
Saint, 69, 208, 209, 216
Saint Francis, 59
Salvation, 235, 245
samabhāva, 57
Sanction, 131
sarvodaya, 14
sat, 27, 65
Satan, 6, 7
sat-cit-ānanda, 27
sattva, 40, 194; —*guṇa*, 198
satya, 26, 34, 93
satya-āgraha, 48
satyāgraha, 19, 22, 24, 30, 35, 40, 48, 49, 51, 56, 61, 76, 79, 84, 90, 95, 102, 107, 119, 127, 149, 151, 161, 180, 190, 197, 219, 220, 238, 240, 253, N210; & A-bomb, NTR; basis, soul's bliss & power, 96; campaigns,

90–92, 112, 140; coercive, 217–227; core, exact conduct, 23; many deaths for large result, 83, 88, 103–104; deduced, 50–52, 78–79; extends domestic life to political, 63; changes energies, 87; exemplars in, 80, 205; failures, 206; faith its basis, 32, 73, 87; discovered in search of God as Force, 61; gains, end of enmity & new friends, 114–15; dependence on God, 73, 89; on grace, 49, 89; helplessness, its condition, 89; individual perfection, its basis, 75; intent to influence, 220–21; innocent suffering in, 87; joy in, 89, 112; only last resort, 158; to link spiritual and practical, 53; methods in, 86; non-embarrassment in, 91–92; in a "nutshell", 65; power of one, 88; origins, 56–57, 130; physical non-retaliation, *sine qua non*, 24; preemptive preparation, 92, 158; prayer, basic means, 67; public opinion in, 92; purity & innocence in, 82, 99–102; invalid, 239; *Rāmanāma*, key, 72–74; reason in, 84; science of, 11, 69, 132, 210; self-immolation, core, 211; recognition of soul, requisite, 32, 83; as soul-force, 10, 53; spiritual basis, 20–52, esp. 83; touchstone, spontaneity, 84; substitute for violence, 25, 62; substitution ethics, heart, 68; based on surrender, 41; no tactical & strategic calculations, 90–91, 92; transmutes hatred, 105; universal, 64; continues Upaniṣads, 26, 33; victory in, 72, 83, 114; vows in, 93; principle weapon, non-cooperation, 43

satyāgrahī, 90, 132, 222–23, N21
satyam, 27
satyam eva jayate, 31, 65
Science, of action, 34, 39; of life, 208; moral & spiritual, 69, 101, 124, 175; physical, 206, 210; of *satyāgraha*, 132
Self-control, 53, 70
Self-deception, 66, 141–42, 173, 251
Self-defense, 25, 32, 101, 122, 146, 202, 204, 238
Self-destruction, 45, 58, 66, 75, 97, 98, 101, 123, 148; atomic escalation, 127; hastened, 145; open question, 129; price to evil of its violence, 147
Self-determination, 16, 232, 241
Self-examination, 22, 37, 71, 85, 188, 252
Self-immolation, 100, 222, 245
Self-interest, 13, 80, 204, 230
Self-purification, 45, 47, 54, 71, 73, 75, 76, 77, 79, 86, 90, 93, 133, 234, N124, N210; service in, 47; in N.V. defense, 101–102
self-realization, 8, 42, 79, 153, 186, 193, 221. *See also*, Realization
Self-sacrifice, 53, 234, 248–49
Self-suffering, 52, 76, 78, 85, 151, 203, 214, 217, 218; derived, 64; core of *satyāgraha*, 211; transmuted to joy, 112
Sense control, 44–45
Sermon on the Mount, 125
Service, 17, 42, 47, 48, 56
Sheppard, Dick, 208
siddhi, 30
Simplicity, 74, 247, 248
Sin, 12, 37, 44, 137, 146, 193, 231, 235; causes, desire & anger, 45; root, I & mine, 197
Sincerity, 157–58, 244
Social action, 238
Social disease (sickness), 55–56
Social identity, 54
Social life, 56, 151; a *sādhana*, 79
Social norms, 176, 223–24
Social relations, 13, 78
Socialism, 61, 244, N125
Socrates, 10, 205
Solidarity, 13
Soul, 7, 15–16, 27, 33, 36, 42, 58, 70, 96, 131, 153, 211
Soul-force, 3, 11, 13, 17, 22, 24, 25, 46, 51, 53, 59, 62, 63, 64, 67, 68, 79, 81–82, 83, 88, 89, 93, 96, 104, 110, 113, 132, 151, 197, 200, 214, 216, 226, 242, 247; discovery, 131; cases of self-defense, 99–102; three-fourths invisible, 63

286/

South Africa, 57, 91, 125, 130, 229–30, 240, 243
Spinning wheel: G. sees God in, 23; measures N.V., 96; symbol of N.V., 187; effective as picketing, 83
Spirit, 156, 224, N74
"Spiritual" vs. "material", 6nb
Spiritual evolution, 96, 129, 178, 196, 209, 226, 238
Spiritual facts, 31, 63, 91, 97, 178, 180, 181, 182, 243, 253; necessary to analysis of peace, 128
Spiritual force, 10, 11, 76, 170
Spiritual growth, 25, 98, 102, 233, 235
Spiritual ideal, 2, 6
Spiritual progress, 156
Spiritual reality, 19, 21, 23, 58, 131, 143, 154, 192, 200, 233
Spiritual realization, 19, 21, 22, 24, 25, 29, 33, 34, 46, 49, 51, 62, 75, 77, 79, 90, 93, 96, 98, 112, 156, 193. *See also*, Realization
śraddhā, 20
Standard, 69, 226; of action, wholly formal, 194; of behavior, 224
State, 70, 231, 233
sthitaprajña, 8, 9, 23, 40, 43, 51, 90, 133, 195; ideal *satyāgrahī*, 44
Strategy, 90–92, 155, 198, 230, 247
Strikes, 224
Struggle, 11, 17, 37, 50, 83, 93, 109, 175, 216, 228, 234, 235, 236, 241, 246; 251; law of, 44; path of realization, 44
Substitution, 21, 23, 29, 68, 71, 72; ethics, 71, 74–75, 76
Suffering, 225–26, 247, N78
Suffragette, 125
Suicide, 127, 170, 178, 235, 245, 252
Superimposition, 30, 108, 192
Superpowers, 244
Suppression, 55
svadharma, 180, 193, 221, 226; duties of stage, station & circumstance, 178
Śvetāśvatara Upaniṣad, 195
swadeśi, 94
swarāj, 15
syādavādi, 5

Tactics & strategy, 90-91, 92, 155, 157, 228, 233
Taittirīyaka Upaniṣad, 138
tamas, 40, 194
Tamilnad, 98
tapas, 52–53, 76, 78, 85, 86, 218, 238
tapaścaryā, 78, 85–86
Technology, as violence, 55
Terrorism, 55, 126, 147, 232
Test cases, 25, 61, 123, 132
Tilak, Bal. G., 69
Tolerance, 222, 242, 251
Totalitarianism, 126
Training, 85, 94, 100, 112, 132, 157, 246
Transmigration, 32, 235
Transcendental identity, 27
Treaty of Versailles, 201, 213, 232
Truth, 5, 14, 18, 24, 27, 38, 40, 42, 51, 58, 59, 72, 93, 96, 110, 132, 149, 154, 179, 220, 228, 229, 242, 249, N125, N157; as God, 22, 48; a practical force, 30; as moral authenticity, 4; as Name, 74
Truth-relation, 29
Trusteeship, 31
Tulsīdās, 102
Tyranny, 215

Uka, 37
Unilateralism, 66, 133, 243, 244, 245
USSR, 247
US, 240, 247
Universality & Infallibility, derived, 108–15
Universalizability criterion, 138–39, 150, 203
Unto This Last, 56
Untouchability, 94, 218
Upaniṣads, 19, 25, 30, 33, 68, 86, 195, 235
Utility, 14, 184, 193, 194, 197
Utopian (picture), N125
Utopianism, 181

vairāgya, 44, 72
Validity, 34, 130–34, 224, 228
Value, 9, 13, 47, 138, 153, 169, 178, 201, 202, 203, 148, 249, 252
vibhūti, 43, 53; —*māyā*, 76

Victory, 9, 37, 77, 91, 112, 151, 177, 187, 201, 232

vikāra, 41, 43

Violence, 4, 9, 12, 62, 63, 65, 66, 107, 112, 119, 120, 122, 123, 124, 125, 129–30, 137, 145, 147, 151, 152, 159, 162, 165, 169, 171, 172, 188, 195–96, 199, 204, 224, 229, 230, 241, 243, 247, 251, N64, NTR; absolute, nuclear, 120, 127; prefers to cowardice, 252–53; essence, exploitation, 56, 232; types, N70; *use* of, 142–44; brutalizes user, 142

Virangam, 98

Virtue, 8, 43, 98, 203–204, 215

Voice within, 220. *See also*, Conscience & Inner Voice

Vows, 93–94

Vykom, 83, 93, 98

War, 36, 50, 88, 101, 125, 156, 164, 165, 166, 168, 170, 175–77, 189, 190, 200, 201, 207, 232, 235–36, N62; N138; G. allows, 164; causes, 231–33; unmixed evil, 168–69, 173; not unmixed, 173, 189; G. prefers to injustice, 164, 170; moral equivalent of, 130; logical steps to, 163–65

War resister, 165, 173, 213; methods, 166

Will, 22, 42, 47, 63, 89, 143, 150, 162, 244, 246

World Wars, 55; I, 171; II, 60, 91, 189

Wrong, 98, 148, 183, 222–23; action, 68

Yādavas, 216

yajña, 35, 44–49, 51, 80, 92, 102, 179

yathā piṇḍe tathā brahmāṇḍe, 28, 29, 37, 39, 63, 67, 69, 72, 80, 94, 111, 163, 166, 178, 179, 200; *advaitic* interpretation, 192–193; commutative use confuses, 180, 183

yoga, 35; of *karma*, 37; of equability, 175

Yogasūtra, 59, 68

Yogeśvara Kṛṣṇa, 48. *See also*, Kṛṣṇa

yogī, 40

Zulu Rebellion, 17